THE
FORMULA
ONE
YEARS

LIFE IN THE FAST LANE FROM 1950 TO THE PRESENT DAY

First published in 1999 (as 50 Years of the Formula One World Championship)
Second Edition 2005
Third Edition 2009
Fourth Edition 2015
This edition published in 2018

Copyright © Carlton Books Limited 1999, 2005, 2009, 2015, 2018

Carlton Books Limited
20 Mortimer Street
London W1T 3JW

A CIP catalogue record for this book is available from the British Library

ISBN: 978-1-78739-193-2

Editor: Martin Corteel
Designer: Luke Griffin
Picture research: Paul Langan
Production: Lisa Cook

Printed in Dubai

Previous page **LEWIS HAMILTON IN ACTION FOR MERCEDES IN 2017.**

THE FORMULA ONE YEARS

LIFE IN THE FAST LANE FROM 1950 TO THE PRESENT DAY

Featuring **exclusive** contributions from:

TONY BROOKS, JOHN SURTEES, JACKIE STEWART, NIGEL MANSELL, DAVID COULTHARD, JARNO TRULLI & MARK WEBBER

BRUCE JONES

CARLTON
BOOKS

CONTENTS

OPPOSITE FERRARI'S SEBASTIAN VETTEL DIVES INTO THE LEAD AHEAD OF LEWIS HAMILTON AT THE START OF THE 2017 UNITED STATES GP.

FOLLOWING PAGES A PITSTOP FOR FERRARI'S KIMI RAIKKONEN IN 2014.

INTRODUCTION

Sixty-eight years have elapsed since the first Formula One World Championship and the cars, drivers and tracks have changed out of all recognition. Rough and ready in the 1950s, with drivers killed in their pursuit of glory, the sport is now a global business. The cars are phenomenal in their complexity, the drivers younger and fitter, and the tracks made safer by barriers and fencing to keep spectators safe, but the pursuit of glory remains the same.

Compare the machinery assembled on the grid for the first World Championship grand prix at Silverstone in 1950 with the cars gracing the tracks as the second decade of the 21st century nears its close and it's a case of crude and front-engined versus, sleek, safe and rear-engined.

Everything bar the pure love of speed has changed, with the development and innovation continual and frequently coming in astonishing jumps as the great technical minds such as that of Lotus founder Colin Chapman came up with yet another way to extract the most from the rules. The engines had been moved to sit behind the driver before the first decade was out, with aerodynamic wings sprouting in the late 1960s and slick tyres being used from the early 1970s. Then came turbocharged engines, ground-effect aerodynamics and carbon fibre brakes. Semi-automatic gearboxes, anti-lock brakes and traction control followed, with developments of many of these trickling down to the cars that we would drive on the road.

Amazing as this progress has been, it raises the most imponderable of all racing questions: how can you compare drivers from different eras? The simple answer is that you can't with any accuracy, although understanding the infinite variables helps when you examine the skills of multiple World Champions Juan Manuel Fangio, Ayrton Senna, Michael Schumacher and Lewis Hamilton, despite the fact that Fangio stopped racing before the 1950s were out, Senna didn't arrive in Formula One until 1984, Schumacher hit the front 10 years later and was the man for another decade, and Hamilton has been leading the charge since then.

To help you understand Formula One's remarkable evolution, I looked to both speed and brains in picking drivers from each of the seven decades to talk about their time in F1. Hopefully the collected and considered thoughts of Tony Brooks, John Surtees, Jackie Stewart, Nigel Mansell, David Coulthard, Jarno Trulli and Mark Webber will enlighten and entertain you as we celebrate Formula One's enduring appeal.

PREVIOUS PAGES **SEBASTIAN VETTEL IN THE THICK OF BATTLE IN 2014.**

LEFT **LEWIS HAMILTON DELIGHTS HIS HOME CROWD AT SILVERSTONE AS HE GUIDES HIS MERCEDES W08 TO VICTORY IN 2017.**

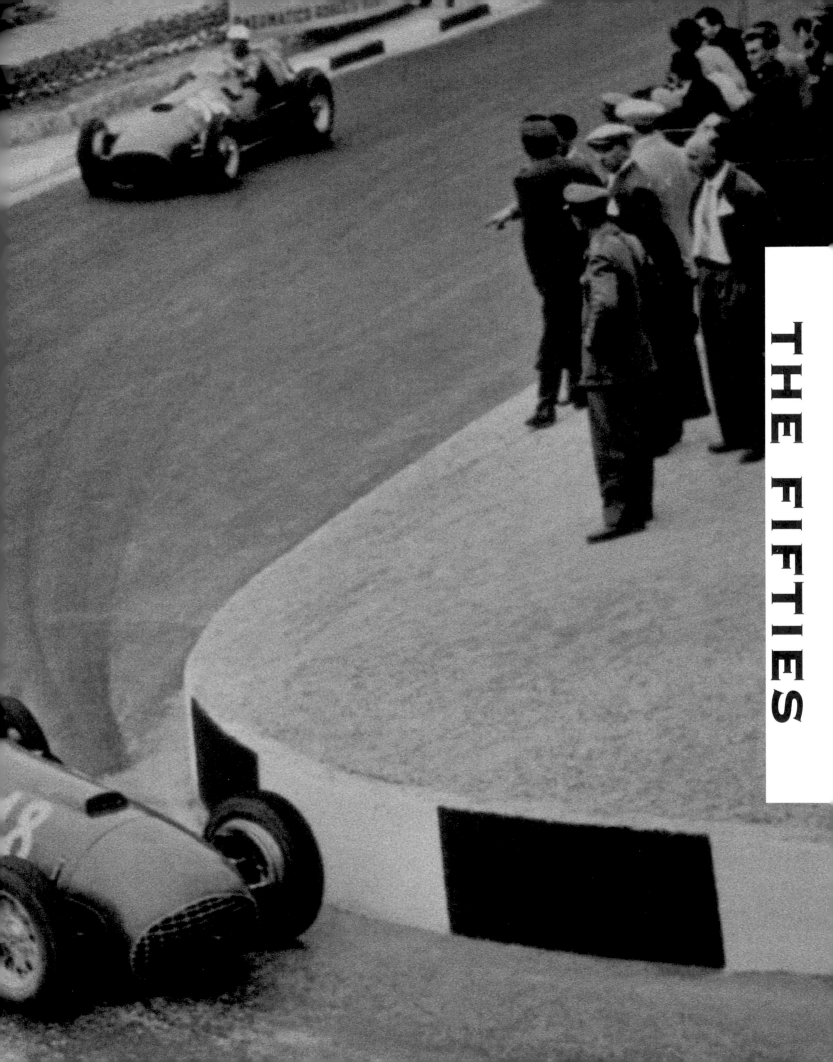

THE FIFTIES

THE FIFTIES

Honours: 2ND 1959, 3RD 1958
Grand Prix record: 38 STARTS, 6 WINS

Tony Brooks was possibly the most talented driver from Britain to race in the 1950s, yet, like his contemporary Stirling Moss he was never to become World Champion, retiring from Formula One with six Grand Prix wins to his name and yet without having brought his career to fruition. However, the fact that he survived it at all in an age when so many of his contemporaries died in action shows that he was an intelligent mastercraftsman.

Most people recall the race that made Tony's name, the non-championship Syracuse Grand Prix in Sicily in 1955. Even today mention of this race elicits a wry smile from Tony. "Yes, it launched my career, but it almost swamped it as people always want to talk about that before talking about anything else." Mind you, this isn't surprising as it was his first race in a Formula One car and he beat the works Maseratis on a circuit that he'd never seen until that weekend.

Tony recalls the race thus: "First I have to tell you how I came to be racing there. John Riseley-Pritchard and I had a successful test with Aston Martin in the winter of 1954 and were invited to join the works team for 1955. John's first drive was at Le Mans, the dreadful one in which 80 spectators were killed, and his family put pressure on him to stop. He had a Formula Two Connaught and he asked me to drive it. I wanted to try a single-seater, so I drove it in four national races and as a result of my performances in these I was invited to race Connaught's Formula One car at Syracuse. I shouldn't kid myself that I was first choice, as it was

after the end of the season and I'm sure they couldn't get anyone else to drive. Secondly, the Connaught was not very reliable and, thirdly, Syracuse was at the far end of Italy.

"I was more concerned with my upcoming dentistry exams than graduating to Formula One. Luckily, the car handled beautifully, and if it had had a good engine it would have been a regular World Championship challenger. As it was, this one had a 2.5-litre Alta which had been bored out from two litres and lost out as it had insufficient power and poor reliability. But it was a lot more powerful than the 1.5-litre Formula Two Connaught I'd raced.

"Worried about the car's reliability and wanting to be sure I started so that the team could claim start money, we limited my mileage in qualifying so that I was still learning the car and the track when I started the race from third on the grid. I went straight into the lead and broke clear, but I soon started thinking that Connaughts didn't often finish and backed off 500 revs to be sure. Luckily the engine had plenty of torque and I scored the first win for a British driver in a British car since 1924."

Not surprisingly, this led to offers and Tony joined Mike Hawthorn at BRM for 1956. But it didn't run smoothly. Although the car was fast with a fantastic power-to-weight ratio, inadequate brakes were the root of the BRM P25's problems, including in the Aintree 200 when fading brakes dropped Tony to second behind Moss's Maserati.

"All in all, 1956 was a disaster, and my first World Championship start was nearly my last. This was the British Grand Prix driving the lethal BRM. Mike turned his over at Goodwood and then I did the same at Silverstone, but at least I did the decent thing and set it on fire. My accelerator stuck at Abbey, this after it had broken earlier and I had lost several laps in the pits as it was lashed up. When I rejoined I knew that it was sticking, but I knew I could take Abbey flat. Trouble was, there was now more oil and rubber down and I needed a quick lift, but the throttle didn't respond and I ran onto the grass. With a decent car I could have run along the grass and eased back onto the track. With the BRM, if there was anything untoward you lost it. So I spun, hit the bank and was flipped out

onto the grass. It was stupid that I was out there trying to go as fast as that even though I was laps down, but I had only raced at Syracuse and wanted to prove that I could drive a Formula One car quickly. With more experience, I would have parked up, but it taught me a lesson, nearly a fatal one and I escaped with a broken jaw."

Tony had started 1957 by having his eyes opened by racing a Cooper in the International Trophy at Silverstone. "This was the defining moment of the 1950s for me, the event that made people take notice of the potential of rear-engined cars when I qualified on pole with a 2-litre engine ahead of the 2.5-litre opposition. It wasn't a World Championship entry, but it showed people that they had to put the weight where it should be, over the back wheels, which makes sense when you're trying to put the power down through these back wheels. Design never looked back after that. The cars were easier to drive, turned better, and being lighter stopped better, as well as being more aerodynamic. This performance proved that they were more than toys."

Tony entered the World Championship with Vanwall and kicked off with second behind Fangio's Maserati at Monaco. But then came a second incident that shaped his thoughts on racing a defective car. This came at Le Mans when he was again racing for Aston Martin.

"I was taking over from Noel Cunnigham-Reid at 3AM with the car lying in second place but stuck in fourth gear. I thought I knew how to fix it and made the mistake of looking at the gear lever rather than the road ahead. When I looked up, I realised I had missed the braking point for Tertre Rouge. I ran wide, clipped a sandbank and flipped, landing upside down in the track. I was trapped and was left to wonder if it would be a simple run-over job or incineration. Umberto Maglioli was the first on the scene, knocking the car off me. I then leapt clear with burned legs. It was sheer stupidity and I should have waited until the Mulsanne Straight before trying to fix it. Hereafter, I made myself a promise never to drive flat-out in a mechanically flawed car. It never affected my attitude to risk, as shown by the fact I scored my six Grand Prix wins after this second mishap, but it modified it when all was not right with a car."

Back in the cockpit for the British Grand Prix at Aintree, Tony wasn't well enough to go the distance and so handed his car over to team leader Moss when his own car had blown its engine, and Moss drove on to give them a combined victory.

So, 1957 saw Tony join the ranks of Grand Prix winners, but latter-day fans often question the level of competition in the late 1950s, especially as the grids were rounded out with Formula Two cars. Tony has views on this: "Even today the races tend to be between three or four people. Certainly, the last third of the field was sometimes made up by Formula Two cars, but this didn't make it any less competitive, it merely provided mobile chicanes for the drivers at the front to steer around. They added to the show. One has to look at the time differential not from the front of the grid to the back, but from the front of the grid to the slowest 2.5-litre car."

There was another factor that has to be considered when trying to compare the merits of drivers across the decades. And this is reliability, something that was poor in the 1950s, requiring drivers to learn how to nurse their machinery to reach the finish.

"Reliability was poor, but it gave drivers a chance to show their skills. Niki Lauda said how easy drivers have it in the 1990s after he drove the McLaren two-seater and found everything was done for the driver in the cockpit. In the 1950s there was much more scope for a driver to demonstrate superiority, whereas it's now down to technology, with a few tenths difference between Michael Schumacher and the rest.

"My philosophy was that you should try to win at the lowest speed possible. It seemed obvious, but not everybody practiced this, to my advantage actually. If you drove a car to the limit all the time, taking it up to maximum revs, hauling the gear lever through, you were going to increase your chance of failure, because the standard of engineering was blacksmith-like compared to today's space-age standards. You had to watch the rev counter as there were no rev limiters. And it wasn't just changing down when you ran the risk of over-revving, as you could do so accelerating out of a corner if you were drifting and trying to watch where you were heading and the rev counter at the same time.

"We also had excess power. This was only around 280bhp, but that was on narrow tyres that were extremely hard. So, if someone had slightly more power than you, you could still do something about it by making sure that you didn't spin your wheels out of a corner and thus would be as quick or quicker up the next straight. Today, with the amazing grip the cars have, you just bang your foot down and 20 extra horsepower will really show. The scope to compensate has long since gone. There was so much scope for a driver to show his skill in the 1950s. Not just in speed, but also in reliability. This point is not always recognised. I'm not going to name names, but there were some people who'd have won a lot more races if they'd had more empathy with the car."

The quality of circuits was something else that could separate the men from the boys, with trees and walls often lining the narrow tracks. They were bumpy, too. Tony continued: "The roughness of the surface was an additional challenge rather than a car breaker as the cars were generally massively-built and suspension failures were a rarity. It was transmissions that tended to go. If you were hammering a car out of a corner over bumps, it was rather like a speedboat on waves with its prop leaving the water, you could do a lot of damage through excess wheelspin then sudden grip.

"The races were longer, too, with distances of 500 kilometres before 1958 before they were shortened to 300 kilometres. To be honest, 500 kilometres was too long for the spectators and for some of the cars. Stamina was crucial, as even though distances were reduced, it took us longer to cover 300 kilometres than it does the same distance today.

"People often talk of how physical it must have been to drive these cars, but it's a myth that the steering was ultra-heavy. What was physically draining was the heat from the engine. It could affect your concentration. The brakes were heavy, though. As to the steering, racing at somewhere like Spa you would caress the steering wheel and the throttle as the car was balanced on a knife-edge with all four tyres sliding. You would alter the angle of the car by delicate inputs, not like today when it's a matter of brute force. I find all this 4-g business gruesome. What's that got to do with ordinary driving? Do we really want to know if we've got Mike Tyson-size neck muscles? If we want to find this out, let's have neck wrestling events... It's anathema to me, as driving should be poetry in motion. Take Spa, apart from La Source, every other corner was taken in a four-wheel drift. Today the whole finesse has gone. I think they're missing so much. But they seem to enjoy it and they get paid a fortune, so good luck to them. In terms of the sensual pleasure of driving I think they're missing out. But I must be careful as I haven't driven a contemporary Formula One car. In fact, I don't think I want to as it would have to be all or nothing for me."

Understandably, drivers in the 1990s have to spend a great deal of time in the gym getting fit enough to survive the g-forces they encounter in a race. Surely this is something that would have been alien to Tony?

"Well, I played a lot of squash and tennis and was always fit, keeping a sensible diet. But I never visited a gym. Stirling (Moss) was probably the first really professional driver. Behind the wheel I took it just as seriously as he did, but out of the car I wasn't tyring to be commercial, whereas Stirling was. Neither Stirling nor I drank, whereas Mike (Hawthorn) was the contrast..."

Safety is another factor that has changed out of all recognition. "There were on average three or four drivers killed each year in the

1950s. It's wonderful that it's so much safer now, but Formula One today is not the same. In my day it was Grand Prix motor racing, today it's Formula One, it's a totally different sport because we knew that one mistake could be our last. It's a different psychological challenge today as a driver knows that if he has a shunt, however big it is, the worst thing will be having to think of an excuse as to why it wasn't his fault while the computer will be producing a print-out that shows it jolly well was... After all, would mountaineering be the same if you had a safety net? Suddenly everyone would manage to climb the North Face of the Eiger without a mistake because of the different psychological approach. I'm not anti-Formula One, but it's show business now."

Staying with Vanwall for 1958, Tony was again number two to Moss but was able to win three times to Moss's four, while Hawthorn won just once and lifted the title for Ferrari.

It was all-change for 1959 and, with the withdrawal of Vanwall, Tony joined Ferrari. "This was my happiest year in racing, especially as I had the same car as everybody else, unlike at Vanwall where I was number two to Stirling and the whole team was run around him, which I accepted. But the fact is that he had the pick of the cars and engines, and I'm not even sure that I didn't sometimes start races in chassis that I hadn't driven in practice. Certainly, engines that I hadn't tried, as Stirling might say he didn't like his engine, try my car and like mine. In theory they were all the same, but in those days they weren't. Sensibly, team manager David Yorke would limit my practice laps, as if I went quicker than Stirling he would feel that he had to beat this time, putting race miles on the car.

"We had equal cars at Ferrari until it became evident which of us was most likely to become World Champion, then I became the number one. However, there was no difference in the cars, rather that if the situation arose that my team-mates would have to back me up. But that moment never came, unlike in 1958 when Phil Hill yielded two second places to Hawthorn.

"The atmosphere in the team was good, too, with our Anglo-American drivers. Phil Hill was a great guy as were Dan Gurney and Cliff Allison. Jean Behra was the odd man out as he couldn't speak English or Italian. Luckily, I could speak Italian, not that I got to use it much with Enzo Ferrari as I met him only twice as he never came to the races.

"I never encountered any political problems, but I'm not a political animal. Amazingly, in the 40 minutes it took to agree on my contract with the team, which also included a full sportscar programme, I managed to negotiate a bye for Le Mans as I had agreed to continue driving for Aston Martin there. That wouldn't happen now.

"Team manager (Romolo) Tavoni may have fallen out with Behra, but he never tried it with me. He recognised that I was always doing my best and that it was either going to be good enough or it wasn't. Although Phil lived in Modena and probably bore the brunt of any politics.

"Enzo was a dictator and very stubborn. Indeed, it took lengthy argument from Hawthorn and Peter Collins in 1958 to convince him to fit disc brakes. And it took a change of formula (to the 1.5-litre formula that came in for 1961) to follow the rear-engined route."

Having won the French and German Grands Prix, Tony went to the final round at Sebring with a shot at the title, having to win with fastest lap to lift the crown. "I should have been on the front row, but Harry Schell was credited with a time that no-one thought he'd done. Well, not legitimately, as the course was marked out with barrels, so he must have taken a shortcut. Trouble was, this put me on the second row with "Taffy" von Trips behind me and he hit me half way around the lap. This put me up the escape road and I had the tremendous dilemma as to whether I should have the car checked over or not, overturning the promise I had made myself after Le Mans in 1957. I came in and instantly threw away my hopes of the title. As it was, I rejoined and finished third, giving the title to Jack Brabham. But if I hadn't pitted for a check-over it could have been a case of third time unlucky... Enzo probably didn't see it that way, but I'd do the same again if faced with the same situation.

"I decided to rejoin Vanwall for 1960, as Tony Vandervell said he'd have a rear-engined car. With Ferrari sticking with a front-engined car this sounded good, especially as I was starting a garage business and wanted to spend more time in England and not having a sportscar programme would enable me to do this. But by doing this I realised that I was putting my post-racing career ahead of my racing career as logic dictated that Ferrari would provide the 1961 World Champion when the rules changed to 1.5-litre engines as they already had the best package around with their 'Sharknose' 156s already running away with all the Formula Two races."

Then the Vanwall deal folded... "I should have taken a sabbatical, but I was offered a drive in a Yeoman Credit Cooper and took it." And this was the start of the decline of Tony's career as it wasn't competitive. The following season with a BRM was little better although he did round it off with third place at the US Grand Prix and then retired from racing to concentrate on his family and his garage business.

Tony doesn't hesitate to rank his contemporaries: "Fangio then Moss, perhaps with Moss the better in sportscars. Behra was next ahead of Hawthorn and Collins, although both the latter had their off days. Of the drivers of today, Schumacher stands out, but the contribution of the driver is far less today so I can't see anything much to chose between the rest. Driving in the wet boosts the drivers' contribution as it gives drivers excess power and this is when Schumacher is even more dominant."

Ask Tony where he sees Formula One heading and this is what he reckons: "The future is dicey. Look at the dramas when Senna died in 1994. If a driver, drivers or, worse still, spectators were killed, one could visualise a terrible public reaction. The other risk is that Formula One is supported by tobacco money, but if it gained a bad image then sponsors wouldn't replace the tobacco sponsorship when it's no longer allowed. So, because of political pressures and the risk of accident, I think its future is not totally assured, even though Bernie Ecclestone has done a marvellous job in making it into show business for an audience of billions."

FARINA THE FIRST

The Formula One World Championship was held for the first time in 1950, linking established Grands Prix from just six countries. Alfa Romeo and its drivers Farina, Fangio and Fagioli dominated, but Ferrari was waiting to pounce.

All was quiet in the years immediately after the Second World War, but it did not take long for motor racing to re-establish itself. By 1950, the governing body had decided that the time was right to bind the various Grands Prix together to launch a World Championship. There was plenty of pre-war racing equipment available, and no shortage of drivers who had raced in the 1930s. True, they had lost some of the best years of their careers during the hostilities but, despite the enforced break, they were still at the top of their game.

ALFA ROMEO TAKES CONTROL

This inaugural year was all about Alfa Romeo, with the great Italian marque's cars winning every race, with the exception of the stand-alone Indianapolis 500 that was included in the World Championship to give it some appeal to the American market but not entered by any of the regular Formula One teams.

Alfa Romeo's squad comprised the legendary "three Fs": Dr Giuseppe "Nino" Farina (then aged 44), Juan Manuel Fangio (a stripling at 38), and Luigi Fagioli (53). Equipped with an update of the pre-war Tipo 158, they steamrollered the opposition, chased by Ferrari.

Ferrari had suffered a disappointing run of results in 1949, and the team was absent from the first race, held at a rudimentary Silverstone on May 13 in the presence of the royal family. There were

21 cars in the field, many of which were a good 15 years old, and Farina had the honour of taking the first pole position. Fagioli led initially, but dropped to third place behind Farina and Fangio. When Fangio's engine failed, Fagioli took second place ahead of local star Reg Parnell, who drove Alfa Romeo's fourth works car.

A week later at Monaco, Farina's luck changed when he triggered a nine-car pile-up on the opening lap, which also took out Fagioli. Fangio was ahead of the carnage, and somehow survived when he came across the pile-up at speed on the next lap, going on to score a memorable win. Alberto Ascari rewarded Ferrari with second place, a lap down.

Farina and Fagioli finished first and second in the Swiss Grand Prix at the tricky Bremgarten road circuit, and once again Fangio suffered an engine failure –

LEFT **THE FIRST WINNER: GIUSEPPE FARINA SET THE WORLD CHAMPIONSHIP BALL ROLLING BY WINNING THE OPENING GRAND PRIX AT SILVERSTONE AND THE 1950 TITLE.**

21

Above A LUCKY AVOIDANCE: JUAN MANUEL FANGIO (34) TAKES A LOOK AT THE CARNAGE FROM THE OPENING LAP AT MONACO.

Left ON A SWISS ROLL: FARINA RACED TO VICTORY FOR ALFA ROMEO IN THE SWISS GRAND PRIX AT BREMGARTEN.

Right FLYING AMATEUR: PETER WHITEHEAD WAS A GENTLEMAN DRIVER, BUT HE WAS QUICK TOO. HERE HE TAKES HIS FERRARI ACROSS THE LINE IN THE ITALIAN GRAND PRIX.

as did all three works Ferraris. In the Belgian Grand Prix, held at the mighty Spa-Francorchamps circuit in the Ardennes hills, Fangio fought back with his second win of the year, this time ahead of Fagioli. Variety was provided by Raymond Sommer, who led in his Talbot before blowing up.

FARINA TAKES THE TITLE

The first championship, like so many to follow, came to a head in the final round at Monza. Fangio arrived at the race with 26 points as opposed to the 24 of the consistent Fagioli and the 22 of Farina. Fangio and Farina had the new and more powerful Alfa Romeo 159 model, but the title was settled when Fangio retired with a seized gearbox. Farina won the race, and with it the World Championship.

Ferrari had been working hard on a new unsupercharged engine during the season, which had been showing well in non-championship races, and Ascari was on the pace with the latest model in the Italian Grand Prix. When his car retired, he took over the machine of team-mate Dorino Serafini and finished second, ahead of Fagioli.

In addition to the establishment of the World Championship, the 1950 season was also notable for the introduction of much new racing machinery. However, the year's most talked-about car never appeared at a Grand Prix. The much-vaunted V16 BRM made an ignominious debut in the International Trophy at Silverstone in August, retiring on the startline with driveshaft failure.

ARGENTINA'S ACE

Alfa Romeo continued to set the pace in 1951, but Ferrari came close to toppling the champions. Mechanical problems had robbed him the previous year, but now Juan Manuel Fangio was dominant and claimed his first world title.

For 1951, Alfa Romeo broke up the "three Fs" team, replacing Fagioli with 48-year-old Felice Bonetto. Jose Froilan Gonzalez, who had previously driven a Maserati, joined Ascari and Luigi Villoresi at Ferrari. The stocky young Argentinian, known as the "Pampas Bull", was to become a major force during the season.

The World Championship was expanded to a total of seven races, with Monaco dropped from the calendar and Grands Prix in Germany and Spain added. This time the championship began in Switzerland, and in soaking conditions Fangio scored a fine win, almost a minute ahead of Piero Taruffi's Ferrari, with Farina a distant third. Meanwhile, a promising young Englishman made his debut in a British HWM, qualifying 14th and finishing eighth. His name was Stirling Moss.

The Indianapolis 500 was the next race, with Lee Wallard controlling proceedings. As in the year before, not one of the Formula One drivers took part. Indeed, ironically, they only started to do so as the race was dropped from the World Championship, a decade later.

FANGIO HITS TROUBLE
Farina and Fangio dominated the Belgian Grand Prix at Spa-Francorchamps, but when Fangio pitted, a rear wheel stuck and his race was ruined. Farina duly won from the Ferraris of Ascari and Villoresi, while a fired-up Fangio set the fastest lap in his recovery drive, but finished last.

Fagioli was back in an Alfa Romeo for the French Grand Prix at Reims and went on to score his first victory – but only after Fangio took over his car when his own mount had retired in a race of high attrition. Another shared car – the Ferrari of Gonzalez and Ascari – took second, ahead of Villoresi. After tyre troubles, Farina was a distant fifth.

FERRARI'S BREAKTHROUGH
A Ferrari win had seemed on the cards, and the first one finally came in the British Grand Prix at Silverstone, where Gonzalez put in a fine performance to take the lead from countryman Fangio when the Alfa Romeo driver pitted and stalled while trying to rejoin. The BRM made its first championship appearance,

Lᴇꜰᴛ **TWO-PART WIN: JUAN MANUEL FANGIO STARTED THE FRENCH GRAND PRIX IN HIS ALFA ROMEO, BUT SWAPPED OVER TO LUIGI FAGIOLI'S CAR WHEN HE HIT TROUBLE AND WON IN THAT.**

25

Above **AND THEY'RE OFF: FANGIO (4) OUTDRAGS ASCARI'S FERRARI (12) AT THE START OF THE FRENCH GRAND PRIX.**

Left **HOLD ON A SECOND: THAT'S FANGIO LATER IN THE SAME RACE AT REIMS AND NOW HE'S IN ALFA ROMEO NUMBER 6.**

with Reg Parnell taking a promising fifth place and Peter Walker finishing seventh.

Ferrari was the dominant force in the German Grand Prix at the Nurburgring, the first championship race held on the long, tortuous circuit in the forests of the Eifel mountains. Ascari notched up his first win, despite a late stop for rear tyres. Fangio, who required an extra non-scheduled fuel stop, took second for Alfa Romeo. Third to sixth places were filled with Ferraris, while Farina retired with gearbox trouble.

The Italian Grand Prix was the penultimate round this year, and Ascari and Gonzalez celebrated a fine one-two result for Ferrari in front of the home crowd. Alfa Romeo had a much-modified car, the 159M, and Fangio was battling for the lead until a tyre failed. His storming recovery drive ended with engine failure. Farina retired early in the race, but took

over Bonetto's car and eventually earned third place.

The final race at Pedralbes in Spain proved to be Alfa Romeo's swansong. Despite his Monza retirement, Fangio led Ascari by 28 points to 25 going into the race, and a dominant win secured Juan Manuel's first crown. The Ferraris suffered tyre troubles, with Gonzalez and pole man Ascari taking second and fourth places, split by Farina's Alfa Romeo.

At the end of the year, Alfa Romeo withdrew from Grand Prix racing, unable to finance a new car to challenge Ferrari in 1952. Partly in response to Alfa Romeo's departure, the Fédération Internationale de l'Automobile announced that for 1952, the World Championship would run to less powerful Formula Two rules. It was hoped that this would encourage a wider variety of cars and avoid a Ferrari walkover.

Right **CHAMPIONSHIP CHALLENGER: ALBERTO ASCARI (SECOND RIGHT) DISPLAYS HIS OPTIMISM PRIOR TO THE ITALIAN GRAND PRIX, A RACE HE WENT ON TO WIN.**

Below **TRUE BRIT: REG PARNELL ON HIS WAY TO A FOURTH PLACE FINISH IN REIMS AT THE FRENCH GRAND PRIX.**

FERRARI'S FAMOUS FIRST

Ferrari responded to the introduction of Formula Two rules changes by dominating. Alberto Ascari won every race he entered to become world champion, while an injured Juan Manuel Fangio could only watch from the sidelines.

Despite the change of regulations, Ferrari entered 1952 as the major force. The marque had already been highly successful in Formula Two, and had a first-class driver line-up. Ascari, Luigi Villoresi and Piero Taruffi were joined by Giuseppe Farina – now on the market after Alfa Romeo's withdrawal. The main opposition should have come from reigning champion Fangio, who had switched from Alfa Romeo to Maserati to drive the new A6GCM. However, the Argentinian was forced to miss the entire season after breaking his neck in a crash during a non-championship race at Monza.

BURGEONING INTEREST
The rule change achieved its aim of attracting a variety of cars to take on the red machines. From France came the Gordinis of Jean Behra and Robert Manzon, while in Britain there was a host of projects underway, including the Cooper-Bristol, Connaught, HWM, Alta, Frazer Nash and ERA. The most successful of these would prove to be the Cooper-Bristol, an underpowered machine blessed with superb handling. Its brilliant young driver was a flamboyant Englishman by the name of Mike Hawthorn, who proved to be the find of the year.

The championship began with the Swiss Grand Prix, a race notable for the absence of Ascari, who was busy with Ferrari commitments at Indianapolis. Taruffi scored an easy win, well ahead of local Ferrari privateer Rudi Fischer. Encouragingly, the Gordini showed promise, with Behra racing to third place. That place had been held by Stirling Moss in the HWM, but his car was withdrawn after two of its sister entries suffered hub failures.

Ascari's trip to the Indianapolis 500 came to naught, as he could qualify his Ferrari only midgrid and was out of the race by one fifth distance. Troy Ruttman triumphed in a Kuzma. Ascari then scored his first win of the new Formula Two era in soaking conditions in the Belgian Grand Prix at Spa-Francorchamps, crossing the finish line almost a minute ahead of team-mate Farina. Manzon gave Gordini another third place, but all eyes were on

LEFT **THREE IN A ROW: ALBERTO ASCARI ROCKETS PAST THE CHEQUERED FLAG AT SILVERSTONE FOR HIS THIRD WIN IN SUCCESSION FOR FERRARI. HE WAS A RUNAWAY CHAMPION.**

29

Below **RISING BRITISH STAR: MIKE HAWTHORN MADE A MAJOR IMPACT BY FINISHING FOURTH ON HIS DEBUT IN BELGIUM.**

Bottom **TO THE FORE: ASCARI LEADS TEAM-MATE FARINA AT THE DOWNHILL START AT ROUEN.**

Right **BIG MAN, BIG RESULT: JOSE FROILAN OVERFLOWS FROM HIS MASERATI AS HE RACES TO SECOND AT MONZA.**

Hawthorn, making his championship debut. He ran third and, after a fuel leak delayed him, finished a fine fourth. It was the highest place to date for a British car, and the first sign of great things to come from John Cooper's small company.

Behra's Gordini surprisingly beat the Ferraris at Reims but, unfortunately for him, in this particular year it was a non-championship race.

FERRARI MAINTAINS ITS DOMINANCE

The French Grand Prix itself took place at Rouen a week later, and Ferrari's Ascari, Farina and Taruffi finished first, second and third, with Manzon fourth. Ascari and Taruffi were then first and second in the British Grand Prix, but Hawthorn was the darling of the home crowd, rising to the challenge and finishing third. Dennis Poore also impressed with his Connaught, leading Hawthorn until he had to make a long fuel stop, finally coming home fourth.

The German Grand Prix at the Nurburgring was a complete Ferrari whitewash, with Ascari heading Farina, Fischer and Taruffi. Ascari had to work hard for his win though, for a late pit stop for oil dropped him to second and forced him to catch and re-pass Farina. The new Dutch Grand Prix among the sand dunes of the coastal resort of Zandvoort was next up, and saw Ascari leading Farina and Villoresi home, with Hawthorn again leading the challenge in a gallant fourth place finish with his Cooper-Bristol.

Ascari had already clinched the championship title before the season's final race, the Italian Grand Prix, but just for good measure he rattled off his sixth win from six starts, this time with a minute's advantage over Gonzalez and a further minute's advantage over Villoresi and Farina.

ADVANTAGE ASCARI

Alberto Ascari claimed his second world title in a row as Ferrari were again supreme in the second and final year of the Formula Two category. However, Juan Manuel Fangio struck back for Maserati, signalling the start of four years of domination by the maestro.

Fangio was back and fit at the start of 1953, and heading a Maserati outfit which looked as if it might upset the Ferrari bandwagon. Joining him in a strong Argentinian line-up were Jose Froilan Gonzalez and Onofre Marimon. Meanwhile, Mike Hawthorn's 1952 performances with the Cooper had not gone unnoticed, and he had earned a seat with Ferrari, alongside Ascari, Giuseppe Farina and Luigi Villoresi. With Hawthorn gone, Cooper lacked a driver of substance, and so Gordini provided the only real opposition to the Italian cars.

A DARK DAY IN ARGENTINA

For the first time, the "World Championship" tag was justified by a race outside Europe that the regulars actually contested - unlike the anomaly of the Indianapolis 500 - with the series kicking off at Buenos Aires.

Unfortunately the race was marred by undisciplined spectators, and Farina was involved in a tragic incident when he hit a boy who crossed the track during the race. Nine people were killed in the mayhem that followed. It was the first fatality in a World Championship race, but sadly it would not be the last. Meanwhile, Ascari and Villoresi finished first and second for Ferrari ahead of debutant Marimon. Hawthorn had a steady race to fourth, while local hero Fangio ran second before retiring.

Over in the US, Bill Vukovich made amends for losing the 1952 Indianapolis 500 with nine laps to go by starting from pole in his Kurtis Kraft and winning this time around.

Maserati's new car arrived in time for the Dutch Grand Prix. It showed promise, but Ascari and Farina took the usual Ferrari one-two, with the best Maserati - shared by Felice Bonetto and Gonzalez - in third. Fangio broke a rear axle and scored nothing.

The Maseratis were the cars to beat in the Belgian Grand Prix, however, and Gonzalez and Fangio led the field until retiring. Inevitably, though, Ascari was there to pick up the pieces, scoring his ninth consecutive win.

A BRITISH FIRST

The French Grand Prix was back at

LEFT **FOLLOW THE LEADER: ALBERTO ASCARI BLASTS CLEAR OF THE FIELD AT THE DUTCH GRAND PRIX AT ZANDVOORT. THIS WAS HIS EIGHTH WIN IN A ROW AND SET HIM UP FOR HIS SECOND TITLE.**

LEFT A WINNING START: ALBERTO ASCARI ACKNOWLEDGES THE OVER-FLOWING CROWD AS HE WINS THE ARGENTINIAN GRAND PRIX.

BELOW LEFT QUIETER SURROUNDINGS: ASCARI ENJOYS THE TWISTS OF BREMGARTEN WHERE HE WRAPPED UP THE CHAMPIONSHIP WITH A ROUND STILL TO GO.

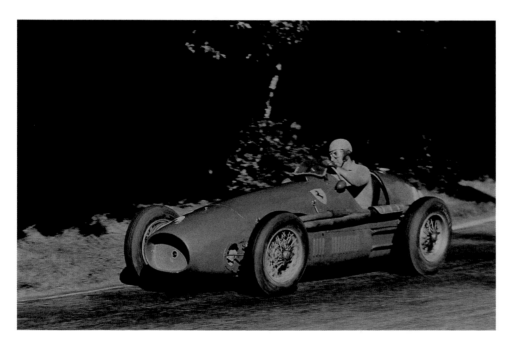

Reims, and it proved to be a classic encounter which saw Hawthorn truly come of age. After taking two fourth places and a sixth in the season's opening races, he emerged as a front-runner, getting the better of a sensational duel with Fangio to score his first win - the first for any British driver. Strangely, Hawthorn could not repeat his French form in the British Grand Prix, where Ascari was utterly dominant. Fangio chased hard, and finished ahead of Farina, Gonzalez and Hawthorn.

Ascari was again the man to beat in the German Grand Prix, but he lost a front wheel early on. However, he made it back around the Nurburgring's lengthy lap to the pits, and later took over Villoresi's fourth-placed car. Farina main-tained Ferrari's record though, winning ahead of Fangio and Hawthorn. In his new car, Ascari was closing in on the British driver when the engine blew.

The Ferrari driver clinched his second title at the penultimate race, the Swiss Grand Prix at Bremgarten, yet it was any-thing but easy. Fangio led Ascari until gearbox and engine troubles intervened,

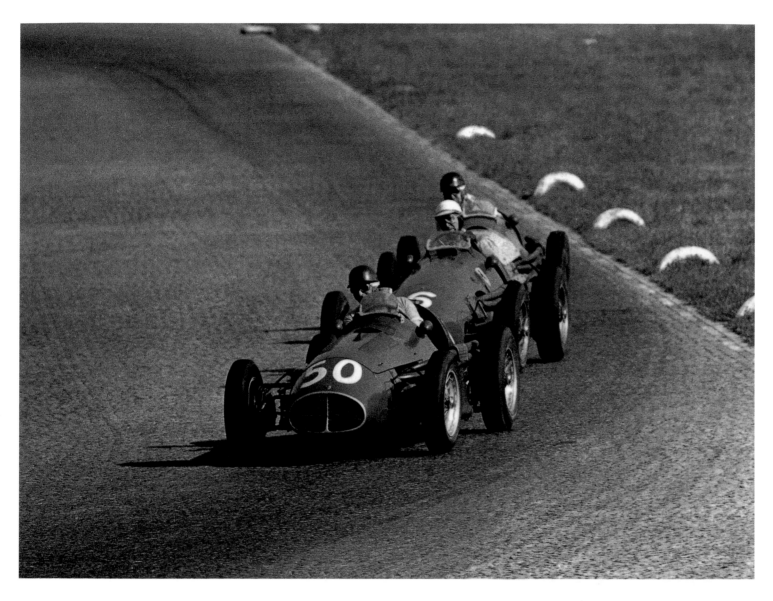

Above **HE'S BACK: JUAN MANUEL FANGIO RETURNED FROM INJURY AND HIT THE VICTORY TRAIL AT THE ITALIAN GRAND PRIX.**

Right **THE SMILE SAYS IT ALL: JUAN MANUEL FANGIO SHOWS HIS PLEASURE AT HIS REFOUND FORM AT MONZA.**

and then Ascari lost the lead with a plug change. He dropped to fourth, but worked his way back to the lead, heading home Farina and Hawthorn.

Maserati had threatened to win all year, and it eventually happened in the finale at Monza, albeit in bizarre circumstances. After a great slipstreaming battle Ascari looked set to win, but on the last lap he spun and forced Farina wide. The lapped Marimon also got involved, and through the dust cloud emerged Fangio, to score his first win since 1951, crossing the line just ahead of Farina. And so Fangio moved above Farina to rank second overall, while fourth place was also enough to give Hawthorn fourth overall ahead of Villoresi.

MERCEDES MOVES IN

Mercedes-Benz finally returned to racing, and their "blank cheque" operation immediately set new standards that transformed Formula One. Juan Manuel Fangio and his wonderful W196 Silver Arrow were unstoppable. Meanwhile, Britain found a new star in Stirling Moss.

After two years of Formula Two it was all change for 1954, with the introduction of new 2.5-litre regulations. The big story was the decision by Mercedes-Benz to return to Grand Prix racing for the first time since the Second World War. The legendary Alfred Neubauer, who had masterminded their dominance in the 1930s, was still at the helm, and he snapped up Fangio to join Hans Herrmann and Karl Kling on his driving force. Mercedes' new W196 was a technical marvel, but was not ready until the

third race of the year. Also on the way was Lancia's new D50. The Italian marque hired Alberto Ascari and Luigi Villoresi to drive it, but it was ready even later than the Mercedes, not joining in until the final race. Thus, after two titles, Ascari effectively wasted the season.

Fangio was luckier, for he was allowed to start the year in the new Maserati, the 250F. An attractive and effective car, it proved to be one of the mainstays of Grand Prix racing over the next few seasons. Ferrari had lost Ascari and Villoresi, but Mike Hawthorn, Giuseppe Farina, Jose Froilan Gonzalez and Frenchman Maurice Trintignant were on hand to drive the latest model.

FANGIO'S WINNING START
Fangio's decision to start the year in a Maserati was a wise one, and he duly

won the opening Grands Prix in Argentina and Belgium. The first race was a rain-hit affair with the track conditions changing several times. Dominant in the wet, Fangio won ahead of the Ferraris of Farina, Gonzalez and Trintignant. Farina led the early laps in Belgium, but when he hit trouble Fangio went by, and headed home Trintignant. Moss showed he would be a force to be reckoned with by taking third in another Maserati. Splitting these two races was the Indianapolis 500, with Bill Vukovich making it two wins on the trot.

Mercedes finally appeared at Reims, with three of the magnificent W196s in streamlined, full-bodied form. The cars were perfectly suited to the fast track, and Fangio and Kling finished first and second, with Hermann retiring after setting fastest lap. However, Mercedes came

LEFT **FLYING START: JUAN MANUEL FANGIO GAVE THE ALL-NEW MERCEDES W196 A WINNING DEBUT IN THE FRENCH GRAND PRIX AT REIMS BEFORE RACING TO HIS THIRD WORLD TITLE.**

down to earth with a bang at Silverstone, as their streamlined bodies did not suit the airfield circuit. Fangio finished fourth, while Gonzalez scored his second British Grand Prix win, again in a Ferrari.

Tragedy struck at the Nurburgring when Marimon was killed in practice; he was the first driver to die at a World Championship event. Fellow Argentinians Fangio and Gonzalez were distraught but, to his credit, Fangio got on with the job and won the race, his Mercedes now using the new open-wheel body. Fangio then led from start to finish in the Swiss Grand Prix. Moss pursued him until retiring, and then Gonzalez took up the challenge.

MOSS MAKES HIS MARK
The Italian Grand Prix established Moss as a star of the future. His performances had earned him a works Maserati seat, and he led until nine laps from the end when the car's oil tank split. He would eventually push the car over the line in 11th place, but he had made his mark. Meanwhile, Fangio swept by to win in his streamlined Mercedes, ahead of Hawthorn.

The Lancia team was finally ready for the last race in Spain, and the radical car showed promise, for Ascari led for ten laps and set the fastest lap before retiring. However, it was to be Hawthorn's day, as the Englishman went on to score his second win, ahead of Maserati's young find, Luigi Musso. Mercedes had a bad day, and Fangio finished only in third place. However, his second title was already in the bag.

ABOVE DRINK THIS LAD: A YOUTHFUL STIRLING MOSS LOOKS BEMUSED AS HE'S OFFERED A PRE-RACE TIPPLE AT THE ITALIAN GRAND PRIX.

LEFT FORMATION FINISH: KARL KLING SHADOWS MERCEDES TEAM-MATE FANGIO ACROSS THE LINE AT REIMS, THE OPPOSITION WAS LEFT STUNNED.

RIGHT RUBBISH COLLECTOR: PAPER STUCK IN FRONT OF MIKE HAWTHORN'S RADIATOR DIDN'T STOP HIM FROM WINNING THE SPANISH GRAND PRIX.

FANGIO'S HAT-TRICK

Mercedes, Juan Manuel Fangio and Stirling Moss dominated the 1955 Formula One season, but the appalling tragedy at Le Mans – which cost over 80 lives – overshadowed everything, and caused Mercedes to announce its withdrawal from racing.

June 11, 1955, is the blackest day in motor racing history. More than 80 people were killed when Pierre Levegh's Mercedes crashed into the crowd during the Le Mans 24 Hours. Formula One stars Juan Manuel Fangio and Mike Hawthorn were both peripherally involved in the incident, which had major repercussions for the sport. As a knee-jerk reaction, the Grands Prix in France, Germany, Switzerland and Spain were cancelled, and motor racing never returned to Switzerland again.

MERCEDES MUSCLE

Mercedes went into the season with morale high. Team boss Alfred Neubauer had signed Stirling Moss to partner Fangio, and now had two top drivers in his Silver Arrows. Maserati signed up Jean Behra to replace Moss, while Hawthorn left Ferrari to drive for Vanwall, with family business pressures dictating that it was better if he was based closer to home.

The season opener in Argentina was run in sweltering conditions, and saw Fangio score a comfortable win. Indeed, he was one of only two drivers able to go the distance solo, and the three pursuing cars were each shared by three drivers apiece as the heat took its toll, with José Froilan Gonzalez, Giuseppe Farina and Maurice Trintignant all taking stints in the second-placed Ferrari.

Alberto Ascari hit the headlines in Monaco by flipping his car into the harbour. Fortunately, he escaped with minor injuries. At the time he was leading – Fangio and Moss had both retired their Mercedes – and this left the way open for Trintignant to become a popular and surprise winner ahead of Eugenio Castellotti's Lancia. Four days later, Ascari's luck ran out when he was killed in a bizarre accident at Monza, whilst he was testing a Ferrari sports car. Already struggling for finance, Lancia announced its withdrawal from the sport, regrettably before the D50 had been able to fulfil its promise.

The Indianapolis 500 remained as part of the championship, and continued to stand apart from the events for Formula One machinery. Bob Sweikert triumphed after Bill Vukovich crashed

Left **TOTAL CONTROL: JUAN MANUEL FANGIO WAS STREETS CLEAR OF HIS RIVALS THROUGHOUT THE 1955 SEASON,
WITH ONLY TEAM-MATE STIRLING MOSS KEEPING HIM ON HIS TOES.**

41

Left SURPRISE WINNER: MAURICE TRINTIGNANT TAKES VICTORY AT MONACO FOR FERRARI IN AN UNUSUAL RACE.

Far Right MASTER AND PUPIL: FANGIO LEADS STIRLING MOSS AT AINTREE, BUT IT WAS THE BRITISH DRIVER WHO WON THE RACE.

Below CHAMPION'S LAST RACE: ALBERTO ASCARI PRESSES ON BEFORE FLIPPING INTO MONACO'S HARBOUR. FOUR DAYS LATER HE WAS KILLED WHEN TESTING.

fatally when heading for his third consecutive win. Mercedes meanwhile bounced back at the Belgian Grand Prix at the tricky Spa-Francorchamps circuit, with Fangio and Moss finishing first and second at their ease. Castellotti was allowed a final fling in a Lancia – as a privateer – and ran third before retiring to leave the spot for Ferrari's Farina.

LIFE AFTER LE MANS
The following weekend came the Le Mans tragedy and, despite the outcry, the Grand Prix circus reconvened for the Dutch Grand Prix at Zandvoort just a week later. Fangio and Moss scored another Mercedes one-two finish at the seaside circuit, chased to the line by Luigi Musso's Maserati. By now Hawthorn had given up on the Vanwall project, and his return to Ferrari was rewarded with a creditable seventh place.

The British Grand Prix forsook Silverstone and moved to Aintree for the first time, racing on a circuit laid out around the outside of the course of the famous Grand National steeplechase. Mercedes scored a crushing one-two-three-four finish. This time Moss headed home Fangio, with Karl Kling and Piero Taruffi following on. It was Stirling's first win, but for years afterwards people wondered if Fangio had allowed him to take the glory at home.

A QUIET REVOLUTION
At the back of the grid that day in a little Cooper was a rookie called Jack Brabham. He failed to finish, but it was the start of an amazing partnership, one that was to change the very face of Formula One beyond all recognition.

With all the cancellations, only the Italian Grand Prix remained to be run, this time on Monza's banked circuit. After Moss retired, Fangio headed Taruffi in another one-two, with Castellotti third in a Ferrari. Fangio's third title was already secure, with Moss a distant second. But both men would be hit hard when Mercedes announced its withdrawal.

A significant result came in a non-championship race late in the season, when Tony Brooks took his Connaught to victory at Syracuse in Sicily. It was the first major victory for a British car in the World Championship era.

FANGIO FOR FERRARI

Following the withdrawal of Mercedes from all motor sport activities, Juan Manuel Fangio switched to Ferrari and landed his fourth World Championship crown. But the Argentinian needed some luck – and the incredible generosity of his sensational new team-mate, Peter Collins.

The two Mercedes stars of 1955 did not spend much time contemplating unemployment, as Fangio joined Ferrari, where another new face that season was talented British youngster Collins, along with Luigi Musso and Eugenio Castellotti. The promising Lancias had also found a new home at Ferrari. They had, in fact, been entered by the Scuderia at the Italian Grand Prix the previous year, but had not started owing to tyre troubles. Modified over the winter, they became Lancia Ferraris for 1956.

Meanwhile, Stirling Moss returned to Maserati to race the still competitive 250F alongside French ace Jean Behra. Prospects also looked good for the British teams as Mike Hawthorn and Tony Brooks joined BRM, while Vanwall had modified cars for Maurice Trintignant and Harry Schell, and Connaught hoped to build on its Syracuse success.

MASERATI HITS BACK

Fangio won the opening round in Argentina, but he did so only after taking over Musso's car when his own retired. The Maseratis struggled in the heat, although Behra took second place. Maserati then hit back at Monaco, where Moss scored a fine second Grand Prix victory. A seemingly very off-form Fangio damaged his own car and this time took over the sister machine of Collins, which

he guided to second place. Over in the US, pole-placed Pat Flaherty avoided a pile-up early in the race to win the Indianapolis 500 in a Watson. Again, no Formula One regulars took part.

Fangio and Moss both hit trouble in the Belgian Grand Prix, and Collins scored a famous victory in his Lancia Ferrari, becoming the third British race winner in as many seasons. Local star Paul Frère earned a fine second place, while Moss took over Cesare Perdisa's car and recovered to finish third. Collins scored his second win at Reims a month later, heading home Castellotti, Behra and Fangio, the champion, who was delayed by a pit stop. The surprise of the race was Harry Schell, who flew to fourth in the Vanwall after an early delay.

Collins went into the British Grand Prix leading the championship from the

LEFT **CONGRATULATIONS, BRAVO: JUAN MANUEL FANGIO RECEIVES THE PLAUDITS AFTER WRAPPING UP HIS FOURTH WORLD TITLE WITH A GIFTED SECOND PLACE IN THE ITALIAN GRAND PRIX.**

consistent Behra and Fangio. His thunder at Silverstone was stolen by Hawthorn and Brooks, who led the field on the return of BRM. Both hit trouble early on, though. Then Moss and Roy Salvadori ran at the front until retiring, which allowed a rather fortunate Fangio to take the honours. Collins took over Alfonso de Portago's Lancia Ferrari and finished as runner-up, ahead of Behra.

Fangio was then an easy winner at the Nurburgring, while Collins was out of luck. With his own car retiring with a fuel leak, he took over de Portago's machine, but crashed out of the race.

A FINAL SORT-OUT

For the first time in several seasons the title fight went down to the wire, at the Italian Grand Prix. Fangio was well placed on 30 points, but Collins and Behra were eight behind – they could only take the title by winning the race and setting fastest lap with Fangio failing to score. Schell again surprised everyone by running at the front in the Vanwall and, when he retired, Moss, Fangio and Collins were left to fight it out. Fangio's

hopes faded with steering trouble, but he was saved when Collins – who could still have won the title – stopped and handed his car over to him. It was a gesture, which Fangio would never forget. Despite a scare when he ran out of fuel, Moss just held on from the Collins/Fangio Lancia Ferrari. With BRM and Vanwall having already shown well during the year, it was Connaught's turn to earn some success. Ron Flockhart took advantage of a high attrition rate to come home third. Further British success seemed just around the corner.

Left **THE TITLE DECIDER: FANGIO IS CHASED BY MOSS IN THE ITALIAN GRAND PRIX.**

Below left **A TRUE GENTLEMAN: PETER COLLINS SPURNED PERSONAL GLORY TO HELP FERRARI TEAM-MATE FANGIO TO HIS FOURTH TITLE.**

Right **MOSS'S MONACO MAGIC: STIRLING MOSS LED EACH OF THE 100 LAPS TO WIN AT MONACO FOR MASERATI.**

FANGIO'S FIFTH AND FINAL

Juan Manuel Fangio acquired his fifth and last World Championship title, this time for Maserati, but Stirling Moss and Vanwall were the true stars of a year during which the all-British team won three times as Ferrari struggled to keep up.

There was plenty of activity during the winter, the most notable news being Fangio's switch from Ferrari to Maserati. It was quite a coup for Maserati to entice the reigning champion back to drive its latest 250F model, and it proved to be an extremely wise choice for the great Argentinian. Meanwhile Moss, always keen to drive British cars wherever possible, headed to Vanwall. Indeed, he had already won the previous year's International Trophy for Tony Vandervell's promising concern. Mike Hawthorn continued to hop back and forth across the

English Channel, rejoining Ferrari for a third spell after a bad time with BRM. He teamed up with his great buddy Peter Collins, plus Luigi Musso and Eugenio Castellotti.

Once again Fangio won his home race in Argentina, heading a Maserati one-two-three-four finish made up by Jean Behra, Carlos Menditeguy and Harry Schell as the Ferrari challenge fell apart. Vanwall did not enter the race, and Moss had trouble at the start in his borrowed Maserati, then set fastest lap as he recovered to seventh. After the Argentinian Grand Prix, the talented Castellotti lost his life in a testing crash at Modena, and he was replaced by Maurice Trintignant. Then the enigmatic Alfonso de Portago was killed in the Mille Miglia. It was a bleak period indeed for Enzo Ferrari.

There was a spectacular pile-up at the

start of the Monaco Grand Prix, which eliminated Moss, Collins and Hawthorn, letting Fangio score an easy win. Brooks took his Vanwall to second after extricating it from the mess. Star of the race was Jack Brabham, who got his underpowered Cooper up to third before the fuel pump failed, then pushed it home sixth. Sam Hanks finally came good to win the Indianapolis 500, a race he had been trying to win since 1940, and promptly retired.

BULLSEYE FOR BRITAIN
The French Grand Prix returned to Rouen, and Fangio stormed to victory ahead of Ferrari men Musso, Collins and Hawthorn. The next race was at Aintree, and it proved to be a memorable day for Britain. After Moss retired his leading Vanwall, he took over the sixth-placed car of team-mate Brooks. The opposition

LEFT **MAKING THEIR POINT: SHE'S SMILING, BUT FRIENDS AND FORMER COLLEAGUES JUAN MANUEL FANGIO
AND STIRLING MOSS LOOK AS THOUGH THEY'RE NOT QUITE IN AGREEMENT.**

49

1957

BELOW LEFT BRITISH DOUBLE: TONY BROOKS CONGRATULATES STIRLING MOSS AFTER THEIR COMBINED WIN IN THE BRITISH GRAND PRIX AT AINTREE.

BELOW RIGHT GIVING CHASE: TONY BROOKS'S VANWALL HEADS OUT OF THE STATION HAIRPIN IN THE WAKE OF FANGIO'S MASERATI.

BOTTOM EPIC VICTORY: JUAN MANUEL FANGIO STORMS AFTER THE FERRARIS TO WIN THE GERMAN GRAND PRIX AT THE NURBURGRING IN HIS MASERATI.

Below **LONG WAY HOME: STIRLING MOSS TRIUMPHED FOR VANWALL IN THE ONE-OFF RACE ON THE ULTRA-LONG PESCARA ROAD COURSE.**

Right **MASSED RANKS: THE FIELD LINES UP FOR THE START OF THE ITALIAN GRAND PRIX AT MONZA.**

wilted, and when Behra blew his engine – and Hawthorn punctured on the debris – Moss swept home to a wonderful victory.

Vanwall was out of luck in the German Grand Prix, with both cars suffering suspension problems. But the race is remembered as one of the all-time classics, as Fangio came storming back to win after an over-long fuel stop, catching up with Collins and Hawthorn and then leaving them in his wake.

Because the Belgian and Dutch Grands Prix at Spa-Francorchamps and Zandvoort respectively had been cancelled, an extra Italian race was added to the series. This was the Pescara Grand Prix, held on a 16-mile circuit of public roads on Italy's Adriatic coast. Enzo Ferrari, supposedly opposed to Italian road circuits after the Mille Miglia disaster, did not enter Hawthorn and Collins, but loaned a "private" car to Musso. He was in front for the first couple of laps, before Moss took the lead and scored his second victory of the year. Fangio finished second, and sealed his fifth and final title.

MOSS FOR VANWALL

The Monza finale, no longer using the banking, saw a spectacular fight between Vanwall and Maserati. Moss headed Fangio home, with promising German Wolfgang von Trips upholding Ferrari honour in third. It was a lame season for the Prancing Horse, as Ferrari had not won a race all year, and clearly needed to resolve that situation in 1958. The job was made easier when Maserati withdrew its works team at the end of the season, citing a lack of funds.

BRITISH BREAKTHROUGH

Mike Hawthorn pipped Stirling Moss to become the first British World Champion, but his success was overshadowed by the death of his team-mate and friend, Peter Collins. Hawthorn then elected to retire from racing, only to lose his life in a road accident before the start of the 1959 season.

The departure of the works Maserati team from Formula One was a major blow to the World Championship, although the cars survived in the hands of privateers. The marque's withdrawal coincided with the retirement of Juan Manuel Fangio. The five-time World Champion would run just a couple of 1958 Grands Prix before calling it a day.

Ferrari abandoned its old Lancia-based 801s, and had a new model, the 246 Dino, with Hawthorn, Collins and Luigi Musso

the star drivers. Moss, Tony Brooks and Stuart Lewis-Evans stayed with Vanwall, while John Cooper mounted a serious effort with Jack Brabham and Roy Salvadori as drivers. Rob Walker entered a private Cooper-Climax for Maurice Trintignant, while Jean Behra and Harry Schell headed a revived BRM effort.

BRITISH GLORY
The season started off with a surprise at the Argentinian Grand Prix. Most of the British teams were absent, including Vanwall, so Moss was free to replace Trintignant in Rob Walker's little rear-engined Cooper. He won the race with a canny display of tactical driving, although his tyres were all but worn out by the end. In the following Grand Prix, at Monaco, Trintignant was at the wheel of Rob Walker's car and, amazingly, he

scored his second success in the street race as, once again, the faster cars hit trouble, including Moss's Vanwall.

The British run of success continued in the Dutch Grand Prix at Zandvoort, where Vanwall swept the front row. Moss won the race, while the BRMs of Schell and Behra finished second and third after the other Vanwalls had retired. Salvadori's Cooper came home fourth, and even the best Ferrari – that of fifth-placed Hawthorn – had a British driver.

Good fortune smiled on Jimmy Bryan as he avoided numerous accidents that marred the Indianapolis 500 to win America's biggest race. The Belgian Grand Prix was next and Brooks came good for Vanwall, giving the team its second win on the trot, followed home by Hawthorn and Lewis-Evans.

Ferrari had been without a win since

LEFT **BRITISH BULLDOG: MIKE HAWTHORN BECAME THE FIRST BRITISH WORLD CHAMPION AFTER WINNING A THREE-WAY
BATTLE WITH FELLOW BRITONS STIRLING MOSS AND TONY BROOKS. HE WAS NOT TO LIVE LONG TO ENJOY IT.**

53

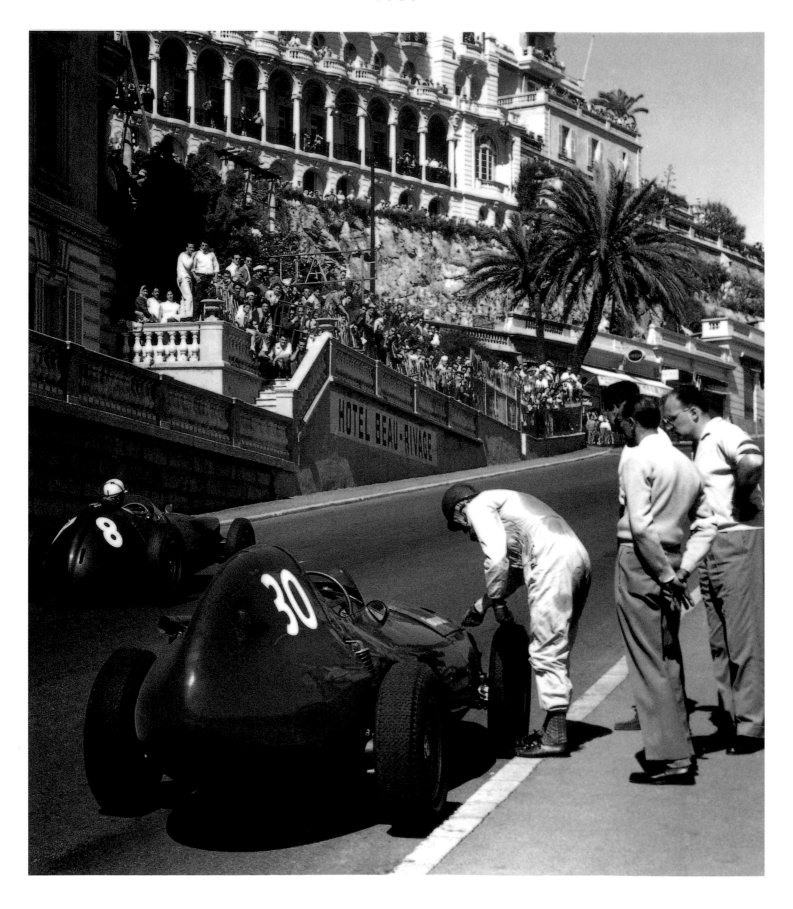

LEFT IT'S BROKEN MISTER: TONY BROOKS EXAMINES HIS VANWALL AT MONACO AS SCHELL'S BRM MOTORS BY.

RIGHT FINAL ADVICE: STIRLING MOSS CHATS WITH THE VANWALL CREW BEFORE THE START OF THE MOROCCAN GRAND PRIX. HIS WIN WAS NOT ENOUGH.

BELOW LEFT THAT'S MORE LIKE IT: BROOKS HIT A WINNING VEIN WHEN HE LED THE WAY FOR VANWALL AT SPA-FRANCORCHAMPS.

BELOW RIGHT CHAMPION'S DRIVE: SECOND PLACE AT CASABLANCA IN HIS FERRARI WAS SUFFICIENT FOR MIKE HAWTHORN TO BECOME BRITAIN'S FIRST WORLD CHAMPION.

1956, but the waiting ended at Reims where Hawthorn scored what would be his only victory of the season. However, there was no celebrating as team-mate Musso, who had qualified second, was killed in the race. Fangio ducked out of the World Championship, after finishing fourth in his last race.

FERRARI IN THE GROOVE

At the British Grand Prix, back at Silverstone, it was the turn of Collins to win for Ferrari, with Hawthorn taking second. But a fortnight later tragedy struck again when Collins lost his life in the German Grand Prix. Brooks went on to score a hollow victory a long way clear of the Coopers of Salvadori and Trintignant. Moss had retired while leading at the Nurburgring, and he gained some revenge at the first ever Portuguese Grand Prix at Oporto, winning from pole position with Hawthorn second.

A GRAND FINALE

The title battle went to the final round – the Moroccan Grand Prix on the outskirts of Casablanca. In one of the closest points battles ever, Moss led all the way and set fastest lap. However, with Brooks blowing up, Hawthorn eased into second place, which was all he required to take the crown. It was a terrible day for both Vanwall and Stirling, made worse when Lewis-Evans crashed and later succumbed to his injuries. The only consolation for Vanwall was the inaugural constructors' title.

After quitting the sport while at his peak, Mike Hawthorn was ironically killed in a tragic road accident in January of 1959. He was just 29 years old.

BRABHAM MOVES UP

The old order changed for ever when Jack Brabham took his Cooper-Climax to the 1959 championship. It was the first title for a rear-engined car, marking a triumph of handling over old-fashioned power. The revolution started here.

The big news of the winter was the surprise withdrawal of the Vanwall team, just as it had reached full competitiveness. However, Cooper, BRM and Lotus upheld British honour. After the previous year's tragedies there were big changes at Ferrari as Tony Brooks joined from Vanwall and Jean Behra moved across from BRM, while Phil Hill – an occasional Ferrari driver in 1958 – went full time. Stirling Moss kept his options open, and appeared in both Rob Walker's Cooper-Climax and a BRM, in the colours of the British Racing Partnership.

SUCCESS FOR COOPER-CLIMAX

In previous years, Climax had given away a few cubic centimetres of engine capacity, but the company's latest engine was a full 2.5-litre unit. Although still a little down on power compared with its rivals, the Cooper chassis' handling proved vastly superior to even up the balance of overall performance.

With the Argentinian Grand Prix cancelled, the World Championship opened at Monaco. Behra's Ferrari led until retiring, and then Moss's nimble Cooper expired, leaving Brabham to score his first win in the works Cooper ahead of Tony Brooks's Ferrari. Meanwhile, the Indianapolis 500 enjoyed one of its most competitive runnings ever, as Rodger Ward fought with Jim Rathmann, Johnny Thomson and Pat Flaherty before winning.

BRM WINS AT LAST

The Dutch Grand Prix saw a major surprise as Jo Bonnier notched up BRM's first victory – nine years after the marque took its first, stumbling steps. The bearded Swede had to work hard to hold off the Coopers, and was helped when Moss retired.

Ferrari fought back with a fine win for Brooks at Reims, team-mate Phil Hill following him home. Moss was in the BRP BRM on this occasion, and was battling for second when he went off the road. Three marques had won the first three races, but Cooper was back in the frame at the British Grand Prix as Brabham scored his second win, ahead of Moss's BRM which crossed the line just ahead of young Kiwi Bruce McLaren in the second works Cooper. Ferrari did not turn up at Aintree, blaming Italian industrial action.

LEFT **THE FACE OF A CHAMPION: JACK BRABHAM SCORED TWO WINS FOR COOPER AS HE PROPELLED THE BRITISH MARQUE AHEAD OF ITS MORE TRADITIONAL RIVALS.**

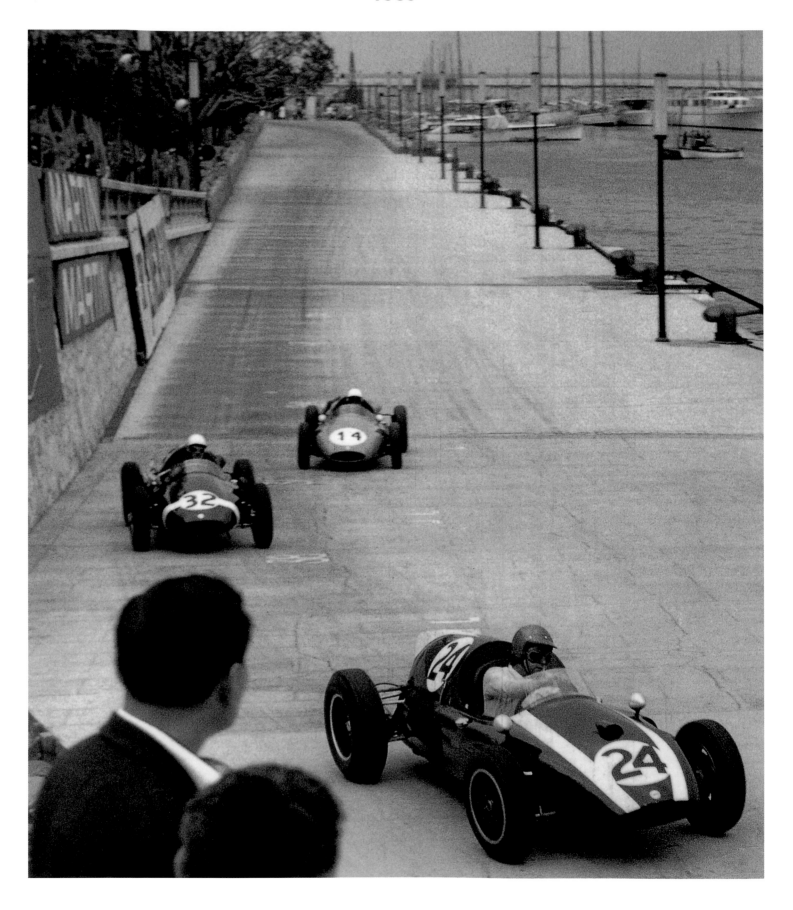

For the first and only time the German Grand Prix was held on the daunting, banked Avus circuit in Berlin and, uniquely, the result was an aggregate of two 30-lap heats. Missing Aintree had obviously done Ferrari some good, for Brooks dominated the event. But, as at Reims the year before, Ferrari's celebration was muted by tragedy. Veteran Behra, who had been a mainstay of the championship since its inception, died after a crash in the sports car support race, just one race after quitting the team to race his own Porsche.

BRABHAM CLOSES IN

Moss had to wait until the Portuguese Grand Prix to pick up his first win of the year in Rob Walker's Cooper. Brabham crashed out, but still led the championship as the circus moved to the penultimate race at Monza. Moss won again, ahead of Hill, while third place for Brabham kept his title challenge alive.

It was then a full three months before the final race, the first ever US Grand Prix, and the only one to be held on the Sebring airfield track in Florida – home of the famous 12 hours sports car race. Moss could still lift the crown and, after taking pole position, he was leading comfortably when his gearbox failed. Brabham ran out of fuel and had to push his car home in fourth place, but the title was his come what may. A surprise win went to his team-mate McLaren, who, at 22 became the youngest Grand Prix winner – a record which still stands. Trintignant was second in another Cooper, ahead of Brooks, with Cooper thus taking the second constructor's cup.

LEFT **COOPERS IN CONTROL: JACK BRABHAM LEADS THE WAY AT MONACO WITH MAURICE TRINTIGNANT (32) HEADING FOR THIRD IN ROB WALKER'S COOPER.**

ABOVE RIGHT **BRM WINS AT LAST: JO BONNIER HOLDS OFF MASTEN GREGORY'S COOPER EN ROUTE TO WINNING AT ZANDVOORT.**

RIGHT **THE PRICE OF GLORY: JACK BRABHAM IS EXHAUSTED AFTER PUSHING HIS COOPER HOME AT SEBRING.**

THE SIXTIES

JOHN SURTEES

Honours: WORLD CHAMPION 1964
Grand Prix record: 111 STARTS, 6 WINS

Asking a motorcycle racer what he thinks of Formula One will elicit an interesting response, particularly if that racer is a seven-time World Motorcycle Champion. However, though John Surtees fits that bill, he is also the obvious person to talk about Formula One in the 1960s as he turned from two-wheeled competition to four and became World Champion in 1964, a unique feat, before going on to form his own racing team.

"I look upon the 1960s in a number of ways," says John. "It was a time of total mismanagement by the governing body as the movement from the 2.5-litre formula to a 1.5-litre formula and then to a 3-litre formula was ludicrous. Secondly, it was the decade of the two Cs: the Climax and the Cosworth, as they governed everything."

Armed with his successes with MV Agusta, John looked at cars in 1960 after some promising tests in 1959 and it went from there: "Apart from watching practice at Monza," John explains, "I'd never seen a car race before I sat in a Formula Junior at Goodwood for my first race. Indeed, the only four-wheeled experience I had before that was driving around Goodwood in first an Aston Martin DBR1 sportscar then in one of the three recently retired Vanwall Formula One cars and a couple of laps in the Aston Martin Formula One car.

"I was a part-timer in 1960, as I was still involved in my motorcycle career and came on the World Championship scene after only three drives – one in Ken Tyrrell's Formula Junior Cooper in which I came second behind Jimmy Clark's works Lotus at Goodwood, another at Oulton Park in my own Formula Two Cooper when I was second this time behind Innes Ireland's works Lotus and then a third in which I set a lap record at Aintree – as Colin Chapman asked me to join Lotus after a test at Silverstone. So I drove in the International Trophy at Silverstone when an oil leak forced me out. Then I went to Monaco for my World Championship debut. This was a totally new experience as I'd never ridden at Monaco, and one major difference when adapting to cars was getting organised to take slow corners. Sadly, we were plagued by gearbox problems.

"The British Grand Prix at Silverstone was next and I came second. Then came the Portuguese Grand Prix at Oporto where I started on pole, set fastest lap and led until I made a mistake passing Stirling Moss when I got my wheels caught in the tramlines. He'd just come from the pits and I suppose I was a bit wound-up as certain people – but not Stirling – were less than happy that I'd joined the four-wheeled scene. I rounded out the year with the

American Grand Prix when after a bad start I tried too hard to get back to the front, spun and took out my team-mate Jimmy Clark.

"Chapman could see that I didn't have much experience, but the fact that the first time I sat in a car I was able to go as quickly as anyone had been in that car was good enough for him. And that's why he asked me to be his team leader for 1961. When he asked me who I wanted as my team-mate, I said Jimmy. Colin said that this was fine as he'd fixed for Innes (Ireland) to drive a UDT Laystall Lotus. Innes then ranted at me down the 'phone, so we went to see Colin to sort it out, there was a big row and I walked away from Lotus, which wasn't the best thing to do with no top-level drives available. And so I joined Cooper instead.

"It's strange when I look back, for in that Lotus 18 I was probably sitting in the most competitive car of my career. The reliability wasn't good, but that aside there was no reason that I couldn't have won three of the four Grands Prix I contested."

This was a time of rapid change in Formula One, and nowhere were the changes greater than in the hotbed of the British teams: "The constructors had modernised Dr Porsche's concepts from the days of his Auto Union racers and hadn't gone along with the standard concept of what a racing car should be. So, what John Cooper had started with Jack Brabham, who provided a nice balance and was very feet on the ground, was followed by the more gifted Chapman.

"The arrival of the Climax engine signalled a new way of thinking. It was engineered so that it had a similar power output to its rivals, but so that it had very useable power which allowed drivers to adjust the car's handling. And this is what set the scene for the 1960s.

"Because of indecision about what format Formula One would adopt in 1961, people weren't prepared for the 1.5-litre formula. You had the Climax still, but they weren't getting a lot of development into them as Climax was working on its V8, while Ferrari had a lot of experience with its V6 and made a 1.5-litre version of it that worked well. The Ferrari chassis wouldn't have been as effective as the Lotus or the Cooper, but when you have a 1.5-litre formula it doesn't give drivers the same amount of opportunity to grab back time." John's best result in 1961 was a pair of fifths in his Yeoman Credit Cooper. For 1962, John insisted on joining a works outfit and thus raced a works Lola under the Bowmaker Racing banner, twice coming second. He also won national races and several in the Tasman series.

"When I went to Ferrari in 1963," John continues, "that was largely due to an engine factor as we'd had the Lola in its first year and had been extremely unfortunate not to win at least one Grand Prix as it broke a few times. Then it was announced that Climax would concentrate on Lotus and Cooper in 1963. Drivers at BRM didn't like the idea of me going there, so I joined Ferrari.

"I had been asked to go to Ferrari in 1961, and had talked to Enzo Ferrari and Carlo Chiti, but felt I wasn't ready for them as they were riding high and overestimating what they could do. They asked again at the end of 1962, when they were down, and from what I'd seen in bike racing I thought this was the best time to join an Italian outfit.

"When I arrived at Ferrari, it was virtually a new team as Chiti and many of the team had left for ATS. Luckily Franco Rocchi had stayed as project engineer, while Mauro Forghieri joined as a co-ordinator. We found bits and pieces of the 1962 car and tested

these with bits we reckoned we needed then took it from there. Michael May was brought in to work on the V6's direct injection to up its power, with the promise that a V8 and a V12 would follow.

"We had a new team manager, Eugenio Dragoni, a maverick who was a link man to Mr Ferrari and, as it subsequently turned out, also to Fiat. We had a 'cat and mouse' game from the very beginning, meaning you had to watch over your shoulder.

"The car was very driveable in a Cooper sort of way rather than in a Lotus sort of way as it could be driven hard and was forgiving, but there were continuous troubles with changing characteristics of the engine, because the fuel injection was too sensitive. To go along and meter it for a whole speed range was very difficult and changing ambient temperatures would affect the way it ran. We agreed that I should see Bosch about their fuel injection. This coincided with the non-championship race at Solitude, just down the road from their base. It should have been our first win of the year, as it was fantastic in the wet, but it dried and Jimmy Clark pipped me. However, I could use the throttle more and be sure it would respond. So we were in good spirits for the next race at the Nurburgring. And we had the edge all meeting, enabling me to be the hare to Jimmy for a change." This was John's first win for Ferrari and boosted his standing within a team that was becoming increasingly important to him.

"When I joined Ferrari, I got on well with the Old Man and so thought that it would be my life," John explains. "But to have done justice to myself I should have behaved as Jackie Stewart did and made sure that I only put my seat in the best possible car. However, that would have meant going back to Chapman and saying that when I turned him down over Innes that I was wrong. Secondly, I enjoyed being part of a team like Ferrari and hauling it back to success. And I liked the environment and the people.

"The V8 came and it was a political thing which I questioned, as all of Ferrari's working had been with 12-cylinder engines. I wanted to know if Ferrari was going to make up enough ground to make a V8 as good as a Climax. But the deal with Fiat was beckoning and the V8 was something like a commercial project that was partly sponsored by Fiat. And again it had direct injection and was a little heavy. The car handled well, but it wasn't as efficient as the Lotus. You were able to push on, but we were lacking that vital mid-range power, an area that British engine builders seemed to concentrate on. On occasions when the atmospheric conditions were right, we were on par with the Climaxes, but it wasn't consistent." However, John won the German and Italian Grands Prix and this was enough to edge out Clark and Graham Hill in a last-round battle for the world title in Mexico.

Staying on for 1965, John was not impressed that Ferrari started off with the V8. This is why: "The only time I felt we could dominate was in the Italian Grand Prix at Monza when Rocchi had come up with a revised cylinder-head for the Flat-12 and it really sung. But I lost the clutch at the start... Unfortunately, I wasn't to drive it again as I had an accident in a CanAm race at Mosport Park. This was a great shame, as I was really looking forward to going to the American and Mexican Grands Prix on an equal footing." John's injuries were life-threatening and he didn't return to driving until 1966.

"I used to return to England to liaise with manufacturers like Lucas and Girling, and I asked Enzo if he minded if I got involved with the Lola CanAm project as I was worried that we were losing out to the gathering momentum of what was happening in England where all the manufacturers were building on each other which is why the industry is so strong here today. The Old Man said that I could try, but with one of our Ferraris rather than with Lola. So I took one of our old sportscars, stripped it, went to the States and did a few CanAm races. I then told him that the engine was too small and the car too heavy. So it was agreed that I would be allowed to stay in communication with other manufacturers. It was very positive, but it was partly the beginning of the end.

"Without going into details as to why I left, part of the reason that Dragoni had been trying to boot me out was that I had upset Forghieri by contradicting him about what worked on the car and what didn't. Secondly, although he wasn't involved in the race programme, I crossed swords with Mike Parkes. As he wanted to get into Formula One and he made a ready ally for Dragoni.

"When I was convalescing, I went out at Modena with what would have been my car for the Tasman series if I hadn't injured myself. This was a Formula One chassis to which we fitted a 2.4-litre V6. I was winched in and it flew. Then came the big day, the new 3-litre Formula One, new for 1966. Everyone said we'd shine,

but our original project engine hadn't been proceeded with and Ferrari had produced a short-stroke version of the sportscar engine which weighed 100lb too much and produced 280bhp rather than 320. I went out and found it 2.5 seconds slower per lap than with the 2.4-litre V6. The engine probably had the same power as Jack Brabham's Repco which was fitted in a car that was 100lb lighter...

"Anyhow, I said that I'd race the 2.4-litre Formula One car, not the 3-litre V12. But they asked me to try the 3-litre in the non-championship race at Syracuse. So I did so and luckily it was a bit wet. I pushed like hell and only just managed to beat (Lorenzo) Bandini who had the 2.4. They asked me to try the 3-litre again in the International Trophy at Silverstone, which I did. And I was passed as though I was standing still by Brabham and by Jackie Stewart's 2.3-litre BRM. Monaco was the year's first World Championship race and I told them that I wanted to race the more agile 2.4-litre car. Furthermore, I told them our V12 wouldn't last and that we were marginal on the gearbox. However, Dragoni said that Ferrari sold 12-cylinder road cars, so I would race the 3-litre V12. I duly led the race until, guess what, the gearbox packed up. I wasn't happy, especially as Lorenzo got to drive the 2.4 and pressed Stewart for victory..

"At Spa, I still had to use the 3-litre, but Rocchi modified the cylinder head to boost power and it made such a difference that I got pole. Then it poured as we came down the hill towards Burnenville. I drove off line there to avoid trouble and the next lap saw that there had been mayhem. I went on to win after a dice with Jochen Rindt's Cooper. The mechanics were delighted of course, but there was not a word of congratulation from Dragoni. People forget, too, that this had been a difficult time for me, coming back from my CanAm shunt.

"However, it all came to a head at Le Mans. We were facing a threat from Ford and the plan was for me to go off like a hare and have the Fords give chase, hoping they would break. However, as I got ready, Dragoni told me that Ludovico Scarfiotti would start the race as his uncle, Fiat boss Gianni Agnelli, was there to watch. Ludovico was going to be a second and a half off my pace and this would blow our plan, so I was furious and told them to forget it and quit.

"So there I was leading the championship with no car to drive. I then finished the season in a Cooper-Maserati. And, if I hadn't had a gear strip at the Nurburgring when I finished second, or the bag tank hadn't popped at Monza, or I hadn't been hit by Peter Arundell at Watkins Glen, then it was quite possible that I could have stolen the title.

"Dragoni finally brought out the proper 3-litre engine – the one we were supposed to have at the start – in time for the Italian Grand Prix, and it flew. But it was a one-off success.

"I rounded out the year with a win in Mexico, but it was here that I discovered that Maserati were doubtful about continuing, even though they eventually did. Shell then asked if I would go back to Ferrari, for 1967, but this wasn't on. I had a slim chance of racing a Lola powered by a BMW V8. Then Mr Nakamura of Honda said that Honda would only stay in racing if I joined them and helped them run the team. I'd seen what Honda had done with its 1.5-litre Formula One engine and in motorcycle racing, so

I decided to give it a chance.

"However, all normal reckoning of what teams were doing that year was affected by the arrival of the Ford Cosworth DFV. This had an even bigger impact than the Climax, as the Climax was more widely available. The Cosworth on the other hand, started only with Lotus."

The first Honda John drove was overweight, but a lighter car-built in association with Lola made its debut in the Italian Grand Prix and John won first time out...

"Sadly, the best years of my racing potential were lost in this period. But I find it a lot easier to live with today as I'm sure that if the programme as it was laid down had proceeded, you would have seen Honda challenging for the title in 1969. You only need to need to look at the overweight 1968 car to see that if the continuous development programme had happened – a lightweight 12-cylinder coupled with a lighter chassis – then it would have been a winner. However, Mr Honda's politics took it over and the impractical air-cooled V8 RA302 was made instead." A disaster, this led to Honda quitting at the end of the year.

"I had no intention of forming my own team, but three things caused it and it all came at the wrong time. Firstly, I had the experience of joining BRM in 1969 at a period when it would have been best forgotten. Secondly, I agreed to get involved in a ridiculous CanAm project with Jim Hall. Thirdly, I agreed to find a project for actor James Garner who wanted to steal a march on Steve McQueen and become a team owner. Between the dreadful political scene at BRM and the situation with Hall's car it nearly brought me to the point of a mental breakdown.

"While I was in America, I'd been approached to find a car for Garner, and I found that Len Terry had a car that he'd designed. So I'd virtually put the deal together, but it didn't exactly work when we tested it and then it broke. Secondly, Garner quit. We were thus faced with sinking our losses, but I decided we'd sort it and after a major rehash it became the Surtees TS5 which ended up winning a number of Formula 5000 races in David Hobbs's hands. We decided to make a few more to amatise costs, so I sent Hobbs over to the US to try and drum up custom. And we sold all the cars we could make after he finished second in the British and American championships. But when I went down with pneumonia at the time of the US Grand Prix I decided that enough was enough and that I would make my own Formula One car. And this, the TS7, ran in 1970.

"The only reason teams like mine could come into existence was because of Cosworth. Look at the top teams today, almost all are there because of Cosworth. It was a wonderful product for people to be able to build cars around and to be able to compete with the world's best. Only Renault have come close to making this sort of impact since."

Despite winning the non-championship Gold Cup in 1970 and 1971, John's driving career came to a close in 1972, with John rounding out his career with wins in the Formula Two races at Fuji and Imola in a year when fellow fomrer motorcycle racer Mike Hailwood guided Surtees to the European Formula Two crown. The team continued in Formula One until the end of 1978, albeit without conspicuous success.

When asked to pick the great drivers from the 1960s, John offers these views: "Comparing drivers of any age is never easy as you had different characters in different equipment. But there were the constants. You could be sure that Jimmy Clark would be quick. He wasn't the world's most aggressive driver, the most forceful or necessarily the fastest. But he was able to come together with the right machine and particularly with Chapman to form a formidable combination. Jimmy was fully appreciative that if you pushed a Lotus too hard it would fail, so he got into the groove as he was able to understand how to get the most out of them.

"However, you mustn't overlook that when I came into Formula One that the most competitive driver was Stirling Moss. He wasn't necessarily the fastest around, either. But there was one thing about Stirling that even if he'd had a pitstop and was out of the reckoning, he'd have a go.

"Jack Brabham would also always have a go, too. He was sometimes travelling more sideways than forwards, but it was partly due to the fact that he was in Coopers. Dan Gurney was another who was quick.

"Then there was Graham Hill, who I always looked on as steady, able to put it all together and relate to his machine well. He wasn't as aggressive as the others, or as fast, but he was someone who could produce. In many ways, there's an awful lot between Graham and Damon that's similar.

"There are always drivers and racers at any time and Jimmy was a driver. He was just on the edge of being a racer, but not consistently. Jack and Dan were racers. Then, later on, you had people like Rindt who were drivers but became racers. Stewart was a very competent driver who came together with Ken Tyrrell and they made a formidable set-up with Cosworth. I always looked on him as a percentage driver who at times surpassed himself, such as when he won at the Nurburgring in the wet in 1968.

"I have a lot of respect for Chris Amon, but he was too easily affected by what happened around him. While I had a lot of time for Lorenzo Bandini who was quicker than people appreciated and I think Ferrari was wrong to put him in the position of having so much responsibility.

"It's crazy to compare people across the ages, but I loved to watch Ayrton Senna. At Donington on that wet day in 1993, I wasn't only interested in watching his progress but also in listening to how he used the throttle. Michael Schumacher's drive at Spa in 1998 was also wonderful. They are real people at work, treading on that narrow line between keeping it on the road and not. It was a pleasure, too, to watch the progress of Mika Hakkinen when he came of age in 1998.

"Formula One today is wonderful. Think of the amount of money put into those cars and what it has achieved in performance with safety. A purist might say that it would be nice to get rid of all the driver aids, but you can't stand still: Formula One must be the pinnacle. Sure, other forms of racing can be controlled to keep costs in check, but Formula One must always be coming up with innovations."

RIGHT: **SURTEES RACES HIS BOWMAKER LOLA DOWNHILL INTO ROUEN'S NOUVEAU MONDE HAIRPIN IN THE 1962 FRENCH GRAND PRIX.**

BRABHAM RESISTS MOSS

Jack Brabham claimed his second consecutive World Championship for Cooper, with Lotus emerging as a major force. Yet, but for a mid-season accident putting him out for several races, Stirling Moss might have won that elusive title.

By 1960 the rear-engined machines were dominant. For one last year, though, Ferrari stuck with its front-engined D246 and won the Italian Grand Prix – but only because the British teams boycotted the event. Colin Chapman's Lotus team had been in Grand Prix racing for two years with very little success, but all that was to change with the new Lotus 18, its first rear-engined model.

BRM also had a new rear-engined car, which had debuted at Monza the previous year. Jo Bonnier stayed on, joined by Graham Hill from Lotus and American Dan Gurney from Ferrari. A further American,

Phil Hill and Wolfgang von Trips remained with Ferrari, while Brabham and Bruce McLaren maintained their successful partnership at Cooper.

McLaren won the Argentinian Grand Prix and Cliff Allison did well to get his Ferrari home second. Bonnier and Moss (still in Rob Walker's old Cooper) had both led before retiring. Allison was then injured in practice at Monaco, breaking his arm when he was flung from his Ferrari and thus ending his season. Meanwhile, Moss got his hands on the new Lotus, and won in fine style in the rain ahead of McLaren and Phil Hill. Once again, Bonnier's BRM led before retiring, while a notable newcomer was multiple motorcycle world champion John Surtees in a works Lotus.

Rodger Ward and Jim Rathmann did battle again in the Indianapolis 500, this time with Rathmann coming out on top

after the latter's tyres went off with three laps to go.

Brabham had failed to score in either of the first two Grands Prix, but he bounced back by winning the Dutch Grand Prix. Innes Ireland guided his Lotus to second ahead of Graham Hill. And for the second race in a row Chapman gave a first chance to a future world champion. At Monaco it had been Surtees and in Holland it was a young Scot called Jim Clark who was battling for fourth when the gearbox broke.

DISASTER IN BELGIUM

The Belgian Grand Prix was one of the blackest weekends in the history of the World Championship. During practice Moss crashed heavily, breaking his legs. Then two young Britons, Chris Bristow and Alan Stacey, were killed in separate accidents during the race. Brabham and

LEFT **ALL SMILES: JACK BRABHAM HAD EVERY REASON TO BE HAPPY IN 1960 AS HE TOOK FIVE WINS ON HIS WAY TO A SECOND TITLE.**

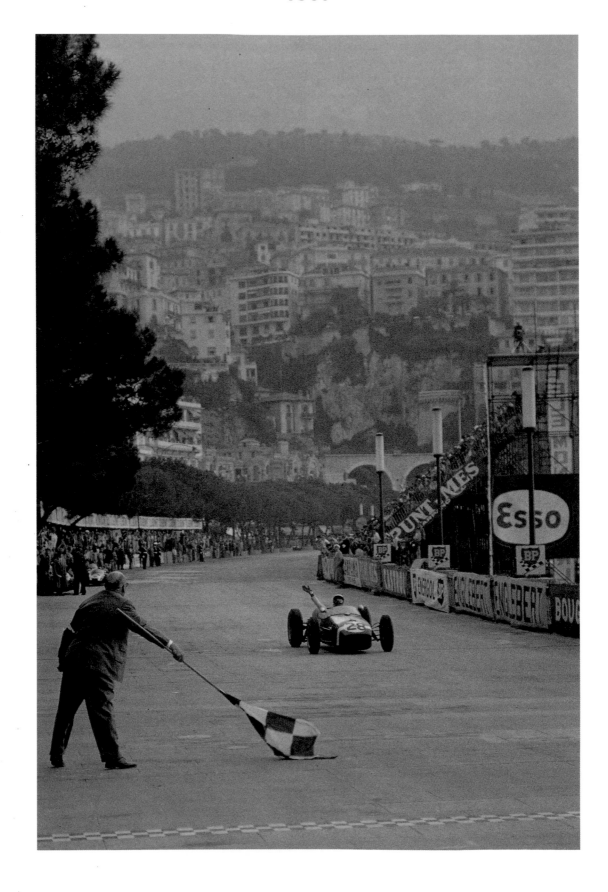

McLaren went on to score a one-two for Cooper, but only after Hill's BRM blew up when second.

At Reims Brabham took a third consecutive win, and on this fast track the front-engined Ferraris of Phil Hill and von Trips gave him a hard time until they broke. Graham Hill was then the star at the British Grand Prix at Silverstone. He stalled on the line, and drove superbly through to the lead before spinning off. Thus Brabham was able to come through to score his fourth straight win, followed by the impressive Surtees and Ireland.

BRABHAM'S SECOND TITLE
Brabham scored a fifth win in Portugal, and with it clinched the title with two Grands Prix to run. After missing two races while his legs healed, Moss was back, and ran second before he had problems.

The Italian Grand Prix was a disappointment. The race was on Monza's banked track, and the British teams boycotted it on safety grounds. Bound by blood ties, Ferrari turned up in force, and Phil Hill scored a hollow victory.

The US Grand Prix moved from Sebring to Riverside in California for the one and only time, and Moss won there to nip past Ireland to be third overall, with the race marking the demise of the 2.5-litre formula which had seen the transition from domination by Mercedes to the success of the British rear-engined machines.

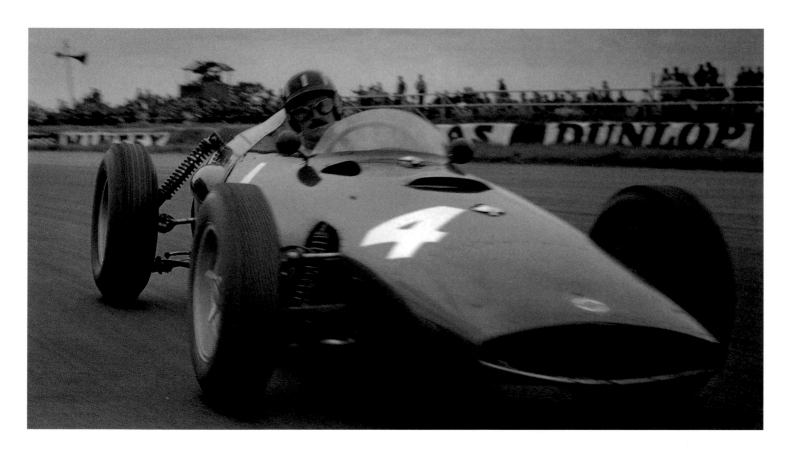

ABOVE **BRM'S STAR: GRAHAM HILL STARRED AT THE BRITISH GRAND PRIX BUT CAME AWAY WITH NOTHING.**

LEFT **A FIRST FOR LOTUS: STIRLING MOSS SCORES LOTUS'S FIRST WIN IN ROB WALKER'S CAR IN MONACO.**

RIGHT **MAIDEN POLE: SURTEES (RIGHT) SITS ON POLE FOR THE FIRST TIME, WITH GURNEY AND BRABHAM ALONGSIDE IN OPORTO.**

FERRARI'S BITTERSWEET YEAR

Ferrari was better prepared than anybody else for the new formula, and dominated the season. Phil Hill took the title, but in the most tragic of circumstances after his teammate Wolfgang von Trips lost his life at Monza.

It was all change for 1961 with the introduction of a 1.5-litre formula. The British manufacturers had been slow to respond, but not so Ferrari. Effectively sacrificing the previous season, the Italian team had developed a rear-engined car, dubbed the "sharknose" – and a new V6 engine. Climax and BRM lagged behind, so much so that the only engine available for the British teams was the four-year-old 1475cc Climax Formula Two unit.

PORSCHE JOINS IN

While von Trips, Phil Hill and fellow American Richie Ginther were in the lucky position of driving the works Ferraris, welcome variety was provided by the arrival of Porsche. Already successful in Formula Two, the German marque signed Dan Gurney and Jo Bonnier from BRM. Lotus had an excellent new chassis, the 21, and the promising Jim Clark and Innes Ireland to drive it. BRM and Cooper used developments of their old cars, with Graham Hill and Tony Brooks leading the BRM attack, while once again Jack Brabham and Bruce McLaren teamed up at Cooper.

More than ever before, the still-uncrowned Stirling Moss had underdog status. Lotus refused to allow Rob Walker to buy a new Lotus 21, and he had to make do with the old 18 model. And yet in the season-opening Monaco Grand Prix Moss turned in one of the drives of his career to brilliantly beat the Ferraris of Ginther and Hill.

Ferrari took its revenge at the Dutch Grand Prix when von Trips scored his first win, with Hill right on his heels in second. The result was reversed in the Belgian Grand Prix, where Ferrari filled the first four places and Hill took his first win against a representative field, following that boycotted Monza race in 1960. Von Trips was followed across the finish line by Ginther and local driver Olivier Gendebien.

The French Grand Prix at Reims was a sensational race. Hill, Ginther and von Trips retired, and Giancarlo Baghetti – making his first start in a privately-entered Ferrari – pipped Gurney's Porsche to the chequered flag. Baghetti remains the only driver to have won on his Grand Prix debut.

LEFT FERRARI TO THE FORE: PHIL HILL HEADS VON TRIPS IN A THRILLING, CONSTANTLY-CHANGING BATTLE FOR THE LEAD OF THE BELGIAN GRAND PRIX.

BELOW LEFT FIRST-TIME WINNER: BAGHETTI RESISTS THE PORSCHES OF BONNIER AND GURNEY TO WIN ON HIS GRAND PRIX DEBUT AT REIMS.

RIGHT CLASSIC POSE: STIRLING MOSS WEARS A MASK OF CONCENTRATION AS HE GUIDES HIS ROB WALKER LOTUS TO VICTORY IN GERMANY.

It was back to normal at the British Grand Prix as von Trips, Hill and Ginther finished first, second and third in the rain at Aintree. Moss had tried to mix it with the Italian cars before his brakes failed, but then struck back at the Nurburgring. As at Monaco, he overcame his Lotus-Climax's power deficiency to beat Ferrari, heading home Hill and von Trips. The race was doubly good for Climax as its new V8 engine was finally ready and Jack Brabham had qualified on the outside of the front row but retired early on.

A FATAL VISIT TO MONZA
Nobody objected to the banked corners at Monza this time. Ironically the Italian Grand Prix, which should have seen the title fight between von Trips and Hill turned to tragedy as Clark and von Trips tangled at the end of the first lap, and the German was killed, along with 12 spectators. Almost unnoticed by stunned onlookers, Phil Hill won the race, and with it the title.

The US Grand Prix moved to a third new venue in as many years in the form of Watkins Glen in upstate New York. With Ferrari not entering in the wake of Monza, Moss and Brabham battled for the lead. When they both retired from the race, Ireland came through to score his one and only win, and the first for the works Lotus team. Gurney was second for the second race in succession, ahead of the BRM of Tony Brooks who announced his retirement, after a distinguished career which was often overshadowed by the heroic exploits of Moss and Hawthorn.

A DIFFERENT HILL

Ferrari's star faded in the most dramatic fashion, as BRM and Lotus battled it out for the World Championship and Graham Hill beat Jim Clark to claim his first world title at the beginning of another golden era for the British teams.

The biggest story of the 1962 season occurred, however, in a non-championship race at Goodwood on Easter Monday. Stirling Moss suffered multiple injuries when he crashed his Lotus head-on into an earth bank. Despite having been at the top of the sport for a decade, Moss had never landed the ultimate prize. And, although he was nursed back to health, after he tried a car again he decided to quit as he'd lost that vital edge.

In addition to this, reigning champions Ferrari self-destructed over the winter, as some of the top staff walked out.

However, the Italian team carried on with virtually unchanged cars and drivers Phil Hill and Giancarlo Baghetti. While promising new boys, Mexican Ricardo Rodriguez and Italian Lorenzo Bandini were also in the squad.

NEW BRM HORSES

BRM had a powerful new V8 engine for the 1962 season, and Graham Hill was joined by Richie Ginther, who had left Ferrari. Meanwhile, the Climax V8 looked good and was the choice of many top teams. Two-time World Champion Jack Brabham quit Cooper to design his own car – although he would start the year with a Lotus – so Bruce McLaren became Cooper's team leader.

Lotus had another new car, the 25, which featured a revolutionary monocoque chassis. Clark and Trevor Taylor were the works drivers. An interesting

newcomer was the Lola, entered by the Bowmaker team for John Surtees and Roy Salvadori, while Porsche had a new flat-eight engine for Dan Gurney and Jo Bonnier.

Unusually, the season opened with the Dutch Grand Prix in May, with Graham Hill scoring his first win, which was also the first for BRM since Bonnier's victory at the same track three years earlier. Taylor finished an encouraging second in only his second Grand Prix, ahead of Phil Hill. Then McLaren won at Monaco, chased home by Phil Hill in what was to prove the Ferrari driver's best race of the year.

The Belgian Grand Prix marked Clark's first win, the Lotus driver coming home ahead of Graham and Phil Hill.

Thus three marques had won the first three races, and it became four when

LEFT **A WINNING START: GRAHAM HILL STARTED THE SEASON IN STYLE BY WINNING THE DUTCH GRAND PRIX. HE WENT ON TO BECOME CHAMPION.**

Left **THE END OF A CAREER: STIRLING MOSS'S WRECKED LOTUS LIES TRACK-SIDE AFTER HE'D CRASHED OUT OF THE NON-CHAMPIONSHIP RACE AT GOODWOOD.**

Below **EMERGENCY ASSISTANCE: AN UNCONSCIOUS MOSS IS TENDED TO WHILE STILL IN HIS CAR AFTER HIS BONE-BREAKING CRASH AT GOODWOOD.**

Gurney gave Porsche its maiden victory at Rouen – but only after three leaders, Clark, Surtees and Graham Hill, had all retired.

Clark then became the first repeat winner, dominating the British Grand Prix at Aintree ahead of Surtees and McLaren. Surtees continued his good form at the Nurburgring, finishing in second place behind Graham Hill's BRM, and just ahead of Gurney's Porsche.

The Italian Grand Prix was the turning point in the title battle, for Graham Hill and Ginther gave BRM a one-two after a thrilling race, and Clark failed to finish. Clark then fought back in the US Grand Prix at Watkins Glen, heading Graham Hill home.

For the first time the finale was held at East London in South Africa, on December 29. Clark took pole position, and was leading the race until his engine failed. And through came Graham Hill to win and lift the championship crown. It was to be BRM's only success. McLaren finished second, and took third behind Clark in the points after a consistent season as Cooper's top man.

It had been a poor year for Ferrari, and the team did not even enter the two final races. To make matters worse, up-and-coming star driver Rodriguez, who had finished fourth in Belgium, was killed in practice for the non-championship Mexican Grand Prix. He was just 20 years of age.

LEFT **KIWI POWER: BRUCE McLAREN ON HIS WAY TO VICTORY IN MONACO.**

BELOW **A PORSCHE WINNER: DAN GURNEY RACED TO THE FRONT AT ROUEN AND GAVE PORSCHE ITS MAIDEN FORMULA ONE WIN.**

THE MAGIFICENT SEVEN

This World Championship proved to be a memorable one for Jim Clark and Lotus, for the uncannily talented Scot won seven races in all. It was simply the most devastating display of craftmanship by a single driver since Alberto Ascari's runaway success 11 years previously.

Absent from the tracks in the 1963 World Championship was the Porsche team, which had withdrawn to concentrate on sports car racing. The German marque would not return to Formula One for more than 20 years before coming back as an engine supplier. The Lotus, BRM and Cooper line-ups were unchanged but, as usual, the off-season had been busy. Having lost his Porsche ride, Dan Gurney teamed up with Jack Brabham to drive the double champion's own cars.

The promising Bowmaker/Lola team withdrew from Formula One, but the cars were not lost to the championship as they were bought by Reg Parnell for the extremely talented young New Zealander Chris Amon.

With Bowmaker out, John Surtees moved to Ferrari, where he joined Belgian Willy Mairesse who had shown flashes of promise in the past. The Ferrari management breakaway of the previous year had spawned a new team, ATS, and a pair of works Ferrari drivers, Phil Hill and Giancarlo Baghetti, both jumped ship. They would come to regret their decision as they failed to score a point between them.

CLARK FALLS AT THE FIRST
Clark led the opener at Monaco, but he retired when his gearbox broke. It was to be his only retirement in an exceptionally reliable year for Lotus. With Clark out,

Graham Hill and Richie Ginther scored a one-two for BRM. And this was to be the first of five successes in the principality for Graham.

Clark's luck changed in the Belgian Grand Prix, and he took a memorable win in the rain, ahead of Bruce McLaren and Gurney, the latter scoring the Brabham team's first top three finish.

It was the same story in the Dutch Grand Prix, where Clark led all the way to win from Gurney and Surtees, and at Reims, where even a misfire could not stop him from winning the French Grand Prix. Clark scored his fourth win in a row at Silverstone, while Surtees took second place after Graham Hill ran out of fuel on the last lap. Another motorcycle star trying four wheels was Mike Hailwood, who finished eighth.

Surtees had threatened to win for a couple of years, and he finally came good

LEFT **SUPER SCOT: JIM CLARK DOMINATED THE 1963 CHAMPIONSHIP, WINNING SEVEN RACES ON HIS WAY TO THE TITLE.**

A STUDY OF CONCENTRATION: GRAHAM HILL FOCUSES ON THE TRACK AHEAD WHILE HEADING FOR THE FIRST OF HIS FIVE WINS AT MONACO.

at the Nurburgring, scoring Ferrari's first success since the 1961 Italian Grand Prix. Clark took second, ahead of BRM's Ginther.

Ferrari had a new chassis ready for the Italian Grand Prix, one which owed a lot to Lotus thinking and was designed to accept the forthcoming 1964 spec V8 engine. Surtees duly battled with Clark for the lead until the overworked V6 gave up. Clark headed home Ginther and McLaren, and clinched the championship

– even though there were still three races to run.

HILL'S MIXED FORTUNES
Graham Hill had suffered from unreliability and sheer bad luck all year, but struck back as he headed Ginther and Clark home in the US Grand Prix. By this time BRM had reverted to using its 1962 model. Clark was stymied by a flat battery, had to start from the back and did

well to finish a lapped third.

The Mexican Grand Prix was part of the championship for the first time, and Clark scored his sixth win of the year. He then added a record seventh victory in South Africa in December to cap an amazing season. Brabham finished second in Mexico and then team-mate Gurney repeated the feat in South Africa, showing that "Black Jack" had got his sums right and would be a force to reckon with.

RIGHT AND THEY'RE OFF: JIM CLARK BLASTS AWAY FROM POLE AT REIMS, CHASED BY GRAHAM HILL (2) AND DAN GURNEY (8).

BOTTOM TWO-WHEELED CONVERT: JOHN SURTEES RACES HIS FERRARI TO SECOND AT SILVERSTONE. HE WAS TO WIN AT THE NURBURGRING.

THE HISTORY MAN

John Surtees made racing history when he became the first man to win a World Championship on both two wheels and four. In a thrilling finale, the motorcycle racing great in his Ferrari just outscored Graham Hill and Jim Clark.

Ferrari hopes looked to be on the up for 1964 as its new V8 engine was mated to the team's 156 chassis which had shown promise in the previous year's Italian Grand Prix. Surtees stayed on to lead the team alongside the highly-rated Lorenzo Bandini. Lotus produced an updated car for Clark, the 33. Peter Arundell was the team's new number two. Hill and Richie Ginther stayed on at BRM, and had a revised car, while Cooper tried desperately to keep up with the new monocoque technology, updating a Formula Three chassis.

HIGHS AND LOWS FOR CLARK

Clark started on a high by leading at Monaco, but he had to pit when his rear roll-bar broke. And so Hill and Ginther scored another one-two result for BRM and a late engine failure for Clark handed third place to team-mate Arundell. Clark made amends with a demonstration run to victory in the Dutch Grand Prix, while Surtees gave notice of Ferrari's championship intentions with second place, ahead of the newcomer Arundell.

The Brabham team did not fare well in the early races, but Dan Gurney led comfortably in the Belgian Grand Prix until running out of fuel with two laps to go. In a farcical turn of events, Graham Hill took the lead and suffered fuel pump failure, then Bruce McLaren also ran out of gas. This allowed a surprised Clark – who had made an early stop – to take vic-

tory. At least McLaren was able to secure the points for second, coasting across the finish line.

Gurney made amends in the French Grand Prix at Rouen by scoring a fine first victory for the Brabham team. Graham Hill pipped Brabham himself for third, while once again Clark led the early stages before his engine failed.

For the first time the British Grand Prix moved to Brands Hatch, and Clark kept up his tradition of winning at home. Hill was second and Surtees was happy to finish third after two consecutive retirements. Surtees then began his surge towards the title by winning ahead of Hill and Bandini at the Nurburgring.

SURTEES'S LATE CHARGE

The first Austrian Grand Prix was held at the Zeltweg airfield circuit, and took a

Above **QUICK AS A FLASH: DAN GURNEY RACES TO THE FIRST VICTORY BY A BRABHAM IN THE FRENCH GRAND PRIX AT ROUEN.**

high toll on machinery. Hill, Surtees, Clark, McLaren and Gurney were among the retirements, leaving Bandini to score his first Grand Prix win, ahead of Ginther. Showing how the top runners were cleared out, third place went to privateer Bob Anderson and he was three laps down. Local hero Jochen Rindt made a quiet debut in his home race in a Rob Walker Racing Brabham-BRM.

Ferrari's run of success continued in the Italian Grand Prix at Monza, where Surtees scored his second win of the year. It was a typically exciting slip-streamer and, after Clark and Gurney fell out, McLaren and Bandini completed the top three. Hill broke his clutch on the line in Italy, but kept his title challenge afloat by winning the US Grand Prix after Clark suffered engine problems. Surtees was second, ahead of an impressive Jo Siffert in one of Rob Walker's Brabhams.

Three drivers went to the finale in Mexico City with a crack at the title. Hill led on 39 points, Surtees had 34 and outsider Clark 30. Hill was soon out of contention for points, and Clark looked set for the title. But with just two laps to go, he struck engine trouble yet again. Surtees had worked his way up, and was waved into second place behind Gurney by team-mate Bandini. And it was enough to take the title from Hill.

PREVIOUS PAGE TOP LEFT AND RIGHT:

END OF THE GAME: JO BONNIER'S
BRABHAM LIES TRACKSIDE AFTER
HIS CRASH IN PRACTICE. HE WAS
NOT IN A GOOD ENOUGH STATE TO
START THE RACE.

ABOVE VICTORY PARADE: JIM CLARK, HIS
LOTUS 25 AND LOTUS BOSS COLIN
CHAPMAN HITCH A RIDE FOR A LAP OF
HONOUR AT BRANDS HATCH.

RIGHT THE ONE AND ONLY: LORENZO
BANDINI WON FOR FERRARI AT
ZELTWEG, BUT NEVER AGAIN BEFORE
HIS DEATH AT MONACO IN 1967.

A PERFECT SCORE

After four straight retirements had robbed him of the world title in 1964, Jim Clark bounced back for Lotus to win the 1965 World Championship – and also the Indianapolis 500 for good measure. Once again a change of engine regulations at the end of the year was the signal of the passing of an era.

The British teams struck back against Ferrari in 1965, with Lotus and Brabham using a new and more powerful 32-valve version of the Climax V8. With Arundell still recuperating from a massive crash in 1964, Clark was joined at Lotus by another new team-mate in the form of Mike Spence, who had driven for the team in the previous year's Italian Grand Prix. Jack Brabham and Dan Gurney were joined in the Brabham line-up by a newcomer from New Zealand called Denny

Hulme, while Rob Walker entered a brace of Brabhams for Jo Bonnier and Jo Siffert.

Ferrari continued with reigning champion John Surtees and Lorenzo Bandini, and there was new competition, too, from Honda, who launched a full effort with Richie Ginther and the little-known Ronnie Bucknum. Ginther's departure from BRM left a seat open alongside Graham Hill, and it was very ably filled by a promising young Scot who had not even driven in a Grand Prix; his name was Jackie Stewart. Talented Austrian Jochen Rindt joined Bruce McLaren at Cooper.

The South African Grand Prix became the first race of the season rather than the last, and Clark, still using the older Climax engine, scored a runaway win. Surtees continued his championship

form with second, ahead of Hill. Debutant Stewart finished sixth.

LOTUS AT INDIANAPOLIS
Lotus was missing from the second race, at Monaco, as the team was competing instead at Indianapolis, where Clark notched up an historic first win for a rear-engined car. In his absence Hill scored a wonderful victory in the street classic, recovering from an early incident to overtake both Surtees and Bandini. Clark came back with a win in a typically wet Belgian Grand Prix at Spa-Francorchamps, ahead of Stewart and McLaren, while Ginther picked up a point in the fast-improving Honda. Clark and Stewart then repeated their double act in the French Grand Prix, held this year on the mountainous Clermont-Ferrand track wih Surtees a very distant third.

LEFT **PORTRAIT OF A STAR: JIM CLARK EPITOMISED FORMULA ONE RACING, WITH HIS PEERLESS DRIVING SKILLS YIELDING A SECOND WORLD TITLE FOR LOTUS IN 1965.**

LEFT **POWER PLAY: LORENZO BANDINI KEEPS HIS FERRARI AHEAD OF GRAHAM HILL'S BRM, BUT IT WAS THE ENGLISHMAN WHO TRIUMPHED AT MONACO.**

BELOW LEFT **POETRY IN MOTION: JIM CLARK POWERS THROUGH THE PUDDLES ON HIS WAY TO ANOTHER WIN AT THE BELGIAN GRAND PRIX.**

RIGHT **POETRY IN MOTION PART TWO: DAN GURNEY FOLLOWS THE BRM PAIRING OF JACKIE STEWART AND GRAHAM HILL AT MONZA.**

Clark won the British Grand Prix at Silverstone for the fourth consecutive time, this time by a short head from Hill with Surtees third again. Clark then continued his winning ways in the Dutch Grand Prix at Zandvoort, and for the third time countryman Stewart followed him home around the circuit amid the dunes. The big surprise at Zandvoort, however, was the performance of Ginther, who led for two laps in the Honda before sliding back to finish in an eventual sixth place.

CLARK TRIUMPHANT

At the Nurburgring Clark scored his sixth win of the year and his first on the daunting German track. With only six scores counting, he had reached maximum points, and the championship was his. He was then in the lead pack at the Italian Grand Prix at Monza and, after he retired with fuel pump trouble, Stewart scored a marvellous maiden win, fractionally ahead of Hill and Gurney. However, with the title sewn up, Clark's luck seemed to

desert him. He retired with engine problems from the US Grand Prix at Watkins Glen, and Hill scored BRM's third win of the year ahead of the Brabhams of Gurney and Brabham.

The season had a twist in the tail, however, as in Mexico City Ginther gave Honda (and tyre maker Goodyear) a first win, leading from start to finish to pip Gurney. It was to remain the Californian's only win. The race also marked the end of the 1.5-litre formula after four diverting years.

JACK IS BACK...

It was all change in 1966 as the 3-litre formula was introduced and there was a race to get new engines ready in time. Jack Brabham was better prepared than most and he earned a deserved third championship title, this time driving his own car powered by the hybrid Repco engine.

Teams and engine builders were furiously busy through the winter as they prepared for the new formula. There was no pukka new engine from Climax, so existing customers had to find their own solutions.

The man who did the best job was undoubtedly Brabham. He announced that he was using a new V8 from the Australian Repco company. The engine was not the most powerful around, but it was reliable, light and compact, and mated well with an updated version of Brabham's existing chassis. Jack had not won a race himself since 1960, and the package was to give his career a new lease of life. With Dan Gurney moving on, Denny Hulme became his number two.

Cooper opted for a more far exotic solution, mating a Maserati V12 to a new chassis. Richie Ginther and Jochen Rindt were the works drivers, and Rob Walker bought one for Jo Siffert.

Former Cooper driver Bruce McLaren followed Brabham's example and set up his own team, initially using a Ford engine sourced from Indy Car racing. Another driver to copy the Brabham example was Gurney, whose All-American Racers concern built the neat Eagle.

It was no surprise to see Ferrari follow the V12 route, and the Scuderia produced a promising new car for John Surtees. Lorenzo Bandini stayed on as his team-mate. Both BRM and Lotus were forced to use uprated 2-litre versions of their V8 and Climax engines. BRM had an unusual H16 under development, but this complicated engine did not race until late in the year. That said, it started very well at Monaco where less powerful cars proved a match for the new more powerful machinery. Clark took pole for Lotus, but he had an unlucky race, while fellow Scot Jackie Stewart won for BRM after Surtees had led with the new Ferrari.

SLIDING OFF AT SPA

There was chaos in the Belgian Grand Prix when eight cars retired on the wet first lap, among them Stewart, who had the worst crash of his Formula One career. He was made to ponder driver

LEFT THREE-TIME WINNER: JACK BRABHAM KEEPS HIS OWN COMPANY AS HE PONDERS THE YEAR AHEAD RACING A CAR BEARING HIS OWN NAME.

1966

LEFT **FLYING SCOT: JACKIE STEWART RACES TO VICTORY FOR BRM IN THE FIRST RACE OF THE SEASON AT MONACO.**

LEFT **SURE-FOOTED: JOHN SURTEES KEPT CONTROL IN THE WET AT SPA-FRANCORCHAMPS TO WIN FOR FERRARI.**

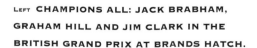

LEFT **CHAMPIONS ALL: JACK BRABHAM, GRAHAM HILL AND JIM CLARK IN THE BRITISH GRAND PRIX AT BRANDS HATCH.**

Above **AUSTRIAN CHARGER: JOCHEN RINDT PRESSES ON TO FINISH SECOND AT WATKINS GLEN IN HIS COOPER-MASERATI.**

safety when trapped inverted in his car soaked in petrol. Surtees stayed on the island that day to win after overcoming a challenge from Rindt's Cooper-Maserati. But a few weeks later John fell out with the Italian team and left to join Cooper.

BRABHAM STARTS WINNING
The new Brabham-Repco came good in the French Grand Prix at Reims, Jack winning after Bandini had retired. Mike Parkes finished a promising second

for Ferrari. Brabham won again in the British Grand Prix at Brands Hatch, with team-mate Hulme coming home second. Brabham then picked up a third win in a row at Zandvoort. And his winning streak continued in the German Grand Prix at the Nurburgring, where he held off the Coopers of Surtees and Rindt. His luck ran out at Monza, however, and he retired. But so too did nearly all the top runners, leaving the way clear for Ferrari newcomer Ludovico Scarfiotti to win.

Despite retiring in the Italian Grand Prix, Brabham had enough of a points advantage over his closest rivals to clinch his third title.

Clearly not backing off, Brabham was on pole for the US Grand Prix at Watkins Glen, but retired and Clark won. Cooper-Maseratis finished in second, third and fourth places in the hands of Rindt, Surtees and Siffert, and their good form continued in the championship finale in Mexico, which was won by Surtees.

95

HULME: THE KIWI KING

Brabham and Repco scored a second win through the efforts of Denny Hulme, but the story of the year was the arrival of the new Cosworth DFV engine. Packaged with the Lotus 49, it marked the beginning of an era.

Lotus had struggled through 1966, but in the March of that year Colin Chapman had persuaded Ford to invest in a new engine, to be built by Cosworth. The British firm duly embarked on an all-new V8 design for 1967, the Double Four Valve (DFV), which would initially be for the exclusive use of Lotus. Chapman drew a simple but effective car, the 49, to exploit it. And he further strengthened his package by bringing Graham Hill back to join Jim Clark.

That elevated Jackie Stewart to be team leader at BRM, where he was joined by Mike Spence. Chris Amon teamed up with Lorenzo Bandini at Ferrari, while former Ferrari star John Surtees was signed to lead Honda's effort and Pedro Rodriguez joined Jochen Rindt at Cooper.

The season opened at the new Kyalami track in South Africa, and the race nearly saw a sensational win for privateer John Love in an old Cooper-Climax. Indeed, with the top names struggling, only a late stop for fuel dropped him to second, behind Rodriguez's Cooper.

DISASTER AT MONACO
Formula One had been through a safe – or lucky – couple of seasons, but Ferrari ace Bandini was to lose his life at Monaco. He crashed out of the lead and his car caught fire, burning him fatally. Hulme won for Brabham, ahead of Hill and Amon.

The eagerly awaited debut of the Ford Cosworth DFV and the Lotus 49 came at the Dutch Grand Prix. And it was an historic day, for Clark took victory ahead of Brabham and Hulme after poleman Hill's engine failed.

Hill also retired next time out, in the Belgian Grand Prix, then leader Clark had to pit for a plug change and Gurney took the often unreliable Eagle-Weslake to a memorable first and only win.

For one time only the French Grand Prix was staged at the Bugatti circuit at Le Mans, a shorter version of the track used for the 24-hour sports car race. The Lotuses were again quick, but both broke their transmissions, making it obvious that their reliability was a weak point. That left Brabham and Hulme to finish first and second ahead of Stewart.

However, Lotus fortunes looked up

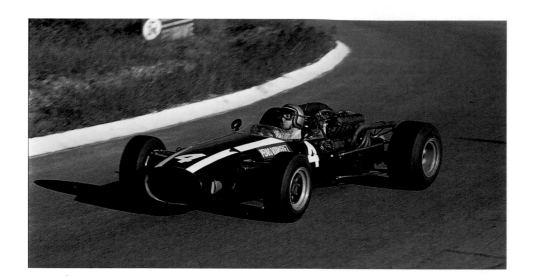

LEFT COOPER'S DAY: PEDRO ROGRIGUEZ
LED HOME PRIVATEER JOHN LOVE FOR
A COOPER ONE-TWO IN SOUTH AFRICA.

at Silverstone, where Clark won the British Grand Prix for the fifth time in six years. Hill led much of the race, but had suspension problems before his engine blew. Hulme and Amon finished second and third.

Lotus gremlins struck again in the German Grand Prix, as Clark and Hill were sidelined by suspension failures. Gurney looked set to win, but when his Weslake blew Hulme and Brabham scored their second one-two.

For the first time the circus moved to the scenic Mosport Park track in Canada. Ignition problems put Clark out and Brabham and Hulme were there to take another one-two, with Hill finishing fourth behind Gurney.

AN ITALIAN SURPRISE

Clark was the hero in the Italian Grand Prix, coming back from problems early on to lead until he started to run out of fuel on the final lap. In a typically exciting

finish, Surtees pipped Brabham to give Honda its first win of the 3-litre age, with Clark spluttering home third. Luck swung to Lotus once again in the US Grand Prix at Watkins Glen, where Clark and Hill managed a one-two finish.

However, Hulme had been a steady performer all year, and he just pipped his boss to the title in the season's final race in Mexico when Clark won from Brabham, but third was enough to keep Hulme ahead.

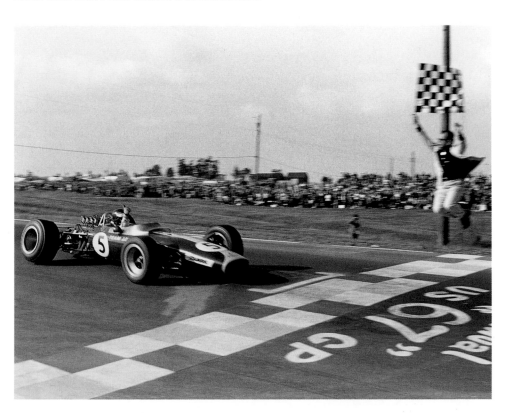

LEFT **READY FOR THE OFF: THE FRONT OF JIM CLARK (3), DENNY HULME, JACKIE STEWART AND DAN GURNEY AWAIT THE START AT THE NURBURGRING.**

BELOW **JUMPING JACK FLASH: JIM CLARK ACKNOWLEDGES HIS VICTORY AT WATKINS GLEN AND THE FLAG-WAVER'S ACROBATICS.**

A YEAR OF CHANGE

Sponsorship and wings arrived on the Formula One scene, but the new developments were overshadowed by the death of Jim Clark. In the sad aftermath, Graham Hill bravely won his second title for the grieving Lotus team.

Several things happened in 1968 which were to have long-term effects on Formula One, but nothing shook the racing world as much as Jim Clark's death in a Formula Two race at Hockenheim. This tragedy withstanding, the season was most notable for the introduction of overt commercial sponsorship. The previously green and yellow Lotuses were now red, white and gold, thanks to backing from Gold Leaf cigarettes. National colours were to become a thing of the past and British Racing Green Formula One cars confined to the history books.

FORD DFVS FOR ALL

Early in the year Lotus, Brabham and Ferrari began to experiment with downforce-enhancing wings, which soon became standard equipment, often in remarkably spindly form. Added to this, Formula One was further transformed as Ford's DFV was made available to all, and for the next 15 years it would be both an affordable and competitive choice for anyone who wanted it, opening the doors for a host of new teams to have a crack at the World Championship.

Other big news was the arrival of Ken Tyrrell to run Matra-Fords. He scooped up Jackie Stewart as his driver, and the partnership would blossom over the next six years. Meanwhile Matra's own team, with Henri Pescarolo and Jean-Pierre Beltoise, became a serious force. Belgian hotshot Jacky Ickx joined Chris Amon at

Ferrari, while Denny Hulme moved to join Bruce McLaren. Clark and Hill continued to lead the Lotus challenge, with Jo Siffert in a private Rob Walker car.

HILL REVIVES MORALE

A sign of what might have been came at the South African Grand Prix, when Clark dominated ahead of team-mate Hill. By the next race, at the new Jarama track in Spain, Clark was dead, with Jackie Oliver his replacement, and Hill revived Lotus morale with his first win with the 49, ahead of Hulme's McLaren. Hill then won again at Monaco, where Richard Attwood finished a fine second in a BRM.

McLaren gave his marque its first victory in the Belgian Grand Prix after Stewart ran out of fuel. It was also the first win for a DFV in something other than a Lotus. The next such win was not

LEFT **THE END OF AN ERA: JIM CLARK SCORES HIS FINAL WIN IN SOUTH AFRICA ON THE LAST OUTING FOR A LOTUS WITHOUT OVERT SPONSORSHIP.**

TOP LEFT **NEW COLOURS: GRAHAM HILL SHOWS OFF THE REVOLUTIONARY GOLD LEAF LIVERY OF HIS LOTUS.**

TOP RIGHT **FIRST-TIME WINNER: JACKY ICKX TAKES THE SPOILS OF VICTORY AFTER TRIUMPHING IN THE FRENCH GRAND PRIX.**

ABOVE **THE KING OF MONACO: GRAHAM HILL RACES CLEAR IN HIS LOTUS EN ROUTE TO HIS FOURTH VICTORY IN THE PRINCIPALITY.**

Above **A MASTERFUL DRIVE: JACKIE STEWART'S MATRA SPLASHES ACROSS THE LINE AFTER AN ASTONISHING DRIVE TO VICTORY AT THE NURBURGRING.**

long in coming, for Stewart guided Tyrrell's Matra-Ford to victory next time out at Zandvoort. There was yet another different winner at Rouen, where young Ickx gave Ferrari its only win of the year in pouring rain. Surtees was second for Honda, but his veteran team-mate Jo Schlesser was killed .

At Brands Hatch the popular Siffert gave Walker his first win in seven years with Rob Walker's Lotus, heading home the Ferraris of Amon and Ickx after early leaders Hill and Oliver both retired.

The German Grand Prix saw one of the greatest drives of all time, Stewart winning with a virtuoso performance in atrocious conditions.

Hulme then showed that his 1967 crown was deserved by winning the next two events at Monza and the Mont Tremblant circuit in Canada. Then new-comer Mario Andretti earned a sensational pole for Lotus at the US Grand Prix, but Stewart took his third win of the year.

Rounding out the season in Mexico City, Stewart and Hill battled for the lead until Stewart fell back with handling problems, leaving Hill to score his third win of the year which was enough to give him his second title.

If the losses of Clark and Schlesser were not enough, BRM's Mike Spence was killed in a Lotus during practice at Indianapolis, and former Italian Grand Prix winner Ludovico Scarfiotti died in a hillclimb.

CONSISTENCY PAYS

Jackie Stewart marched forward to take the world title with Ken Tyrrell's Matra-Ford in a season in which virtually no one else who could offer a consistent challenge. And it clearly established Stewart as the man to beat in Formula One.

Stewart had come close to the title the previous year, when he had been in with a shout until beaten by Graham Hill in the final round, but in 1969 everything went his way. With Matra withdrawing its own team, all efforts were concentrated on Tyrrell's Ford-powered outfit. Stewart and team-mate Johnny Servoz-Gavin – who had impressed in 1968 – were joined by Jean-Pierre Beltoise.

Jochen Rindt took up a golden opportunity and joined Hill at Lotus, while Jacky Ickx left Ferrari to replace the Austrian at Brabham, a team that had finally given up on Repco and joined the DFV bandwagon. John Surtees was available because Honda had withdrawn from Formula One at the end of 1968 as the DFV supremacy had taken its toll, and he joined ex-Lotus driver Jackie Oliver at BRM. Also gone from the scene were Eagle-Weslake and Cooper-Maserati.

The big development of the year, though, was four-wheel drive. Matra, McLaren and Lotus all tried it, but it was a white elephant and none of the cars really worked and were thus put to one side.

A DREAM START

Stewart started the season in fine form, dominating the South African Grand Prix at Kyalami. American ace Mario Andretti, who would have occasional drives in a third works Lotus, gave him a hard time early on in the race but retired and Hill claimed second with Hulme third.

Stewart won again at Montjuich Park circuit in Barcelona, but this time he was helped by retirements ahead as Amon's Ferrari broke when leading, while Lotus had a bad break. First Hill and then Rindt had huge crashes after their wings failed, the latter being hospitalised.

The still-injured Rindt would have to miss the next race, at Monaco, where the FIA announced an immediate ban on the high-mounted aerofoils which had proliferated. They soon crept back in, but in a new and less outrageous form, attached to the bodywork. Stewart and Amon both led but retired, allowing Hill to score a historic fifth Monaco win. While Piers Courage finished in second place in a Brabham entered by Frank Williams, giving the British team owner his first significant result.

LEFT **A STORMING START: JACKIE STEWART WON FIVE OF THE FIRST SIX GRANDS PRIX TO SET HIMSELF UP FOR THE WORLD TITLE.**

STEWART ON SONG

The Belgian Grand Prix was cancelled, and Rindt was fit enough to return at Zandvoort. He took pole and led until retiring, so Stewart scored another win, this time ahead of Siffert. Stewart's fourth victory came at Clermont-Ferrand in France, where team-mate Beltoise did a good job to finish second by a nose from Ickx.

Stewart won once more at Silverstone, where he battled hard with Rindt until the Austrian had to pit with a loose wing. Ickx had a good run to second with the Brabham, and two weeks later he went one better at the Nurburgring, where he gave the team its first win since 1967.

TITLE CLINCHER

The Scot clinched the title with a sixth win in an epic, slipstreaming battle in the Italian Grand Prix at Monza, where he headed home Rindt, Beltoise and McLaren. But, after such a run of success, Stewart failed to win any of the last three races. Ickx triumphed in Canada, Rindt scored his first success at Watkins Glen and Hulme provided more variety with a win for McLaren in Mexico. Missing from the Mexican race, though, was Graham Hill, who had broken his legs in a massive accident at Watkins Glen. He was fit for the following season, but would never again win a Grand Prix.

Above Left **WING FAILURE: GRAHAM HILL DISCOVERS IN SPAIN WHAT HAPPENS WHEN A WING COLLAPSES AND DOWNFORCE IS REMOVED.**

Left **JUMPING JACKY: JACKY ICKX GETS AIRBORNE IN HIS BRABHAM ON HIS WAY TO VICTORY IN THE GERMAN GRAND PRIX.**

Opposite **TAKING IT EASY: JOCHEN RINDT AND JACKIE STEWART LISTEN ON AS EX-FORMULA ONE DRIVER INNES IRELAND CHATS TO THEM IN MEXICO.**

THE SEVENTIES

JACKIE STEWART

Honours: WORLD CHAMPION 1969, 1971, 1973
Grand Prix record: 99 STARTS, 27 WINS

Although Jackie Stewart is talking us through the 1970s, as World Champion twice in that decade – in 1971 and 1973 – his World Championship debut came back at the start of the 1965 season. But there is no-one alive with a greater understanding of the myriad factors that influence Formula One, which is fortunate now that he runs his own team.

"I remember going to a drive-in cinema with Jochen Rindt on the night before my first Grand Prix, the South African in 1965," recalls the tidy Scot. "We were in East London, it was New Year's Eve and it was too noisy in our hotel because of all the partying, so we had to get out. We were probably the only two men together in the drive-in... Of the race itself, I finished sixth in my BRM, but it wasn't a very good performance and I ran out of fuel.

"Considering the level of competition then, I thought of the established drivers as gods. Don't forget, I had come straight from Formula Three and hadn't raced a single-seater until just nine months before my Formula One debut. So, I wasn't surprised about the strength of the competition, but I was surprised that I was able to qualify in the top half of the grid.

"The parity of the equipment was very close and it became closer still as my career progressed from the 1960s to the 1970s. The Lotus-Climax was the combination to have in 1965. Ferrari was a contender, as it always is. BRM was obviously a leading team in 1965 and Cooper was still a contender as it still had

Climax engines. These were all factory teams, the big players.

"From 1968 on, the parity was fantastic as the Ford Cosworth DFV engine became available to all. Don't forget that a brand new DFV cost just £7500. And by 1969 just about everybody had them. Amazingly, they offered great equality as I don't think there was ever more than 10bhp difference between any of them. On top of this, the chassis weren't that different either as there weren't any real aerodynamics until 1969 after some small-scale wings appeared either side of the nose in 1968. So we knew that the cars were pretty much equal. It was up to the driver to find the time."

This considered, how was there so much overtaking then? "Well, with parity of power and with the cars having very little grip, people made mistakes and lost time. Also, there was plenty of drafting as there weren't chicanes every three seconds."

Known as a campaigner for safety in Formula One following an accident at Spa-Francorchamps in the 1966 Belgian GP, when he was left dangling upside down, soaked in petrol and waiting for an explosion, Jackie offers a surprising point-of-view about

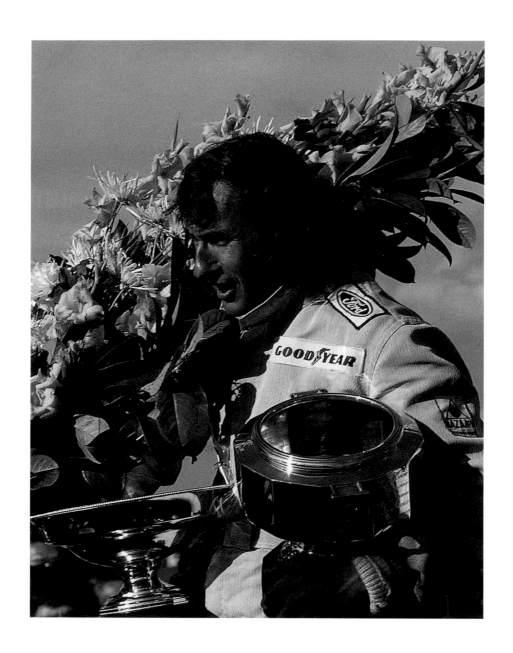

dicing wheel-to-wheel with his contemporaries on circuits that fall a long way short of today's safety standards.

"You knew who to dice with," Jackie explains. "You were 100% safe with Jim Clark, Jochen Rindt, Francois Cevert, Chris Amon, Dan Gurney, Graham Hill and Denny Hulme. Neither Jack Brabham nor John Surtees were as easy to pass, but that's not a criticism as it was their business. As to safety, this didn't affect my psyche at all. You have to understand that it was no good looking over your shoulder and saying that it wasn't safe then, as this was the best that we had. It was changing radically, as when I started we wore open-faced helmets with handkerchiefs covering our mouths below our goggles; we had no seatbelts; we wore overalls with no thermal underwear that were about as useful as a pair of pyjamas.

"I went to Indianapolis in 1965 and saw that the drivers wore seatbelts, which I thought made a good deal of sense and immediately had them fitted to my BRM. My contemporaries still wanted to be thrown clear of the car, but I was concerned that the cars were now such a tight fit that you'd get thrown halfway out and mash your legs. And that's what happened to Graham Hill in the 1969 US Grand Prix at Watkins Glen when he had pitted and rejoined without his belts done up, with his knees being bent the wrong way as he half came out of his car. Jochen Rindt didn't like wearing the thigh straps and he might not have died at Monza in 1970 if he had been wearing them."

So, although the quest for safety wasn't perhaps as all-encompassing to Jackie as observers would have you believe, his calculated approach to the sport soon saw him winning at the highest level, with the first of his 27 wins coming at Monza before his debut season was out after a magnificent scrap with Graham Hill's sister BRM. Third overall in 1965, his next two seasons with BRM weren't as successful, with race finishes a rarity with the BRM H16 in 1967, but then he moved back under the wing of mentor Ken Tyrrell who ran him in a Matra in 1968, ending up runner-up to champion Graham Hill after missing two races having broken a wrist in a Formula Two race. But it all came together in 1969 when Jackie won five of the first six Grands Prix and cruised to his first world title.

When it became clear that Tyrrell would be obliged to fit a Matra engine in place of a Cosworth for 1970, he bade farewell to Matra and struck out with his own team, starting the season with a March chassis. However, before the season was out, the first Tyrrell chassis had hit the grids. Although only equal fifth overall that year, Jackie and Ken struck back and steamrollered the 1971 title. Runner-up to Lotus's Emerson Fittipaldi in 1972, Jackie rounded off his career with another five wins and his third world title in 1973, although his retirement from the sport was brought forward by a race when the team withdrew from the season-closing US Grand Prix as a mark of respect for Jackie's number two Cevert who died in qualifying.

So, Jackie had a lengthy but extremely successful World Championship career, emerging not only intact but with three world titles and a clear understanding about who and what were good. "It's very hard to pick one moment as a highlight of my career, but I suppose that winning the Italian Grand Prix at Monza in 1969 to clinch my first world title was special. I won my

second title parked on the grass by the side of the track at the Osterreichring in 1971 after losing a wheel. And my third and last world title was won by finishing fourth at Monza.

"Equally, when I raced at Monaco in 1973 I knew that it was going to be my last race there, so winning that one was special to me. As was winning the German Grand Prix at the Nurburgring in 1968. But that was more a case of just wanting to get the race over with as the weather conditions were so diabolical.

"There were several defining moments in the 1970s for me. One was the realisation in 1973 that I no longer wanted to be a driver. I was too busy and the aggravation of all my extra business was burning me out. I also saw that unless I retired at a certain time that I might just be tempted to go on and 'Play It Again Sam' like everybody else seemed to be doing and ending up unsuccessful after a career that had diminished. I didn't want that. I wanted a life after driving a car and, at 34, thought that I had a five-year life as Jackie Stewart, three-time World Champion. Luckily, I was heavily used for promotional activities by Ford, Goodyear, Elf and others, sponsors from my racing days. And I also did a lot of commentary work with ABC TV which I enjoyed. And I couldn't have had a better tutor than Jim McKay who ran 'Wide World of Sports', the best sports show of its time. So, the 1970s were a good time for me and my life was expanding when it could have been contracting.

"When you consider the technology, the 1970s were no different to any other decade in that the acceleration of technology was just that little bit faster than before, as it always is in each succeeding decade. Suddenly you had aerodynamics playing a big role. And with aerodynamics you are creating ground effects. Colin Chapman of Lotus could well be put down as the greatest designer in the history of motor racing as he created more radical changes than anyone else. John Cooper created the rear-engined car, but Chapman was the ultimate rear-engined initiator, whether it was the Lotus 18, the early Lotus Indycars that showed the American roadsters the way, the 25 which was the first monocoque car, or the later ground effects cars. I'm sure that Jim Hall tried aerodynamics to a greater degree, but Chapman started the real ground effects and then Patrick Head and Gordon Murray became his disciples at Williams and Brabham respectively."

Acknowledging that the cars had progressed enormously with the introduction of ground effects in 1978, what did Jackie think when he tested one? "It was like being glued to the road. What was going on beneath the car was much more important than what was happening where I was sitting above it.

"The next most important thing was composite carbon brakes which were introduced in the late 1980s. They were amazing. And then came electronics, such as electronic gear shifting, fly-by-wire, telemetry and so on.

Right **FOLLOWING THE LINE: STEWART GUIDES HIS TYRRELL 003 TO VICTORY IN THE 1972 FRENCH GRAND PRIX AT CLERMONT-FERRAND.**

"The last time I drove a Formula One car was when I drove the Stewart SF-1 at Silverstone in 1997. I found it just the same to drive as cars had been in my day. Mind you I drove it to low limits as I wasn't prepared to go into Copse flat and left-foot brake. I was always competitive when I drove cars five or even 10 years after I'd retired, but then I drove a Williams with composite brakes at Paul Ricard in the late 1980s and although I was very close to the then Grand Prix drivers' times, I wouldn't go through Signes at the end of the back straight flat in top as I was older and wiser I suppose.

Certainly, the paddles have helped the gearshift, and that's a major issue as there are no missed gearchanges as this used to be one of the major ways of going past somebody. Nobody did a race in the 1970s without missing a gearchange."

"Looking at the teams, I've always viewed Ferrari as excitingly vulnerable. It's always been such an important name, ever since the early 1950s with Ascari and Villoresi, then later with Fangio in the late 1950s. Ferrari were always seen to be a serious player, as they are in 1999. And yet for 20 years they haven't won a World

Championship. Even when they ran Niki Lauda in the mid-1970s, they weren't dominant as James Hunt won the title in 1976. Yes, you could say that James won because Niki had his accident at the Nurburgring and pulled out of the final race in Japan, but Ferrari hadn't dominated. So, how is it that Ferrari have never actually dominated Formula One? They're simply excitingly unpredictable, then as now. Ferrari has an enormous budget and it's been a consistent threat, yet it has found ways of failing. It's even been beaten by teams who were makeshift at the start of their careers.

"I would say that my key rivals in Formula One were Jim Clark, Dan Gurney, Jochen Rindt, John Surtees, Jack Brabham, Denny Hulme, Francois Cevert and Chris Amon. Graham Hill sometimes drove some unconventional lines through corners, but this wasn't in an attempt to block you, it was just that this was the way that he did it.

"Compare the mental attitude of drivers in the 1960s and 1970s compared to that of those today, and I don't consider there to be any difference. Then as now, some grew horns, as people do in all sorts of contact sports. Driver input versus mechanical input has changed little, too, while the driver as an animal has stayed very similar. Take Jacques Villeneuve for example. He would have corresponded to a Tazio Nuvolari, while Lauda was much more like a latter-day Rudolf Caracciola. However, I don't think driver input has changed much since the 1970s. Michael Schumacher is very demanding, like Ayrton Senna was very demanding, as was Prost, Lauda, myself, Clark and Fangio. The natural leaders are not soft individuals with regards to his list of requirements to do the job.

"If you look back to Fangio, he was a cold and calculating man who knew that he had to have the best car to win and just went where he thought he wanted to go. He was ruthless and there was no emotional commitment to the teams that he drove for, either to Enzo Ferrari or to the Maserati brothers, or even to Mercedes-Benz. Actually, he stayed with Mercedes-Benz in later life even though he finished his career at Maserati as he saw the benefit to his long-term future to be allied to a multi-national corporation. If you think nowadays that somebody is totally commercial as he has Willi Weber or Mark McCormack behind him, just take a look at Fangio who is my idol to this day. He was well ahead of them in terms of professionalism and single-mindedness. He demanded in order to perform his art. Suddenly, Schumacher is starting to look slightly soft in suggesting that he will see his days through with Ferrari. Fangio wouldn't have done that."

So, was Jackie a latter-day Fangio when he left BRM at the end of 1967 and followed the guidance of Tyrrell to Matra in order to get a DFV behind his shoulders for 1968? And was he too taking professionalism and focused direction a stage further when he moved into the 1970s not only sponsored by Ford, Goodyear and Elf, but also working for them and forging long-term relationships that would see him through to the end of the millenium?

Certainly, he was seen as being the most professional driver of his time, both in and out of the cockpit. But, as he explains, it wasn't all a question of money.

"I did a lot of things as it gave me an extra edge, something I felt I needed at the time as I didn't feel that I was better than the other drivers. So, out of the cockpit, I tried to endear myself to designers, engineers, mechanics, gearbox people tyre people and so on. I felt that if was going to be a professional racing driver, then I would have to deliver. And if I delivered better than anyone else, then I'd be more valuable than anyone else and would thus have a better chance of driving for a better team and thus earning more money.

Money wasn't actually the driving issue, though: this just came through success, but had I not done that and laid those foundations by doing things like taking bus tours around Monte Carlo or doing breakfasts, lunches and dinners every day of a Grand Prix weekend, then I wouldn't be here now running my own Formula One team. In fact, it helped extend my life as a three-time Formula One World Champion well beyond where I thought it would stretch to."

Stewart Grand Prix has been on the World Championship grid for three seasons with, fittingly, Ford support and engines.

"I wouldn't have dreamed in 1973 when I retired that I'd have started a team. I might have done something with Ken (Tyrrell), but I'd never have entertained the thought of doing it on my own. However, I own a team because of creating Paul Stewart Racing when my son Paul went racing. I built it up because of him and it became obvious to me that it was economically sound to run two cars rather than one. Then I considered what Paul would do the following year and that's why we launched the 'Staircase of Talent', running three teams for six drivers in three different formulae – Formula Opel, Formula Three and Formula 3000. It was a very professional little operation which was no different to Jackie Stewart the racing driver. Here I was seeing my son participating and working with me. And that was nice, as blood is thicker than water and it's great working with Paul. Also, I thought it would give him something beyond driving. Then it seemed obvious that we should move on up after we'd clinched five Formula Opel titles in a row and six British Formula Three titles in seven years. We looked at the International Touring Car Championship and at Indycar racing, but as our eventual goal was going to be Formula One it seemed sensible to go straight there. But I'd never have done it if I hadn't had Paul as a son."

So, looking at Formula One today both as a former World Champion and as a team owner, what does Jackie think of it?

"Formula One today is incredibly complex and very expensive, but not to the detriment of the sport. Actually, it's been a plus and in a way it has been a plus as it has brought the sport to a level of perceived quality, whether it's hospitality, whether it's presentation, it's become unique. A Grand Prix paddock is now a very impressive arena. It doesn't matter who you are or what your interest, when you go into the paddock you can't fail to be impressed by the quality of the technology, the transporters, the tractor units, the motorhomes, the garages and the Paddock Club. And the new Sepang circuit in Malaysia is going to take the whole matter to an even higher level."

Left: **NEAT AND TIDY: STEWART AND HIS BRM TEAM-MATE GRAHAM HILL WERE TOGETHER IN BOTH 1965 AND 1966.**

A TRAGIC YEAR

Jochen Rindt was leading the World Championship for Lotus when he lost his life at Monza, but no one overhauled his score and the popular Austrian became the sport's first posthumous champion. In a dark year, Bruce McLaren and Piers Courage were also killed.

The big story of the winter was the arrival of March Engineering. Seemingly out of nowhere, the British company appeared at the first race with no fewer than five DFV-powered cars. March scored a coup by getting Ken Tyrrell to run a pair of its chassis after Matra decided to come back with its own team and V12-powered cars. Added to Tyrrell's two for Jackie Stewart and Johnny Servoz-Gavin, the works March team had strong drivers in Chris Amon and Jo Siffert, with Mario Andretti turning out for them occa-

sionally. Ferrari looked well placed with the all-new 312B, and Jacky Ickx returned to drive it. BRM attracted backing from Yardley, and produced the much-improved P153.

Jack Brabham had not won since the 1967 Canadian Grand Prix, but he started the year with a fine win in South Africa with his new BT33. Stewart led before dropping to third place behind Hulme's McLaren.

MARCH TAKES GOLD

Stewart gave March a win in the marque's second ever race, the Spanish Grand Prix at Jarama. He was hounded by the rejuvenated Brabham, until Jack's engine broke. Brabham was to the fore at Monaco too, holding off Rindt in a fine battle for the lead. But the Australian slid off at the last corner,

allowing Rindt past to win. Tragedy struck before the next race in Belgium, though, when Bruce McLaren was killed while testing one of his CanAm cars at Goodwood and so the sport lost a great driver who had been a mainstay of Formula One since 1959.

BRM had not won since Monaco in 1966, but Rodriguez gave the team a sensational victory in the Belgian Grand Prix after holding off Amon's March. The delayed appearance of Chapman's slick new Lotus 72 came at the Dutch Grand Prix, and it scored a debut win in the hands of Rindt. Alas, Piers Courage perished when his De Tomaso crashed and caught fire.

Another new face was dashing young Frenchman François Cevert, who joined Tyrrell when Servoz-Gavin abruptly quit the sport. Rindt and the 72 won at

LEFT **A DRINK MADAM: JOCHEN RINDT ENJOYS THE BUBBLY ON THE PODIUM AT BRANDS HATCH WITH WIFE NINA AFTER QUALIFYING ON POLE.**

Clermont-Ferrand, and then again at Brands Hatch after Brabham ran out of fuel, while leading rookie Emerson Fittipaldi drove a works Lotus 49C to eighth place on his debut.

Ickx was having a bad season, with just four points on the board. But he fought back with second place in the German Grand Prix, held for the first time at Hockenheim, while Rindt took his fifth win. Ickx gave Ferrari a much-needed victory in the Austrian Grand Prix, heading home new team-mate Clay Regazzoni.

RINDT DIES AT MONZA
Tragedy struck again in practice for the Italian Grand Prix at Monza when Rindt crashed fatally after a mechanical failure; he was just 28 years old. The race went ahead without Lotus, and Regazzoni scored a fine win on only his fifth start. Rindt had led the title race comfortably prior to Monza, and the only man who could usurp him was Ickx. He led Regazzoni in a Ferrari one-two in Canada, finished fourth in Watkins Glen and then won in Mexico. But it was not enough, although even he really did not want to win the title by default.

The Canadian Grand Prix marked the first appearance of another new marque for Ken Tyrrell had built his own car to replace the March. It showed promise in Stewart's hands and qualified on pole, but would have to wait until 1971 for its first success.

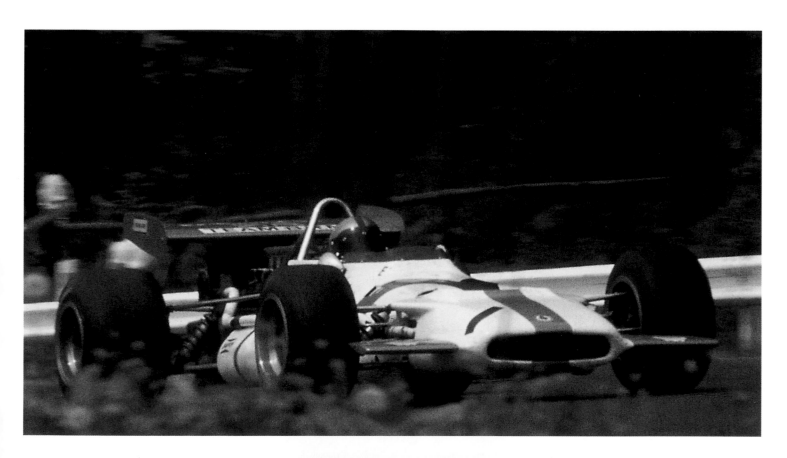

ABOVE **PEDRO RODRIGUEZ PUT BRM BACK INTO THE WINNER'S CIRCLE FOR THE FIRST TIME SINCE 1966 BY WINNING IN BELGIUM.**

LEFT PAGE **A MONZA SLIPSTREAMER: OLIVER LEADS REGAZZONI, STEWART, ICKX ET AL IN A WONDERFUL LEAD-SWAPPING RACE.**

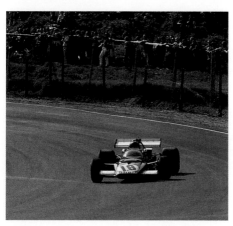

LEFT: **ON THE WINNING TRAIL: JACKY ICKX HEADS FOR VICTORY IN THE CANADIAN GRAND PRIX, HIS SECOND WIN OF THE YEAR.**

STEWART'S SECOND

Jackie Stewart earned his second world title with a dominant performance for Tyrrell. But once again, the year was tinged with sadness as racing recorded the deaths of two of the fastest and most popular stars on the circuits.

If the Formula One grids appeared to be missing one of their staple ingredients, they were, for Jack Brabham was no longer racing, having retired at the end of the previous year after 126 starts and three world titles in a Formula One career that began way back in 1955. However, he settled into life as a full-time team owner, and Graham Hill was signed up to drive.

The works March team had had a poor first season in 1970, and the star drivers left, with Jo Siffert joining Porsche sports car colleague Pedro Rodriguez at BRM,

while Chris Amon went to the promising Matra-Simca outfit. The third STP March driver, Mario Andretti, joined Jacky Ickx and Clay Regazzoni as Ferrari's third driver. Sadly, early in the year the Italian team lost Ignazio Giunti in a sports car crash in Argentina. To replace them, March signed up Ronnie Peterson who had done a solid job in a privately-entered March in 1970 and soon emerged as a leading contender.

FERRARI STRIKES FIRST
Ferrari drew first blood in the South African Grand Prix when Andretti scored his maiden triumph, although Denny Hulme had looked set to win for McLaren until his right rear wheel came loose with four laps to go and he limped home sixth. Jackie Stewart finished second and followed it up with wins in the Spanish and Monaco Grands Prix, with Peterson scor-

ing a fine second place in the latter.

Stewart struggled at a wet Zandvoort, finishing a disappointing 11th in the Dutch Grand Prix while Ickx won for Ferrari.

The French Grand Prix moved to the modern Paul Ricard facility in the south of France, where Stewart and team-mate Francois Cevert scored a fine one-two. Not long afterwards, BRM star Rodriguez, who had finished second in Holland, was killed in a minor sports car race at the Norisring.

Stewart won again at Silverstone, followed home by Peterson, and then at the Nurburgring he and Cevert picked up their second one-two result. This was a repeat of the Scot's 1969 form. BRM bounced back in fine style with a sensational win for Siffert in Austria and an even more spectacular one for Peter Gethin at Monza, where he won by just 0.01s, the closest margin ever. In Austria few noticed the

LEFT **CHAMPION ON THE MOVE: JACKIE STEWART PROPELS HIS TYRRELL TOWARDS VICTORY AT THE FRENCH GRAND PRIX.**

low-key debut of Niki Lauda in a rented March, while at Monza Amon looked set to score his first win in his Matra-Simca after years of being thwarted – until he accidentally ripped off his visor in the closing laps and dropped to sixth.

STEWART WRAPS IT UP

Stewart's engine had broken in the Italian Grand Prix, but he bounced back with a win in Canada, with Peterson again coming second. In the finale at Watkins Glen it was the turn of Cevert to score his maiden win, after Stewart slipped to fifth place with tyre troubles. The title was long since in his pocket, though.

Peterson was adjudged the big find of the year, however, finishing second in the championship thanks to his consistent results. Cevert, another brilliant youngster, finished third overall.

Lotus had a disappointing year, the marque failing to win a race for the first time since 1960. A lot of effort was wasted with an Indy-derived gas turbine car, which never lived up to expectations. In October tragedy struck again and Siffert was killed when his BRM crashed and caught fire in a non-championship race at Brands Hatch. It was a sad end to the season.

"EMMO" TAKES OVER

Lotus returned once again to the top of the podium and its rising star, Emerson Fittipaldi, who had shown much promise the previous year, became the youngest champion as there was no-one else able to offer a season-long challenge.

Lotus went into the 1972 World Championship armed with an updated version of the rather appropriately named Lotus 72 chassis, plus a dramatic new colour scheme. Gold Leaf's red, white and gold colours had been replaced by the black and gold hues of John Player Special and over the next few years the cigarette brand would become completely synonymous with the team, with its car soon becoming known car, which would soon be known as a JPS. Other team sponsors had been in the news as well, as Yardley left BRM to join a revitalized McLaren effort, in which Hulme was partnered by Peter Revson, the latter returning to Formula One some eight years after a shaky debut in the mid-1960s.

Meanwhile, BRM found major backing from Marlboro and, in what proved to be an over-ambitious plan, ran up to five cars per race. There were some changes at Brabham, too, as the team was bought by businessman Bernie Ecclestone. Graham Hill was joined in the team's line-up by Argentina's Carlos Reutemann, the first talent to emerge from that country since the 1950s.

REUTEMANN IMPRESSES
Newcomer Reutemann stunned the field when he took pole for his debut at Buenos Aires, but it was back to normal in the race when he had to pit for tyres and Tyrrell's Jackie Stewart won from McLaren's Denny Hulme. The Kiwi went one better in South Africa, giving McLaren its first win since the 1969 Mexican Grand Prix.

Fittipaldi then gave JPS its first win in the non-championship Race of Champions at Brands Hatch, and then dominated the Spanish Grand Prix at Jarama. The Monaco Grand Prix brought a total surprise when, in wet conditions, Frenchman Jean-Pierre Beltoise drove a fine race for BRM. It was to be the marque's last ever win.

Fittipaldi won at the new and boring Nivelles track in Belgium, and Stewart triumphed in the French Grand Prix at Clermont-Ferrand after Chris Amon again lost a race in the late stages – this time with his Matra-Simca suffering a puncture. Jacky Ickx's Ferrari led the British Grand Prix at Brands Hatch until the

LEFT **SPANISH SUCCESS: EMERSON FITTIPALDI FINISHED FIRST IN SPAIN TO SET UP HIS WORLD CHAMPIONSHIP CHALLENGE.**

Above MOTORBIKE ACES: MIKE HAILWOOD RACED TO SECOND PLACE IN THE ITALIAN GRAND PRIX IN A CAR ENTERED BY FELLOW MOTORCYCLE CHAMPION JOHN SURTEES.

Below FLYING KIWI: DENNY HULME LEADS FITTIPALDI IN THE EARLY LAPS AT KYALAMI.

Belgian was stricken with an oil leak, allowing Fittipaldi to win. Ickx fought back with victory in the German Grand Prix at the Nurburgring, ahead of team-mate Clay Regazzoni. Fittipaldi won the next race in Austria and then triumphed again in the Italian Grand Prix at Monza to clinch the title with two races still to run. Emerson also rewrote the record book by becoming the youngest ever champion, at the age of 25 years, eight months and twenty-nine days.

MIXED FORTUNES FOR STEWART

Stewart had not had much luck through the season, but a new car that was introduced in the Austrian Grand Prix improved his form. And he finished the season with wins in the Canadian and US Grands Prix, heading home McLaren's Revson and Hulme in the first race and Cevert and Hulme in the latter. It was enough for Jackie to make a late run to second place in the championship, ahead of Hulme. The previous year's runner-up, Ronnie Peterson, had a poor season. March's new car failed and a slightly more successful replacement was hastily built. However, Peterson had impressed the right people: for 1973 he earned himself a Lotus ride, alongside champion Fittipaldi.

But there was sad news for Ronnie's country as well. In June veteran Jo Bonnier was killed when his Lola crashed at Le Mans. He raced from 1957 to 1971, but never matched the form which had given him BRM's first win in 1959.

BELOW **EMERSON FITTIPALDI: ROARING TOWARDS WORLD CHAMPIONSHIP SUCCESS.**

STEWART STRIKES BACK

Jackie Stewart landed his third Formula One title after a season-long battle with Lotus and decided to quit while he was at the top. Once again the season was blighted, though, with the deaths of François Cevert and newcomer Roger Williamson.

Lotus boss Colin Chapman's fortunes looked good as in Emerson Fittipaldi and Ronnie Peterson the team had two top drivers. However, some people remembered the previous time the team tried to run two top drivers, Jochen Rindt and Graham Hill in 1969, and it didn't yield the desired championship.

Stewart and his Tyrrell team-mate Cevert had developed into a fine partnership in 1972, and Denny Hulme and Peter Revson looked good at McLaren. Jacky Ickx was joined at Ferrari by Arturo Merzario, who had run a few races in 1972,

while Clay Regazzoni left to join Marlboro BRM. An intriguing new marque was the American-financed Shadow, whose sinister black cars were handled by Jackie Oliver and George Follmer, an American veteran with no Formula One experience. Meanwhile, Hill quit Brabham to set up his own team, Embassy Racing.

FITTIPALDI'S DOUBLE THROW
Fittipaldi had a dream start, winning in both Argentina and his native Brazil. The first win was by no means easy, since Regazzoni and Cevert both led the race before having problems. Then McLaren introduced the sleek and modern-looking M23 in the South African Grand Prix, which would ultimately have a lifetime of six seasons. Hulme put it on pole, but fell to fifth as Stewart bounced back from a heavy crash in practice to score a fine

win. Mike Hailwood became a hero in the race as he rescued an unconscious Regazzoni from his burning car after a massed accident on the third lap.

Fittipaldi scored a third win in Spain, and then Stewart added a second to his tally in Belgium, where the track broke up and many cars skated off. Jackie won again in Monaco, to make it three each, in a race that saw the debut of British driver James Hunt in a March run by flamboyant aristocrat Lord Hesketh.

For the first time Sweden hosted a race at Anderstorp and, although local hero Peterson was on pole, Hulme gave the M23 its first victory. Ronnie gained his revenge in France, finally scoring his first win after suffering appalling luck in the early races. It did not help him much at Silverstone, where the race was stopped after a multi-car pile-up was triggered by

LOST TALENT: FRANCOIS CEVERT FINISHED SECOND ALMOST EVERYWHERE, THEN WAS KILLED AT WATKINS GLEN.

McLaren's third driver Jody Scheckter at the end of the first lap. Revson won the restarted race after Stewart spun out, with Peterson second home.

DUTCH DISASTER

Tragedy returned to the scene at Zandvoort, when Roger Williamson – in only his second race – was killed in a fiery crash. Stewart and Cevert scored a one-two, a feat they repeated in Germany.

In Austria, Peterson waved Fittipaldi through, but won anyway when Emerson retired. Then at Monza Peterson and Fittipaldi finished one-two, but the title went to Stewart who, after an early stop, charged through the field from 20th to an amazing fourth place.

Revson won the rain-hit Canadian race, which saw the first use of a pace car in Formula One, but there was general confusion as the pace car had come out

ahead of Howden Ganley's Iso Williams which certainly wasn't in the lead.

The circus then moved to Watkins Glen for the US Grand Prix at which Stewart planned to have his 100th and last Grand Prix. But Cevert was killed in practice and Tyrrell withdrew. It was a bitter end to a fantastic farewell season for Stewart. In the race, Peterson picked up a fourth win, but he was pushed hard by the fast-improving Hunt.

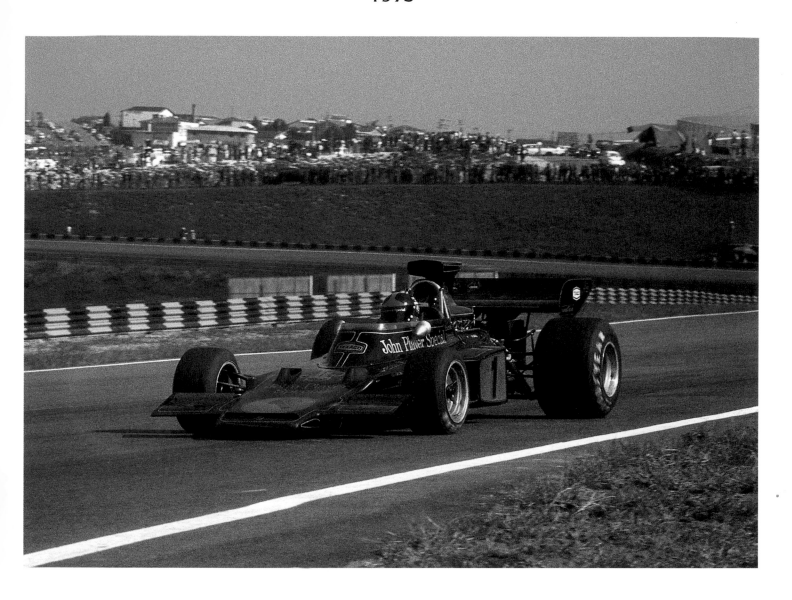

ABOVE **FLYING START: FITTIPALDI STARTED HIS TITLE DEFENCE BY WINNING IN ARGENTINA AND ON HOME GROUND IN BRAZIL (ABOVE).**

LEFT **AMERICAN ACE: PETER REVSON WON THE BRITISH GRAND PRIX.**

"EMMO" AT THE LAST

The 1974 season saw one of the closest Formula One World Championships in years, and in a highly dramatic finale Emerson Fittipaldi landed his second world title – and the first for the McLaren marque.

The winter of 1973–74 had been one of the busiest in memory, and the major news was that Fittipaldi had quit Lotus to join McLaren, along with substantial new backing from Texaco and Marlboro. Denny Hulme stayed on as his team-mate, while a third car – this in Yardley colours – was entered for Mike Hailwood.

Jacky Ickx left Ferrari to join Ronnie Peterson at Lotus, filling the seat left vacant by Fittipaldi, while Ken Tyrrell found himself needing two new drivers. He hired South African hot-shot Jody Scheckter from McLaren and French newcomer Patrick Depailler. Peter

Revson also left McLaren, joining French youngster Jean-Pierre Jarier at Shadow.

Graham Hill's team swapped from Shadow to Lola chassis, while Hesketh built its own car for James Hunt. BRM had new French sponsors in Motul, and Jean-Pierre Beltoise led a squad of three French drivers. Chris Amon's career took another dive when he tried to run his own team with his own car.

ALL CHANGE AT FERRARI

Perhaps the biggest shake-up was at Ferrari, though, where personnel changed and a totally new car was produced. Clay Regazzoni rejoined the Italian team after a year at BRM, and brought with him Niki Lauda who had shown some promise but was not particularly highly thought of. All that was to change once the races got underway.

From the start, the revised Ferrari line-up was competitive. Hulme won the first race in Argentina, but Regazzoni qualified on the front row and Lauda took second in the race. However, the real hero was Carlos Reutemann, who led in the neat new Brabham BT44.

Peterson and Fittipaldi duelled for the lead in the Brazilian Grand Prix until the Swede punctured, leaving Fittipaldi to score McLaren's second win. Reutemann led that race too, and finally came good by winning the South African Grand Prix at Kyalami – Brabham's first success for precisely four years. Sadly, in pre-race testing Revson was killed when he crashed his Shadow, the talented American having emerged as a frontrunner the previous season.

At the Spanish Grand Prix at Jarama, Ferrari's promise produced dividends when Lauda won. Peterson led briefly in the wet in Chapman's new 76, but the car was generally uncompetitive and Lotus soon switched back to the faithful 72. Fittipaldi scored a second win in the Belgian Grand Prix at Nivelles, and then Peterson triumphed at Monaco. Two weeks later, Tyrrell new boys Scheckter and Depailler scored a one-two in Sweden; it was that sort of season, with no one taking a clear lead.

Lauda and Regazzoni finished behind Peterson in the French Grand Prix at the new Dijon-Prenois track, and then Scheckter took his second win at Brands Hatch. Lauda led until puncturing near the end, and his exit from the pitlane was controversially blocked by hangers-on and an official car; he was eventually

awarded fifth place.

In the German Grand Prix at the Nurburgring, Lauda threw it away on the opening lap, leaving Regazzoni to save face for Ferrari. Reutemann won at the Osterreichring, and then Peterson was on top at Monza when the Ferraris failed. Still no one emerged as a likely World Champion.

FITTIPALDI GETS SERIOUS
Fittipaldi staked his claim in the penultimate race at Mosport Park, winning the Canadian Grand Prix ahead of Regazzoni. Amazingly, they went into the final race on equal points, while Scheckter was also in with a shout. In the end a fourth place at Watkins Glen was enough for Fittipaldi to take the honours, with nei-

ther of his rivals scoring. McLaren also beat Ferrari to the constructors' title. Unfortunately the race was marred by the death of Austrian rookie Helmuth Koinigg, who crashed his works Surtees early on.

The North American events saw the debut of two intriguing new marques from the USA, which had long been without representation in Formula One. Both Penske and Parnelli had ambitious plans to compete in Europe and, in Mark Donohue and Mario Andretti, each had a driver who could do the job.

The end of the year marked the retirement of Hulme, just a year after Stewart departed the scene, leaving Hill and Fittipaldi as the only World Champions still competing.

1974

Left TYRRELL TWINS: SCHECKTER HEADS DEPAILLER TO A ONE-TWO IN SWEDEN.

Above THREE DRIVERS, ONE SMILE: CLAY REGAZZONI IS THE HAPPY ONE AFTER BEATING SCHECKTER (LEFT) AND PETERSON AT THE NURBURGRING.

Left MAKING BRABHAM SMILE: CARLOS REUTEMANN SCORED HIS MAIDEN WIN AT KYALAMI AND BRABHAM'S FIRST SUCCESS FOR FOUR YEARS.

A FRESH FACE

Niki Lauda dominated the 1975 World Championship. Amazing to record, it was Ferrari's first title since John Surtees had taken the world crown 11 years earlier. Sadly, Graham Hill's death in a plane crash brought the year to a tragic close.

The close-season saw few changes apart from McLaren streamlining its operation to just one two-car team for Emerson Fittipaldi and Jochen Mass, while Graham Hill's Embassy Racing team switced from Lola chassis to its own Hill chassis. Then, following the first two races, Hill announced his retirement after a then record breaking 176 starts.

Jean-Pierre Jarier stunned everyone by giving Shadow its first pole position in the Argentinian Grand Prix, but then non-started when the transmission broke on the warm-up lap, leaving Fittipaldi

to win for McLaren ahead of James Hunt's Hesketh after the Englishman surrendered the lead by sliding wide when under pressure.

Jean-Pierre Jarier was again on pole in Brazil, and duly led for 28 laps before retiring when his fuel metering unit failed. And this left Brabham's Carlos Pace to score a popular first win in his home race ahead of local hero Fittipaldi. Pace and Brabham team-mate Carlos Reutemann then shared the front row in South Africa, but Jody Scheckter came through to score a home win for Tyrrell.

DISASTER AT MONTJUICH
The Ferraris were the pacesetters at the Spanish Grand Prix, with Niki Lauda and Clay Regazzoni on the front row. But the event was beset by a dispute over safety standards at Barcelona's Montjuich Park.

Eventually a boycott was avoided, but the race turned to chaos. Half the field crashed in the first half of the race, including the Ferraris. And this left Rolf Stommelen leading, but his rear wing broke and his Hill vaulted over the barriers to kill several onlookers. The race was stopped with Mass leading, and half points were awarded.

In a wet race at Monaco, Lauda and the Ferrari 312T came good, winning from Fittipaldi. Lauda followed that with wins at Zolder and Anderstorp, then the Dutch Grand Prix at Zandvoort brought a first win for Hunt and Hesketh. Neither were taken seriously when they started in 1973, but James had developed into a top-rank driver, and in Holland beat Lauda in a dramatic wet/dry fight. The result was reversed in France when Lauda won at Paul Ricard.

LEFT **FERRARI'S HERO: NIKI LAUDA SCORED FOUR WINS MID-SEASON TO CLINCH HIS FIRST WORLD TITLE.**

SLIP SLIDING IN THE RAIN

The rain returned at Silverstone, causing 15 cars to crash out. Shadow's Tom Pryce stunned everyone with pole and he, Pace, Regazzoni, Jarier and Hunt all took turns in the lead. When a sudden rash of crashes finally forced a red flag, Fittipaldi was ahead. Surprisingly, it was to be his last ever Formula One win.

In Germany, Reutemann survived as most of the front runners had punctures, and then in Austria rain and confusion struck once more. The popular Vittorio Brambilla was ahead when the race was curtailed to give the works March team its first win – and the first for any March since the 1970 season. Tragically, however, American driver Mark Donohue crashed his Penske-entered March in the warm-up and subsequently succumbed to head injuries.

Lauda had been quietly racking up the points, and clinched his first title with third place at Monza, as team-mate Regazzoni won. Just the US Grand Prix remained, and Lauda added yet another win. Lotus had its worst season to date, Peterson and Ickx wasting their time with the ancient 72.

November brought a further tragedy which shocked the racing world. On the way back from a test session at Paul Ricard, Hill crashed his light plane. The double world champion, his protege Tony Brise and several team members were killed.

Above **BRITISH BREAKTHROUGH: JAMES HUNT GUIDES THE PATRIOTICALLY LIVERIED HESKETH TO ITS ONE AND ONLY WIN IN HOLLAND.**

Left **DISASTER: THE WRECK OF STOMMELN'S HILL IS WINCHED BACK OVER THE BARRIERS IN BARCELONA'S MONTJUICH PARK .**

RIGHT TO THE END

This season will go down as one of the most dramatic in the long history of Formula One. Reigning champion Niki Lauda survived a terrible accident in Germany and was quickly back in harness, but James Hunt pipped him to the title by a point in the Japanese finale.

As in 1974, Emerson Fittipaldi was at the centre of the news over the close-season for, after two years, he decided to quit McLaren and join his brother Wilson's team, Copersucar. McLaren was left stranded without a number one driver, but the timing was perfect for Lord Hesketh had decided to pull the plug on his very competitive team, and Hunt was unemployed. Understandably, it did not take long for him to join McLaren. Ferrari, Shadow, Brabham and Tyrrell continued as before, but there were a couple of novelties on the car front.

Brabham secured Alfa Romeo engines, while Tyrrell stunned everyone by announcing a six-wheeled car, the P34, with four small wheels at the front and two large ones at the rear. There was confusion at Lotus as Chapman had designed a new car, the 77, but Jacky. Ickx left for the Wolf-Williams team and Ronnie Peterson was joined at the first race by Mario Andretti, a Lotus driver back in 1968–69. Neither was certain to stay, though, and matters were not helped when they collided in the first race in Brazil.

Once again Shadow's Jean-Pierre Jarier shone in Interlagos, while Hunt repaid McLaren's faith with pole. But Lauda started, as he had finished the previous season, with a win. Hunt was on pole for the South African Grand Prix,

but again Lauda won, while Peterson had quit Lotus to rejoin March. An exciting addition to the calendar came next, this being a street race at Long Beach in California, dubbed the US Grand Prix West. And Ferrari's Clay Regazzoni led the whole way.

HOME TO EUROPE
The European season began at Jarama, and all the cars looked different since new rules banned their tall airboxes, with the race also seeing the debut of Tyrrell's six-wheeler. Hunt beat Lauda, but was disqualified when his car was found to be fractionally too wide. Lauda won in Belgium and Monaco, and at neither race did Hunt score. Sweden saw a fabulous one-two for the six-wheelers, Scheckter heading home Depailler. Hunt's luck turned at the French Grand Prix at Paul

LEFT **BRITAIN IS BACK: JAMES HUNT JOINED McLAREN AND RACED TO SIX WINS AND THE TITLE.**

Ricard when the Ferraris broke and he won easily. The same week he was reinstated as Spanish winner, but at the British Grand Prix at Brands Hatch fortune did not favour him. Lauda and Regazzoni collided at the first corner, Hunt became involved and the race was stopped. He won the restart in brilliant style, but was disqualified because he had not been running at the time of the red flag, giving Lauda another win.

LAUDA'S LUCKY ESCAPE

Disaster struck in the German Grand Prix when Lauda crashed heavily and was badly burned. Hunt won the race, but the world waited for news on Lauda. Somehow he pulled through and began a remarkable recovery. Unbelievably, Lauda was back in Monza, where Peterson won for March and Niki finished fourth. Hunt scored nothing, but struck back with wins at Mosport Park and

Watkins Glen. That put him to within three points of Lauda as the circus moved to Fuji for the first Japanese Grand Prix. The weather was atrocious, and Lauda immediately pulled out as he considered the conditions too dangerous for racing safely. In a thrilling chase, Hunt came storming back from a tyre stop to take the third place he required for the crown as Andretti made Lotus smile again in winning by a full lap.

LIKE A PHOENIX...

Niki Lauda was most not the fastest driver, but he was consistent and his Ferrari proved to be extremely reliable. He succeeded in beating off strong challenges from Andretti, Hunt and Scheckter to win his second world title.

After three years with Tyrrell, Jody Scheckter quit the team to join an intriguing new team, Walter Wolf Racing, a team financed by Canadian oil millionaire Walter Wolf who had backed Williams in 1976. James Hunt and Jochen Mass stayed at McLaren to drive the new M26, the replacement for the ageing M23 and, even before the end of the 1976 season, Carlos Reutemann had left Brabham to join Ferrari, taking over from Clay Regazzoni. In addition, Ronnie Peterson replaced Scheckter at Tyrrell, and John Watson left the defunct Penske team to replace Carlos Reutemann at Brabham.

INTRODUCING "GROUND-EFFECTS"
Lotus boss Colin Chapman had pulled off another surprise, providing Mario Andretti and new team-mate Gunnar Nilsson with the stunning 78, the first "ground-effects" car. The car had prominent sidepods with sliding skirts which produced masses of downforce.

The latest Brabham-Alfa proved quick, with Watson leading the Argentinian Grand Prix until it broke. Team-mate Carlos Pace and Hunt also led, but victory went to Scheckter and the new Wolf. Ferrari's Reutemann won in Brazil, and then at Kyalami Lauda scored his first success since his accident in the 1976 German Grand Prix. Sadly, the race was marred by the death of Tom Pryce who hit a marshal who ran across the track just over a blind brow. Formula One's grief was magnified when Pace lost his life in a plane crash before the next race.

Scheckter led most of the way at Long Beach but, when he suffered a puncture, Andretti gave the Lotus 78 its first win. He quickly added a second win in the Spanish Grand Prix, this time ahead of Reutemann.

Scheckter took his second win of the season in Monaco, which marked the 100th win for Ford's Cosworth DFV. In the Belgian Grand Prix at Zolder there was a typically confusing wet race and it resulted in victory for Nilsson. Hunt had had no luck in his title defence, but he beat Watson in a splendid duel at Silverstone in a race that marked the debut of the first turbocharged engine to race in Formula One, with Jean-Pierre Jabouille at the wheel of Renault's RS01.

LEFT **THE MAIN MEN: SCHECKTER TAKES THE CHEERS AT HOCKENHEIM, BUT IT WAS LAUDA (LEFT) WHO WON THE RACE AND THE TITLE.**

Left **WOLF ON THE PROWL: JODY SCHECKTER WON FIRST TIME OUT ON THE WOLF TEAM'S DEBUT IN ARGENTINA.**

Below **V FOR VICTORY: SCHECKTER CELEBRATES AFTER THAT MAIDEN WIN IN BUENOS AIRES.**

Right **CASTING NO SHADOW: ALAN JONES'S MAIDEN WIN IN AUSTRIA WAS ALSO THE FIRST FOR THE ARROWS TEAM.**

LAUDA MAKES IT TWO

Lauda scored Goodyear's 100th win in Hockenheim, and once again the Austrian Grand Prix produced an unusual result, Alan Jones giving Shadow its first win in another damp encounter.

The summer was notable for a spate of DFV failures, with Andretti having four in a row, while Hunt and Scheckter also suffered. Meanwhile, Lauda racked up points, scoring another win at Zandvoort.

Andretti's car held together to win in Monza. Then at a wet Watkins Glen Hunt won after Pace's Brabham replacement Hans-Joachim Stuck crashed from the lead, but Lauda's fourth place clinched the title. And, with that, he left Ferrari.

There were still two races left. Scheckter won in Canada, after Mass tipped team-mate Hunt off. But Hunt ended on a high note with a win in Japan. Tragically, the race was marred by the deaths of two spectators after Ferrari new boy Gilles Villeneuve tangled with Peterson and flipped over the barrier.

Fittipaldi had another bad season with his own car, although he occasionally broke into the top six, while Peterson and Patrick Depailler struggled with the latest six-wheeler before Tyrrell ditched the concept. In contrast, Regazzoni did great things with the little Ensign team, picking up a few points along the way.

LOTUS CONTROLS ALL

Mario Andretti won the World Championship title after a brilliant run with Chapman's outstanding Lotus 79. But it was a year of mixed feelings, as teammate Ronnie Peterson died from injuries received in the Italian Grand Prix.

Nobody seemed to cotton on to the secrets of the Lotus 78, and rivals were in for a shock when Colin Chapman introduced its successor, the beautiful 79. Chapman had a new second driver, too, with Peterson back at Lotus for the first time since the start of 1976. Meanwhile, the outgoing Gunnar Nilsson joined Arrows, a team formed by a breakaway group from Shadow. Sadly, hit by cancer, he was unable to start the season, and was replaced by former Shadow driver Riccardo Patrese. Fellow former Shadow driver Alan Jones also linked up

with what was effectively a new team: Williams, as Frank Williams and partner Patrick Head produced their first car after fielding a March in 1977.

Didier Pironi joined Patrick Depailler in the four-wheeled Tyrrell 008, while Patrick Tambay replaced Jochen Mass at McLaren. Gilles Villeneuve landed a full-time seat at Ferrari, alongside Carlos Reutemann. The 312T3 proved to be a superb machine, and Ferrari switched to Michelin which had been introduced to Formula One by Renault in the hope of finding a performance advantage over their Goodyear-shod rivals.

LOTUS STARTS WINNING
Starting with the old 78, Andretti won in Argentina, with Lauda coming second just ahead of Depailler and Hunt. Then Reutemann won the Brazilian Grand Prix

for Ferrari, and Emerson Fittipaldi came good with second place in the 'family car'. The South African Grand Prix was a classic as Patrese led for Arrows, and the race culminated in a fabulous duel between Peterson and Depailler, the Swede just edging the Frenchman. Villeneuve starred at Long Beach, leading until he hit backmarker Regazzoni and allowed Reutemann to score.

Seemingly forever the bridesmaid after finishing second eight times, Depailler finally earned his first win by beating Lauda in the Monaco Grand Prix. Andretti debuted the Lotus 79 in the Belgian Grand Prix, and gave notice of his intentions by disappearing into the distance, with Peterson finishing second in the 78. They scored another one-two in the Spanish Grand Prix when Peterson had his first run in the 79.

By now the other teams were reacting to Lotus's lead. Scheckter had a proper ground-effects Wolf, and Brabham responded with the amazing 'fan car'. Lauda dominated in its only race at Anderstorp before it was pushed into a garage and never raced again as team owner Bernie Ecclestone respected calls that it was outside the spirit of the regulations and thus enjoyed an unfair performance advantage. Andretti and Peterson scored a one-two in France. At Brands Hatch they both retired, and Reutemann dived past Lauda to take his third win of the year.

TRAGEDY AT MONZA

Rain struck in Austria, and Peterson drove brilliantly to win the red-flagged race after Andretti crashed on the first lap. At Monza, only Peterson could now beat Andretti to the title, but he was happy to obey orders and support team leader Andretti's title bid. He had to take the start in the old 78, and became entangled in a massive pile-up. After a long delay the race was restarted. Andretti won from Villeneuve, but both were penalized for jumped starts, allowing Lauda to take the honours. Peterson died in hospital the following morning from complications to his injured legs – it was a death which stunned the racing world.

Jean-Pierre Jarier replaced Peterson, and was the star of the last two races, although he and Andretti retired in both the US East and Canadian Grands Prix. Reutemann held off the improving Jones in Watkins Glen, while Villeneuve scored a popular win on a new track in Montreal.

There was more sadness when Nilsson succumbed to cancer 12 days after the Canadian Grand Prix. He was just 29 years old.

ᴛᴏᴘ **FAN POWER: LAUDA PEDALS HIS BRABHAM "FAN CAR" AFTER ANDRETTI'S LOTUS EN ROUTE TO VICTORY IN SWEDEN**

ᴀʙᴏᴠᴇ **HIS FINAL WIN: PETERSON RACES TO VICTORY IN AUSTRIA AHEAD OF REUTEMANN AND THE PACK.**

1978

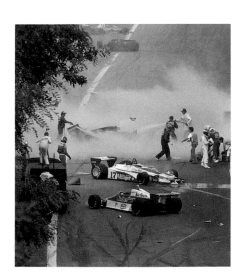

LEFT **THE AFTERMATH: A MASSIVE PILE-UP AT MONZA INVOLVED HALF THE FIELD.**

BELOW **MEDICAL EMERGENCY: PETERSON IS TENDED TO AFTER BEING EXTRICATED FROM HIS LOTUS (6). NO-ONE THOUGHT IT WOULD BE FATAL.**

FORZA FERRARI

Ground-effect cars took over the Formula One scene in 1979, although some of these worked better than others. In a very competitive season the reliability of the Ferraris put them in control and helped Jody Scheckter to scoop the title.

Things looked good at Lotus as Carlos Reutemann joined Mario Andretti, Martini replaced John Player Special as the team's title sponsor and team owner Colin Chapman still had the inside line on new technology. Or did he? The wingless Lotus 80 was supposed to be a leap forward, but it didn't work.

By way of contrast, Williams was spot-on with its FW07. It was not ready at the start of the season, though, so Alan Jones and new team-mate Clay Regazzoni started out in the FW06. Ferrari was also late introducing the 312T4, and while the Ferrari 312T4 didn't prove to be as a good a ground-effect car as its rivals, it was powerful and reliable and thus masked some of its shortcomings to the benefit of Scheckter who arrived from Wolf to join Gilles Villeneuve.

Meanwhile, after 18 months in the background, Renault expanded to a second entry for René Arnoux alongside Jean-Pierre Jabouille and built the very effective RS10.

LIGIER SPRINGS A SURPRISE
There was a major surprise when the little-fancied Ligier team started with a bang, and Jacques Laffite won the Argentinian and Brazilian Grands Prix with team-mate Patrick Depailler second in the latter. The new Ferrari arrived at Kyalami, and Villeneuve and Scheckter finished first and second. Significantly, Jabouille's Renault took its first pole, but retired from the race. Villeneuve and Scheckter repeated the result at Long Beach, where they were chased by Jones. Ligier bounced back in Spain, sweeping the front row before Depailler led throughout. Lotus had a rare good day, with Reutemann and Andretti taking second and third.

The Belgian Grand Prix marked the debut of the Patrick Head-designed Williams FW07, and the goalposts suddenly moved, for Jones led easily until retiring, leaving victory to a grateful Scheckter who won again in Monaco, chased home by Regazzoni's FW07. After retiring in this race, James Hunt decided that he had had enough, leaving the Wolf team to sign fiery Finn Keke Rosberg to replace him, as he quit the sport.

LEFT **A WINNING START: JODY SCHECKTER HIT THE WINNING TRAIL WHEN HE WAS TRIUMPHANT IN BELGIUM.**

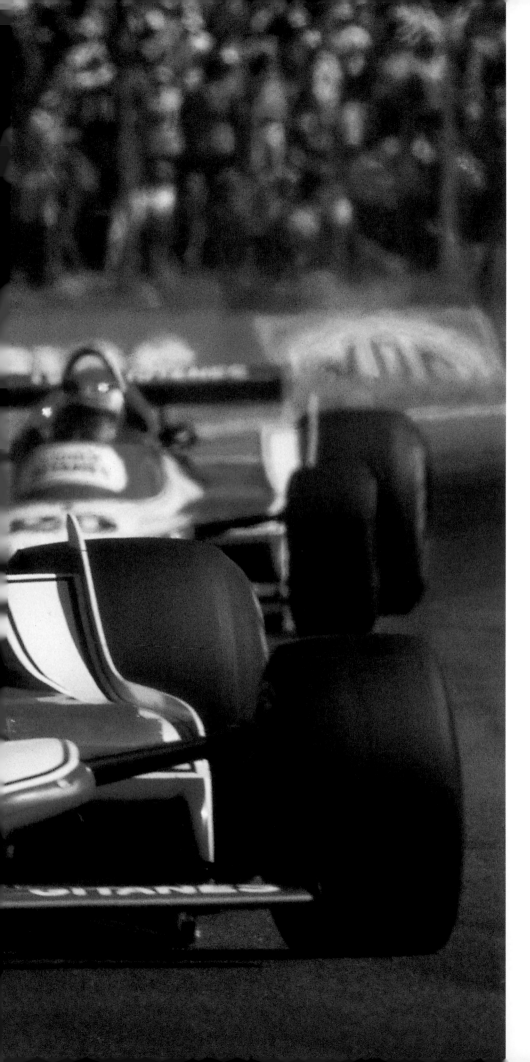

RENAULT COMES GOOD

Renault's dreams came true when Jabouille gave the team its first win, fittingly in the French Grand Prix at Dijon-Prenois. And, in a thrilling finale, Villeneuve just edged Arnoux out of second after the pair banged wheels all the way around the last lap. Then luck went the way of Williams as Regazzoni gave the team a fabulous first victory at Silverstone, which was followed by wins for Jones at Hockenheim, the Osterreichring and Zandvoort. In Holland Villeneuve dragged his three-wheeled wreckage back to the pits after he had blown a tyre while leading, but the damage was too severe for him to rejoin.

Scheckter kept collecting points, though, and by winning at Monza he had amassed enough to claim the title with two races to go. Villeneuve, under orders, followed dutifully in his wheel tracks.

By Montreal, Brabham had abandoned the awful BT48 and replaced it with the neat DFV-powered BT49. It did not interest Lauda, though, and he announced that he was quitting. The race saw a fine battle between Jones and Villeneuve, which went the way of the Williams driver as he took his fourth win of the year. The pair fought again at a wet Watkins Glen finale, but Jones lost a wheel after a pit stop, and the gutsy little Canadian won thanks to another display of Ferrari reliability.

LEFT **A FALSE DAWN: THE LIGIER PAIR OF LAFITTE AND DEPAILLER CONTROL THE ARGENTINIAN GRAND PRIX.**

THE EIGHTIES

NIGEL MANSELL

Honours: WORLD CHAMPION 1992
Grand Prix record: 187 STARTS, 31 WINS

No driver sums up the story of Formula One in the 1980s better than Nigel Mansell. For here was a man who experienced it all, from the highest high to the lowest low and, in doing so, brought Formula One a new following, especially in Britain.

"I was in Formula One for 15 years and in that time saw an incredible amount of change," explains Nigel. "If the 1990s is to be remembered, it will be for improvements in safety. The 1980s, though, will be remembered for massive changes in aerodynamics and transmission. Well, changes in every aspect really. Formula One took a major jump forward in the 1980s."

Nigel started in a small way with Lotus in 1980 after a promising but interrupted passage through the junior formulae, but came on strong and once with Williams hit a winning trail that seemed destined to make him Britain's first World Champion since James Hunt in 1976. Somehow, this didn't happen in the 1980s, with Nigel taking until 1992 to land his crown, but the experience he gained along the way offers an excellent insight.

"I'm very privileged that my career in Formula One spanned a spell that started with just over 400bhp and rose as high as 1400bhp in the turbo era," Nigel enthuses. "I also went from full ground effects to non-ground effects to flat bottoms, and from wide tyres to narrow tyres, so I sampled an enormous spread

of changes. And you must remember that ground effects were banned as drivers were blacking-out in fast corners. The drivers were going, otherwise, to have to start to wear g-force suits.

"My first Grand Prix – the Austrian in 1980 – is one that I'll never forget, because it was one of sheer excitement. Indeed, it was one of accomplishment, as with 10 minutes to go in qualifying I still hadn't qualified the third Lotus. Then to qualify with just one lap to go and only two or three minutes left was something very special as it could have gone each way. The race itself is one that left me with first and second degree burns on my legs and buttocks as I had been sitting in a bath of fuel all race until my engine expired. Afterwards, I remember being in hospital in Birmingham having my burns deroofed, so it was eventful.

"The competition was intense then and the learning curve a very steep one as almost all the cars on the grid had the same engine and we all had the same tyres, making it a more level playing field than it is now. Certainly, the car designs were different, but there was greater parity then. However, like now, it was

far better then to be a team's number one driver than the number two, and that was better than being the team's number three... However, like now, it came down to budgets."

Thanks to Lotus supremo Colin Chapman, Nigel not only raced in two more Grands Prix that year but signed up for a full campaign in 1981, his selection based on Nigel's talent alone as he had no budget to offer. Not a penny...

"When I look back at what I thought when I was trying to break into Formula One, it's amazing," Nigel muses. "I have no idea where I got the strength and direction, but I never thought that I wouldn't get in as others had money and I didn't. I simply thought that I couldn't compete on the money front and so I would have to get in through talent, dedication or sheer skill. I never thought I was in competition with them, as I pigeon-holed them in a different category. I had nothing on offer but just raw talent and that's why I got on so well with Colin Chapman."

So, his years of struggle were rewarded: "I think that in the 1970s it was far more difficult to rise to the top in motor racing than it is today. It was far more competitive as there was far less money around for racing. Sure, it was relatively less expensive, but there is more money around now because of a greater awareness of racing in Britain now since James Hunt, myself and Damon Hill became World Champion. Also, there are a lot more opportunities to make a career in racing, with so many other branches of the sport in which they can earn a living, such as Indycars and sportscars.

"You can always say that people today don't have to make the sacrifices we did, but I look at the positive side and the best have still got hunger. It doesn't matter what background they come from. Specialist writers talk of some drivers having natural talent and others not having it. But you have to have talent full stop to drive a Formula One car. Yes, people can say drivers have flair or are racers. I certainly was a racer and so was Ayrton (Senna), while others, including World Champions, were drivers rather than racers. But it sorts itself out at the pinnacle whether a driver has had an easy route to Formula One or not. The people who haven't got the dedication, haven't made the sacrifices and aren't prepared to put it on the line aren't going to achieve a lot."

On the podium at Zolder with third place at the fourth race of 1981, Nigel ended the season 14th overall, a feat he repeated the following year, both times classified behind team-mate Elio de Angelis. In 1983 Nigel pulled ahead of the Italian. But by then, Nigel had lost his mentor when Chapman died at the end of 1982. It was a loss that hit Nigel hard.

"I think of Colin every day," Nigel reminisces. "He did so much more for me than giving me my break in Formula One. He treated me as a son, taught me things as a father, consoled us when we had downs and helped us progress as human beings. For instance, the first year I drove for Lotus I couldn't afford for (my wife) Rosanne to give up work. When Colin found out how much we were struggling, he doubled my salary overnight then. It wasn't much, but it was enough to let Rosanne give up her job and come to the races. It was such a rewarding relationship that I reckon I would have won another couple of World Championships if Colin was still alive today, and I would have probably won my first World Championship a lot sooner."

However, world titles were still some way off as Nigel had yet to score his first win. It looked on the cards at Monaco in 1984, but he skidded into the barriers in the wet when leading. Then a move to Williams in 1985 came good with two wins, with his breakthrough coming at Brands Hatch.

"My first win didn't change me, but it was simply such a relief," says Nigel. "It was so rewarding to drive for Frank (Williams) and Patrick (Head), and especially with Keke (Rosberg) as a former World Champion. He was the best team-mate I ever had. He was very honest."

And then the wins started flowing. Indeed, Nigel went into the 1986 finale at Adelaide with five wins under his belt and a six-point lead over McLaren's Alain Prost, with his own team-mate Nelson Piquet a further point behind. But then it all went wrong and he crashed out of the lead with a 180mph blow-out.

"The blow-out was not a favourite moment. I had a healthy advantage with 18 laps to go when it happened. With Nelson having hit tyre trouble, I asked to pit. But they told me to stay out and it blew..."

Six wins followed in 1987, but Nigel ended up second again, this time behind Piquet. Still, that was good next to what happened in 1988: "The 1988 season was a letdown as we lost an engine deal with Honda at the last minute when they went to McLaren and this left us with Judd engines. I finished only twice, but at least both times I finished I finished second."

And so it was time to change team, with Nigel moving on to Ferrari for 1989: "It was a sheer delight to drive for Ferrari," says Nigel, eyes bright at the memory. "Yes, there were a lot of politics, but I still have a great relationship with the team and a lot of respect for them. I would have been very disappointed if I'd never been able to drive for Ferrari. I have the accolade of winning my first race for them, a feat only one other driver achieved (Giancarlo Baghetti) and this means a lot to me as they have had some very special drivers drive for them. I hope that the team will land the success in 1999 they have been striving for for 20 years now. I certainly think things are much better at Ferrari than they were when I raced for them. Italians are very emotional people and in the past a lot of emotional decisions were taken that might have been for individuals but for the competitiveness of the team wasn't the correct thing to do. There's a better balance now."

After two years there, Nigel returned to Williams and ended up runner-up for the third time, this time finishing second behind McLaren's Senna. But then it all came good in 1992 and he raced away to win the first five races and then added four more before the season was out, wrapping up the title in Hungary with five races still to run. Yet, for all that, he was not kept on for 1993...

"The way I left Williams at the end of 1992 was a major disappointment," Nigel relates, "as everybody seemed to tell different people different things. I was sad that I wasn't offered a chance to defend my title, as they asked me to halve my salary. There was also pressure from Renault for Williams to run a French driver, thus Prost. This opened the door for my move

RIGHT **PIPPED AT THE POST: AYRTON SENNA HOLDS OFF MANSELL'S WILLIAMS TO WIN THE 1986 SPANISH GRAND PRIX AT JEREZ BY JUST 0.014 SECONDS.**

JUST WILLIAMS

Alan Jones won the 1980 title after overcoming a strong challenge from Nelson Piquet. But, just as Colin Chapman failed to follow up on his 1978 success, so Enzo Ferrari's team lost its way in 1980. Scheckter and Villeneuve would struggle, with Jody's title defence consisting of a solitary fifth place.

In contrast, Williams maintained its momentum with the updated FW07B and Reutemann moved on from Lotus to join Jones. Ligier regained form with the JS11/15, and Pironi joined Laffite to be the find of the season.

Brabham fortunes picked up, and with Lauda and Alfa Romeo gone, Piquet assumed team leadership. Andretti stayed on at Lotus, with Elio de Angelis joining him, while Nigel Mansell was test driver. Renault continued with Jabouille

and Arnoux, while Alain Prost joined Watson at McLaren. Alfa Romeo entered cars for Bruno Giacomelli and Depailler, who was still recovering from his hanggliding accident.

Jones kicked off by dominating the Argentinian Grand Prix in an old-spec FW07. Piquet was second, while Rosberg gave a hint of his potential with third.

Jabouille and Pironi shared the front row at Interlagos, but a heroic effort from Villeneuve earned third. After that it was an all-French battle and, when both Jabouille and Laffite had problems, Arnoux raced away to his first win.

Arnoux repeated his success in South Africa. Laffite and Pironi followed the Renault home. Long Beach saw the end of Clay Regazzoni's career, the Swiss having left Williams to rejoin Ensign. He crashed heavily, and was subsequently

confined to a wheelchair. Meanwhile, Piquet took pole and scored his first win, ahead of Patrese and Fittipaldi.

The FW07B made its bow at Zolder, and although it was quick, Jones and Reutemann were led home by Pironi, another first time winner. Pironi was on form again at Monaco, but after he hit the barrier Reutemann scored his first Williams win.

Politics and racing collided head-on at Jarama as FOCA was in dispute with FISA. A confusing weekend ended with a "Formula DFV" race going ahead without Ferrari, Alfa and Renault. Laffite and Reutemann collided, Piquet's gearbox broke and Pironi lost a wheel – leaving Jones to win a race that was later declared non-championship.

At Paul Ricard, Jones delighted in beating Ligier and Renault on home ground, Pironi and Laffite following him home. The Ligiers were superb at Brands Hatch, but they suffered wheel problems and Jones came through to win.

The Renaults were quick but fragile in Germany, and when leader Jones had a puncture Laffite took the victory. Sadly, in pre-race testing Depailler crashed fatally.

France took another win in Austria, Jabouille scoring his second success as he held off the determined Jones. Mansell was finally given his chance in a third Lotus, only to have to start the race in a fuel-soaked race suit.

In Holland, Jones damaged a skirt and Piquet won ahead of Arnoux. The Italian GP moved to Imola, and Piquet won and took a one-point lead from Jones in the championship.

WILLIAMS'S FIRST TITLE
The situation was tense going to Montreal, and it blew up when Piquet and Jones triggered a huge pile-up. For the re-start, Piquet had to start in the spare, and his engine failed. Pironi led throughout, but was penalized for a jumped start, so Jones took maximum points and the title. It was the first title for Williams. Jabouille broke his legs after a suspension breakage.

Jones went off at the first corner at Watkins Glen, then recovered to win from Reutemann and Pironi. Two big names drove their final races. Having failed to qualify in Canada, Scheckter finished 11th and last, while Fittipaldi broke his suspension, ending another disappointing season with his own team.

Above **FLYING START: RENE ARNOUX WON TWO OF THE FIRST THREE GRANDS PRIX FOR RENAULT BEFORE HIS SEASON TAILED OFF.**

Right **FLYING THE ENSIGN: CLAY REGAZZONI CAME BACK FOR MORE WITH ENSIGN, BUT CRASHED AND WAS CONFINED TO A WHEELCHAIR AFTER A CRASH AT THE US GRAND PRIX WEST.**

PIQUET FOR BRAZIL

Nelson Piquet turned the tables on Alan Jones in 1981, winning his first World Championship title and the first for Brabham since Bernie Ecclestone took control. Unfortunately, off-track disputes dominated the headlines.

After the disaster of 1980, Ferrari switched to a new V6 turbo engine, becoming the first to follow Renault's pioneering route.

The other big news was Ron Dennis's takeover of McLaren, for whom John Barnard set to work on a revolutionary carbonfibre chassis, while Alain Prost left to replace Jean-Pierre Jabouille at Renault.

The season began at Long Beach and Riccardo Patrese took a surprise pole for Arrows, but victory went to champion Jones, ahead of Williams's Carlos Reutemann and Piquet. The Ferraris were quick but fragile. In Brazil the decision to ban sliding skirts turned to farce as Brabham had a perfected a hydro-pneumatic suspension system – the car was legal in the pits, but on the track it squatted and the skirts touched the ground. Piquet took pole, started the wet race on slicks and blew it. Reutemann controverisally led Jones home after reneging on a pre-race deal.

In Argentina Piquet made no mistake, winning easily, while unrated team-mate Hector Rebaque ran in second place until his car broke.

The European season started at Imola with the new San Marino Grand Prix – an excuse to have two races in Italy. Gilles Villeneuve and Didier Pironi both led the wet race early on, but Piquet came through to win from Patrese and Reutemann.

In the Belgian Grand Prix at Zolder, a mechanic from the Osella team died after being struck by a car in practice and an Arrows mechanic had his legs broken when hit attending Patrese's stalled car on the grid – just as the race started. Pironi led until his brakes went, Jones crashed out after earlier knocking Piquet off and victory went to Reutemann.

Nigel Mansell was in great form at Monaco for Lotus, qualifying third behind Piquet and Villeneuve. Piquet led, but Jones put him under pressure and he crashed. Then Jones suffered a fuel pick-up problem and Villeneuve sped by for a superb win in the unwieldy Ferrari. Amazingly, he repeated that success at Jarama. After Jones fell off, Villeneuve led home a train comprising Ligier's Jacques Laffite, McLaren's John Watson, Reutemann and Lotus's Elio de Angelis.

LEFT **THE SECOND BRAZILIAN CHAMPION: VICTORY AT HOCKENHEIM HELPED NELSON PIQUET FOLLOW IN COMPATRIOT FITTIPALDI'S FOOTSTEPS.**

RIGHT **McLAREN'S DAY: JOHN WATSON RACES TO VICTORY AT SILVERSTONE.**

BELOW **THE FIRST OF 51: ALAIN PROST FIRES THE BUBBLY AFTER SCORING HIS FIRST WIN, ON HOME GROUND IN DIJON-PRENOIS.**

RIGHT **TWO-BIT WONDER: PROST'S SUCCESS IN FRANCE WAS AN AGGREGATE ONE AS THIRD IN PART ONE WAS IMPROVED ON WITH A VICTORY IN PART TWO.**

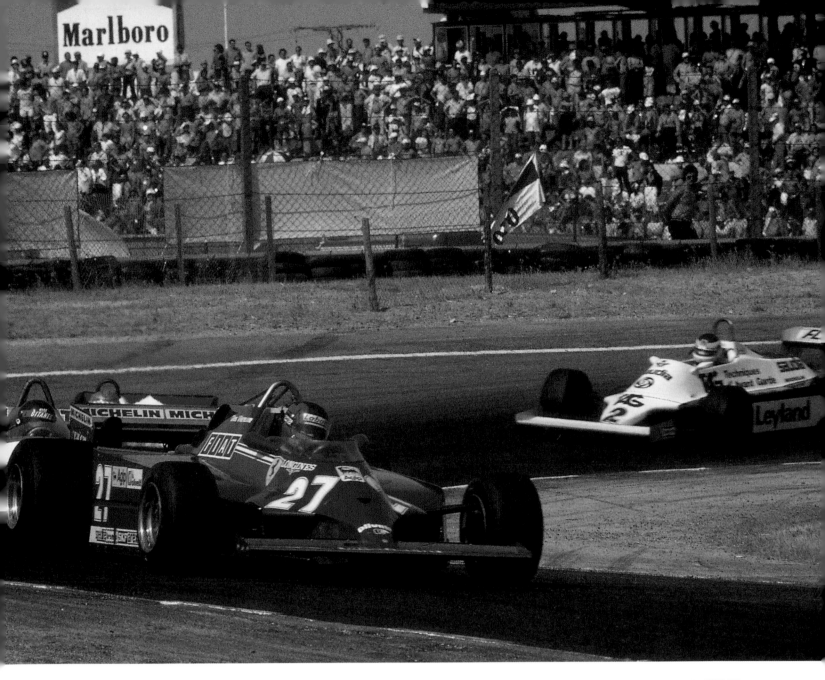

Above **DRIVING A WIDE CAR: VILLENEUVE HAD TO USE EVERY TRICK TO KEEP LAFFITE, WATSON AND REUTEMANN BEHIND HIM IN THE SPANISH GRAND PRIX.**

The French Grand Prix at Dijon-Prenois was another odd race, for rain split it into two parts, and Prost scored his first win in the Renault ahead of Watson and Piquet.

WATSON TAKES GOLD
Watson's big day came at Silverstone. Prost and team-mate Rene Arnoux took turns leading, but when they failed Watson won. It was his first win since Austria in 1976.

Villeneuve, Prost and Arnoux all took turns to lead in Germany, but Piquet took a canny win, with Prost second. Then Austria brought a popular win for Laffite.

At Zandvoort Prost and Jones fought hard in the early stages, until Jones's tyres went off and Prost pulled away to win from Piquet, with Jones third. With Reutemann tangling with Laffite, Piquet took the title lead. Prost then led all the way at Monza, winning from Jones and Reutemann, the latter passing Piquet

when his engine blew on the last lap.

The Canadian Grand Prix was an exciting, wet event. Jones spun off while leading, Prost took over, then Laffite got to the front and held on to win. So they headed for the finale with Reutemann on 49, Piquet on 48, and Laffite on 43. The race was held in a car park in Las Vegas. Reutemann took pole, but faded away as Jones won with Piquet taking fifth and Laffite sixth, which gave Piquet the title by a point.

ONE WIN IS ENOUGH

The 1982 season proved to be one of the most turbulent – and tragic – in the history of Formula One. And Williams's Keke Rosberg became the first man since 1964 to secure the World Championship with just a single victory to his name.

Niki Lauda was back racing again after two years out of harness, joining John Watson at McLaren; Williams replaced Alan Jones with Keke Rosberg; and Brabham looked well set with Riccardo Patrese as Nelson Piquet's team-mate.

Piquet crashed in the opening race at Kyalami, and the Renaults dominated until Alain Prost had a puncture. But he charged back from eighth to win from Carlos Reutemann's Williams and Rene Arnoux's Renault. Piquet made amends by winning the Brazilian Grand Prix from Rosberg and Prost, but the first two were then disqualified for being underweight. They had both had their water tanks for brake cooling topped up after the race, and this was adjudged an illegal way of bringing them back to the minimum weight.

Lauda won at Long Beach from Rosberg. The disqualifications of Piquet and Rosberg in Brazil led the FOCA teams to boycott the San Marino Grand Prix, and it was a half-hearted event with just 14 cars entering. Tyrrell, bound by Italian sponsors, broke ranks to join the manufacturer outfits. Ferrari's Didier Pironi and Gilles Villeneuve traded the lead in what many thought was a show for the fans. Pironi passed Villeneuve on the last lap to win, and since Villeneuve thought he had broken an agreement, a deadly feud began.

A BLACK DAY AT ZOLDER
The feud rumbled on to the Belgian Grand Prix at Zolder where, in final qualifying, desperate to outgun Pironi, Villeneuve hit the back of Jochen Mass's March and was launched into a roll and thrown from his car. The most entertaining driver of the era was killed. The race went ahead without Ferrari, and Watson won.

Monaco was unbelievably dramatic. Arnoux led until spinning, Prost took over until crashing heavily with three laps to go; Patrese then led, but spun, and Pironi and Alfa Romeo's Andrea de Cesaris went by. With one lap to go, Pironi stopped with electrical problems, de Cesaris ran out of fuel and Williams replacement Derek Daly retired after clouting the barrier. Patrese recovered to win a race that no-one seemed to want to win.

LEFT **THE START OF THE END: PIRONI DISOBEYS A SUPPOSED PRE-RACE AGREEMENT TO BEAT VILLENEUVE AT IMOLA.**

In Montreal, now named the Circuit Gilles Villeneuve. Pironi stalled on pole and was hit by newcomer Riccardo Paletti, who was killed. Piquet won the race, Patrese came in second. Then Ferrari finally had some good news, Pironi winning the Dutch Grand Prix in fine style ahead of Piquet and Rosberg.

Brands Hatch saw Lauda win but the star of the race was Derek Warwick, who got the tank-like Toleman up to second before retiring. Pironi went to Hockenheim leading by nine points. But in wet practice struck the back of Prost's Renault in a career-ending accident that broke his legs. In the race, Patrick Tambay scored his first win in the second Ferrari, ahead of Arnoux and Rosberg.

In the Swiss Grand Prix, held at Dijon-Prenois in France, the Renaults led, but Rosberg came through to score his first win from Prost. After Arnoux won at Monza from Tambay, Watson then had to win the final race in the car park of Caesar's Palace at Las Vegas, to deprive Rosberg of the title. Arnoux and Prost both led, but a shock victory went to Tyrrell's Michele Alboreto. Watson was second, but it was not enough and fifth-placed Rosberg took the honours.

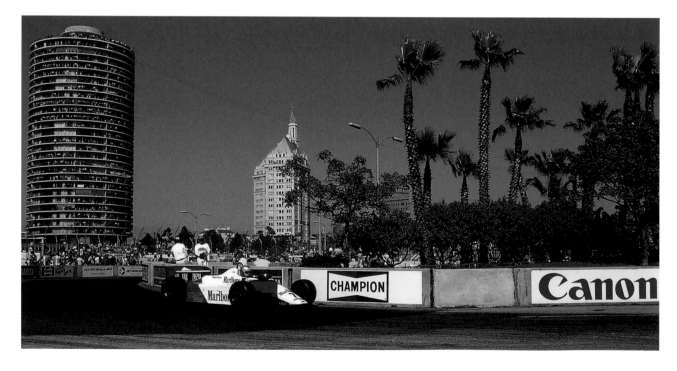

ABOVE **COMEBACK KING: NIKI LAUDA CAME BACK FROM RETIREMENT, WINNING HERE AT LONG BEACH FOR MCLAREN.**

RIGHT **FALLING BACK: NELSON PIQUET HAD A DREADFUL TITLE DEFENCE WITH HIS BRABHAM-BMW.**

PIQUET DOES IT AGAIN

Nelson Piquet notched up his second world title as Alain Prost and Renault threw away their chances during what was a safe season that was also without strikes or technical squabbles.

New flat-bottom regulations cut downforce and got rid of the sidepods, while turbos (and pit stops) became essential. And Williams, for whom champion Keke Rosberg was joined by Jacques Laffite, wasn't ready and would have to spend another year with Ford Cosworth DFV power until its Honda-powered car was ready, with the Japanese manufacturer back after a 15-year break making a low-key start with the small Spirit team. McLaren, too, had to be patient. It had arranged for sponsor TAG to pay for Porsche's V6 and, until that was ready, Lauda and Watson were also stuck with the DFV. Colin Chapman secured Renault engines for Lotus. Although he died suddenly, Lotus carried on: Elio de Angelis had the new car for race two, while Nigel Mansell used DFV power until mid-season.

PIQUET STARTS IN STYLE

Piquet won in impressive style in Rio, but Rosberg drew all the attention. He led, had a fire at his pit stop, recovered to second and was then excluded for a push start. McLaren's Niki Lauda and Laffite finished second and third.

Long Beach was a rare opportunity for the DFV cars to shine. John Watson and team-mate Lauda qualified 22nd and 23rd, but they got the race set-up right and came charging through to finish one-two, with Ferrari's Rene Arnoux third.

Unusually, the European season kicked off at Paul Ricard and Renault continued its habit of winning at home, with Prost coming first.

Patrick Tambay scored an emotional win for Ferrari at Imola, well aware that a year earlier his friend Gilles Villeneuve had been robbed by Didier Pironi.

Rosberg qualified sixth behind the turbos at Monaco, but it rained and he chose to start on slicks. He was in the lead by the lap two and pulled away as the others pitted.

After a 13-year break, the Belgian Grand Prix returned to the Spa-Francorchamps circuit in rebuilt and shortened form. Alfa Romeo's Andrea de Cesaris took the lead, but retired with engine problems. Prost took over and held on to the flag.

Detroit saw Michele Alboreto score his second win for Tyrrell, taking the lead

LEFT **DOUBLE CHAMPION: PIQUET FOUND BMW POWER MORE TO HIS LIKING AND WON THREE RACES EN ROUTE TO THE TITLE.**

Above **SLEEK AND MEAN: THE GORDON MURRAY-DESIGNED BRABHAM BT52 WAS AN EFFECTIVE CHASSIS IN PIQUET'S HANDS.**

Right **SURPRISE, SURPRISE: WATSON UNCORKS THE CHAMPAGNE IN LONG BEACH AFTER HE AND LAUDA CAME THROUGH FROM THE BACK.**

Above Right **FERRARI'S FRIEND: TAMBAY GAVE FERRARI AN EMOTIONAL WIN AT IMOLA AND WAS PLACED FOURTH OVERALL.**

Left **FALLEN AT THE LAST: PROST WON HERE IN FRANCE, BUT LOST THE TITLE AT THE LAST ROUND.**

when Piquet pitted with a puncture. This was the 155th and last victory for the Ford Cosworth DFV. In Canada, Arnoux dominated for Ferrari, ahead of Renault's Eddie Cheever and Tambay.

The Ferraris led at Silverstone, but Prost pushed them as they used up their tyres. Piquet came through to take second, with Tambay third.

Arnoux won again at Hockenheim, although he defied team orders at the start when he was supposed to let Tambay stay ahead. Tambay retired, while Piquet lost out with a major fire and de Cesaris took a lucky second place.

Prost had to work hard to win in Austria, passing Arnoux with six laps to go. Piquet kept his title hopes alive with third, and Prost's lead was now 14 points. He got it wrong in Holland, sliding into Piquet, putting them both out, leaving Arnoux to win from tenth.

Monza brought the worst possible result for Prost: retirement, while Piquet won and Arnoux was second. Brands Hatch hosted the Grand Prix of Europe and Piquet won again, but Prost kept his hopes alive with second.

Just South Africa remained, and Piquet was quick in the first half, while Arnoux stopped early and Prost became stuck in a battle for third. But his turbo was failing and he retired. Piquet dropped to third, as Patrese won from de Cesaris, but ensured that he scored the vital points needed for the second title.

McLAREN MEN DOMINATE

Niki Lauda displayed his judgement and guile when he beat his faster and younger McLaren team-mate Alain Prost to take the world title. This was to be the first of many great years for Ron Dennis's team.

Alain Prost stunned Formula One when he joined McLaren, after falling out with Renault. Indeed, it was all-change at Renault, with Patrick Tambay and Derek Warwick joining as Eddie Cheever found a new home at Alfa Romeo, where he was joined by Riccardo Patrese.

Ligier had sourced Renault engines and attracted Andrea de Cesaris. Arrows had a BMW deal, although Thierry Boutsen and Marc Surer, would start the year with Ford DFVs. Tyrrell was blessed with two great rookies in Stefan Bellof and Martin Brundle.

Ferrari's Michele Alboreto led in Brazil, but spun off, letting Lauda and Warwick take turns in front, but Warwick's suspension broke and Prost came through to win, while Rosberg was second.

Piquet led at Kyalami until hitting turbo problems, and Lauda grabbed an easy win from Prost who'd started in the spare and stormed up from the back. Toleman's Ayrton Senna scored his first point.

Alboreto led all the way from pole at Zolder for his first win in a Ferrari, with Warwick second.

Prost led all the way at Imola, despite a spin. Lauda's engine blew and Piquet held second until a turbo failed, so Arnoux inherited the place. Tambay led for Renault at Dijon-Prenois, but had brake and clutch problems, letting Lauda by to win.

Monaco was wet, and Tambay and Warwick crashed at the first corner, while Prost led Nigel Mansell's Lotus. Then Mansell took the lead, only to crash. Prost regained the lead and was still in front of the fast-closing Senna and Bellof when the race was red-flagged.

Piquet was back on form in Montreal. The Brabham had a new oil cooler in the front, intended to help with weight distribution, but it burned his feet while leading from start to finish...

Detroit started with a shunt between Piquet, Prost and Mansell, for which Mansell got the blame. All three were back for the restart, and Piquet led throughout. Star of the race was Brundle, who climbed from 11th to second.

CRACKING IN THE HEAT
Next was Dallas. It was ragingly hot, the track broke up, many crashed and Formula One never returned. Rosberg dominated after passing Mansell who

then hit gearbox trouble and collapsed while pushing his car to the line for sixth.

Sanity returned at Brands Hatch, although the race was stopped after Jonathan Palmer crashed his RAM. Prost led until his gearbox failed, leaving Lauda to win from Warwick and Senna.

Lotus's Elio de Angelis and Piquet retired while leading the German Grand Prix, leaving Prost to win from Lauda. Prost spun off in Austria when second, and Lauda won from Piquet and Alboreto.

Piquet led in Holland until he suffered an oil leak, so Prost and Lauda completed another demo.

LAUDA NICKS ONE
Prost's engine blew in Monza, and once Piquet did his usual trick of retiring while leading, Lauda cantered to victory from Alboreto.

By now Tyrrell had been banned for irregularities found in Detroit, losing their points. Many saw sinister undertones in the way the sole "atmo" runner was thrown out.

For the first time Formula One went to the new Nürburgring for the European Grand Prix. Prost led all the way, while Alboreto and Piquet – both out of fuel at the finish – were second and third. Lauda was fourth after a spin.

Prost won the finale at Estoril, but Lauda did all he needed to do and came second to secure the title by the closest ever margin: half a point.

LEFT MAN FOR THE MOMENT: WHILE THE
TRACK AND THE DRIVERS FLAKED IN
DALLAS, ROSBERG RACED TO VICTORY
FOR WILLIAMS.

ABOVE NOT LIKE THE ORIGINAL:
FORMULA ONE RETURNED TO THE
NURBURGRING, BUT THE NEW TRACK
WAS NOTHING LIKE THE OLD. PROST
WON.

PROST'S FIRST OF FOUR

Alain Prost secured his first World Championship after a highly competitive year in the McLaren-TAG. Driver moves included Nigel Mansell joining Williams. Meanwhile, Ayrton Senna got out of a commitment to Toleman to join Lotus, alongside de Angelis. François Hesnault moved from Ligier to Brabham, so once again Piquet had a team-mate who was no threat. He also had the novelty of Pirelli rubber.

The McLaren, Ferrari and Renault line-ups went unchanged. Jacques Laffite returned to Ligier alongside de Cesaris. Tyrrell finally joined the turbo club, landing a Renault deal for Brundle and Bellof. However, they'd have to start with the DFV.

Several new teams appeared, with Pierluigi Martini handling the Minardi. From Germany came touring car specialist Zakspeed, while Indycar entrant Carl Haas had backing from Beatrice and enticed Alan Jones out of retirement to drive a Lola.

Alboreto put Ferrari on pole in Rio. Rosberg was alongside, and both led, but Prost won with Alboreto second. Senna stormed to his first win in the wet at Esttoril with Alboreto a minute behind in second and Tambay's Renault third.

Senna led at Imola until running out of fuel, then Johansson looked set to win, but he too ran dry. Prost won – only to be disqualified for being underweight and victory was awarded to de Angelis. Prost won in Monaco, with Alboreto second from de Angelis.

In Canada Lotus swept the front row. De Angelis led before Alboreto took over to win. Johansson made it a Ferrari one-two, with Prost third.

COSWORTH SCORES FINAL POINTS
Senna was on pole in Detroit, but he was one of many to crash, along with Mansell and Prost. Rosberg gave Williams its first win of the year. Ferrari's Johansson and Alboreto filled the podium. History was made by the car in fourth; Bellof's Tyrrell gave the Cosworth its last top-six finish, 18 years after its debut.

Rosberg was on pole at Paul Ricard, but it was Brabham's day. Piquet won and gave Pirelli its first success since Monza 1957! Rosberg took second, ahead of Prost.

Senna led the British Grand Prix at Silverstone, until he ran out of fuel. Prost then won by a lap, from Alboreto, Laffite and Piquet. The new Nurburgring played host to the German Grand Prix for the first time. Teo Fabi took a surprise pole for Toleman. Ferrari's Alboreto and

LEFT **WHEN FOURTH IS ENOUGH: PROST WAS SO DOMINANT THAT HE WRAPPED UP THE TITLE AT BRANDS HATCH WITH TWO RACES TO GO.**

185

Above **KING OF THE DELUGE: SENNA WAS IN A CLASS OF HIS OWN AT ESTORIL, SCORING HIS FIRST WIN FOR LOTUS.**

Right **HOW NOT TO DO IT: PIQUET AND PATRESE GET IT ALL WRONG AT STE. DEVOTE. NEITHER CONTINUED.**

Johansson tangled at the first corner, but Alboreto recovered to win with Alain Prost coming in second.

The Austrian Grand Prix was restarted after a first lap crash. Lauda led and, after he retired with turbo failure, Prost went on to win. Senna and Alboreto completed the top three.

Zandvoort hosted a Grand Prix for the last time. Piquet took pole, but Rosberg led, then Prost took control when Rosberg retired with a failed engine, but Lauda came through to score his first win of the season – and what turned out to be his last.

Senna took pole at Monza and Rosberg starred. But victory went to Prost, ahead of Piquet and Senna. Prost was on pole at Spa, but Senna won from Mansell. Prost took third, and put himself within reach of the title.

Brands Hatch hosted the European Grand Prix and Mansell won in front of his home crowd ahead of Senna and Rosberg. Meanwhile, fourth place clinched the title for a cautious Prost. Then Mansell took pole at Kyalami and led Rosberg home, with Prost third.

The season ended with a new race in Adelaide. Senna took pole, but Prost won the high-attrition event. Ligier ended on a high, with Laffite and Streiff second and third. Lauda retired from racing, but this time permanently. The Renault team quit too, after an awful season.

Although Formula One had enjoyed a relatively safe season, two drivers lost their lives in sportscars: Manfred Winkelhock died at Mosport, while Tyrrell's Bellof was killed at Spa.

OUT WITH A BANG

This championship saw one of the most dramatic conclusions ever. Williams team-mates Nigel Mansell and Nelson Piquet had fought hard all year for the championship lead, but in the final race Mansell blew a tyre, Piquet made a precautionary stop, and McLaren's Alain Prost sped through to the title.

Having lost Niki Lauda to retirement, McLaren replaced him with another former world champion: Keke Rosberg. The Finn was also replaced at Williams by a champion with Nelson Piquet moving across from Brabham. Lotus wanted to hire Derek Warwick, but Ayrton Senna did not want a top name alongside him, so they chose newcomer Johnny Dumfries. Meanwhile, Elio de Angelis left Lotus for Brabham. Over the winter Toleman turned into Benetton, and

Gerhard Berger joined Teo Fabi with BMW engines, perhaps the most powerful in the field.

Piquet won his home Grand Prix at Rio. Senna took pole, and he and Prost led before Piquet took over.

Spain had a Grand Prix again, this time at Jerez. And it produced a thrilling race, with Senna holding off Mansell by 0.014 second.

Senna was on pole at Imola, but a jammed wheel bearing forced him out, while Rosberg fell from second to fifth, his tank dry. Piquet and Rosberg led, but the reliable Prost was there to win from Piquet.

Prost broke Senna's string of poles at Monaco, and led Rosberg home after Senna led briefly, but fell to third.

Then tragedy struck when de Angelis was killed in testing at Paul Ricard.

Piquet took pole for the Belgian

Grand Prix, but Mansell came through to win from Senna and Johansson. In a black weekend in June, former Osella driver Jo Gartner was killed in the Le Mans 24 Hours, while Arrows star Marc Surer was badly injured in a rally.

Brabham was back to strength in Canada, Warwick returning from the Jaguar sports car team. But Mansell took pole and won from Prost.

Senna won from pole in Detroit, but both Ligiers took a turn in the lead, with Jacques Laffite finishing second.

Mansell won at Paul Ricard, ahead of Prost, Piquet and Rosberg. And nobody was going to stop him at Brands Hatch, although Piquet pipped him for pole. Mansell had a driveshaft break, but his day was saved by a red flag as Laffite hit a barrier and broke his legs. Mansell won the restart after a fierce tussle with Piquet.

LEFT **MANSELL IN A FLAP: THIS BLOW-OUT AT ADELAIDE WAS PROBABLY THE MOST DRAMATIC LOSS OF A CHAMPIONSHIP EVER.**

Above **NOT THIS TIME: NELSON PIQUET WON FOUR RACES FOR WILLIAMS, BUT IT WASN'T ENOUGH FOR HIS THIRD WORLD TITLE.**

The German Grand Prix returned to Hockenheim. On this power track it was a surprise to see Rosberg and Prost on the front row, but the Finn led before Piquet took over and won to keep his title challenge alive.

LOOKING TO THE EAST
The twisty Hungaroring circuit made its debut, as Formula One made its first visit to the Eastern bloc and Piquet outran Senna to win.

BMW power ruled in Austria as Fabi and Berger filled the front row for Benetton. Berger led until his turbo blew, and in a race of high attrition it was inevitably Prost who kept it flowing to win from Ferrari's Michele Alboreto.

Fabi took pole at Monza with what was possibly the most powerful car ever seen in Formula One, but Piquet led Mansell to a Williams one-two. Senna was then on pole for the Portuguese Grand Prix, but Mansell led all the way to win from Prost and Piquet.

The campaign's third new track was in fact an old one – but the circus had not visited Mexico City since 1970. Benetton came good and Berger scored his first win.

In a dramatic finale in Adelaide, Mansell was perfectly placed to take the title when a rear tyre blew. Williams made Piquet pit for a precautionary tyre change, and he fell to second behind Prost, with victory giving the little Frenchman his second title.

RIGHT RUNNING ON EMPTY: PROST
CRUISED TO VICTORY IN AUSTRIA, HIS
ENGINE CUTTING OUT AT THE END.

PIQUET MAKES IT THREE

Williams team-mates Nelson Piquet and Nigel Mansell fought for the title until an accident sidelined Mansell in Japan. And Piquet thus accepted the laurels for the third time.

With the turbo era getting out of hand, a new formula was announced. From 1989, Formula One would revert to atmospheric engines, but at the larger 3.5-litre capacity. There would be two interim years, and to encourage teams to change, a separate classification was introduced, with "atmo" drivers battling for the Jim Clark Cup. Cosworth produced the DFZ, for which Tyrrell was the first major team to build cars. They hired Jonathan Palmer and Philippe Streiff, and would dominate. Their opponents were AGS and a new team from former Renault Sport boss Gerard Larrousse.

After a year as just an engine supplier Renault had withdrawn, and Lotus landed on its feet by attracting Honda, with Satoru Nakajima as part of the package. With Haas out, Ford teamed up with Benetton and Thierry Boutsen joined Teo Fabi there, as Gerhard Berger had moved to Ferrari, where he partnered Michele Alboreto as Stefan Johansson left Ferrari to join Alain Prost at McLaren.

Mansell and Piquet shared the front row in Rio and, although Piquet led early on, Prost won, with Piquet finishing second and Johansson third.

In Imola, Piquet crashed in practice and didn't start. Senna led, but Mansell powered past to win.

The Belgian Grand Prix was stopped after the Tyrrells crashed on lap two, then Prost won after Piquet retired, with Johansson clinching a McLaren one-two

and Andrea de Cesaris taking third place for Brabham.

Mansell led at Monaco until his turbo broke. Then Senna took over with Piquet second ahead of Alboreto and Berger. Mansell was hit by cramp in Detroit and Senna took over to win from Piquet and Prost. Things went Mansell's way at Paul Ricard, where he won from pole.

Despite losing ground after a late tyre stop at Silverstone, Mansell beat Piquet after a charge which culminated in a famous passing move into Stowe.

PIQUET COMES ON STRONG
Mansell was on pole in Germany, but his engine failed and Piquet won, while Johansson came second with a flat front tyre. Just seven cars finished as the turbos fell apart, with three DFZs in the top six.

LEFT **WILLIAMS'S WINNER: NELSON PIQUET FOUGHT LONG ANS HARD WITH TEAM-MATE MANSELL BEFORE CLAIMING HIS THIRD TITLE.**

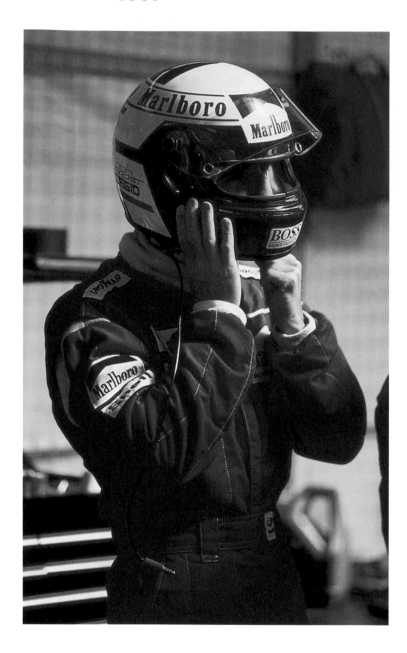

RIGHT **READY FOR ACTION: PROST DONS HIS HELMET, BUT IT WASN'T HIS BEST YEAR WITH McLAREN.**

FAR RIGHT **IN THE SHADE: SENNA WAS THE MAIN THREAT TO THE WILLIAMS DUO, BUT ENDED UP THIRD OVERALL FOR LOTUS.**

Mansell took pole in Hungary and failed to finish, as Piquet won ahead of Senna and Prost.

The circus visited the Osterreichring for the last time and the Austrian Grand Prix was stopped twice by pile-ups on the pit straight before Mansell won easily from Piquet.

Then at Monza Piquet won from Senna and Mansell. Berger took pole in the Portuguese Grand Prix then led most of the way but Prost won. Piquet took four vital points with third, while Mansell collected none. Mansell was back on the title trail after a win at Jerez, ahead of Prost, Johansson and Piquet. Then he won in Mexico, a race split in two by a huge accident from which Arrows' Derek Warwick emerged unscathed. Piquet was second ahead of Patrese.

For the first time since 1976 Japan had its own Grand Prix, this time at Suzuka. And all was resolved when Mansell hurt his back in practice, putting himself out for the weekend. And neither did he go to Adelaide. Ironically, Piquet didn't score in either race. Instead, victory in both went to Berger. Senna and Johansson followed him home in Japan, and in Australia he led all the way to win from Senna. But the Brazilian's Lotus was disqualified for having illegal brakes, and it cost him second overall to Mansell. Alboreto took second from Boutsen. Just nine cars made the flag, with Jim Clark Cup winner Palmer fourth.

Williams replacement driver Jean-Louis Schlesser, driving in place of Mansell who had a viral infection. They met at the chicane, and they touched, sending Senna into retirement. The crowd went wild. Eddie Cheever and Derek Warwick were third and fourth for Arrows.

The Portuguese Grand Prix had to be restarted and Senna led the first lap and swerved at Prost when he pulled alongside. But Prost kept his foot in and took the lead. Senna fell back and Ivan Capelli became Prost's challenger. Driving his March like never before, he was the star of the race, but settled for second, with Boutsen third.

Prost won again in Spain while and Senna was troubled by a computer that gave confusing fuel consumption readings and fell to fourth behind Mansell and Nannini.

Senna stalled on pole in Japan and fell to 14th. Capelli had the temerity to lead briefly, but Prost regained control. Then Capelli's electrics failed. By this time Senna was up to second, with 31 laps to go. He passed Prost eight laps later, then motored for his eighth win and lift the title. Prost was second with Boutsen third.

Prost completed the year by winning in Australia from Senna and Piquet, bringing an end to the turbo era.

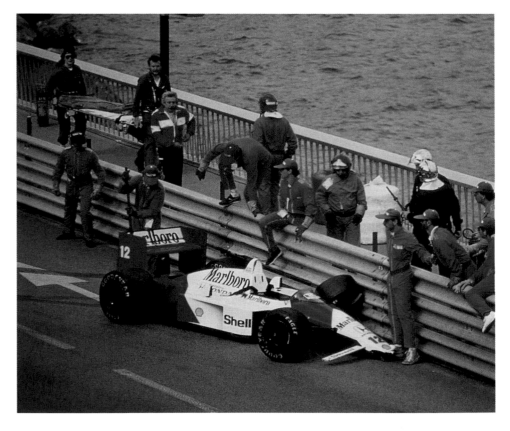

ABOVE **HOW NOT TO DO IT: SENNA'S MCLAREN LIES ABANDONED AFTER HE CRASHED OUT OF THE LEAD AT MONACO AND FLED THE SCENE.**

RIGHT **HOME WIN: BERGER BROKE THE McLAREN STRANGLEHOLD BY WINNING FOR FERRARI IN THE TEAM'S HOME RACE AT MONZA.**

BELOW **WATCH OUT: SENNA AND BOUTSEN SET ABOUT PROST ON THE PODIUM AT CANADA.**

SENNA PLAYS ROUGH

It was Ayrton Senna versus Alain Prost again. As in 1988, Senna took the spoils. But at one time it looked as though he wasn't going to be allowed to start the championship at all.

The trouble between Senna and the authorities stemmed from his disqualification from the 1989 Japanese Grand Prix. He accused FISA President Jean-Marie Balestre of ruling in Prost's favour and was refused entry for 1990. It was only with the season approaching that Senna was readmitted.

Kicking off at Phoenix, Senna tracked down Jean Alesi's Tyrrell, took the lead, was re-passed by the Frenchman, then pulled in front for good. Thierry Boutsen was third in his Williams.

Senna had been set for his first home win at Interlagos when Satoru Nakajima collided and forced him to pit for a new nose, confining him to third behind Prost and Berger.

Williams's Riccardo Patrese won at Imola, ending a seven-year drought. Senna led from pole but a stone jammed in his brakes and he spun off, while Prost was classified fourth behind Berger and Benetton's Alessandro Nannini.

Senna won at Monaco, chased home by Alesi. Prost ran second, but retired with Berger finishing third. Berger jumped the start in Canada and was given a one-minute penalty. With rain falling, McLaren called Berger in and then Senna. Berger was faster and Senna waved him past. Yet, charge as he did, Berger could make up only enough time for fourth, behind Senna, Nelson Piquet's Benetton and Nigel Mansell's Ferrari.

Senna led in Mexico, but had a puncture, handing the race to Prost. Mansell and Berger banged wheels around the banked Peralta corner, with Nigel on the outside, but Mansell held on to complete a Ferrari one-two.

CAPELLI PRODUCES A SHOCK

Prost won at Paul Ricard, but Ivan Capelli led for 45 laps for Leyton House, a team that had hitherto not scored. Team-mate Mauricio Gugelmin ran behind Capelli until his engine blew. Then Prost took the lead three laps from home with Capelli second.

Mansell stole the headlines at Silverstone by announcing his retirement. Victory on the day went to Prost, once Mansell had retired with gearbox problems and Boutsen snatched second, with Senna third after a spin. Germany was next, and it was Senna's turn to win after struggling to re-pass Nannini who

LEFT **PLAYING HARD BALL: IT WAS WIN AT ALL COSTS FOR SENNA AS HE CLAIMED HIS SECOND TITLE AMIDST CONTROVERSY IN JAPAN.**

ran a non-stop strategy. Senna was pipped by Boutsen in Hungary, then beat Prost to win at Spa.

Derek Warwick's Lotus destroyed itself against the barriers at the end of lap one at Monza. Amazingly, he ran back to the pits and climbed into the spare for the restart. For the records, Senna won from Prost.

Mansell left his mark in Portugal by not assisting his team-mate. He chopped across at the start, causing Prost to lift off and fall to fifth. In an instant, the way was clear for Mansell to race untroubled to win from Senna and Prost.

Martin Donnelly was lucky to survive at Jerez when his Lotus disintegrated on impact with the barriers in qualifying. This time Prost won, with Senna retiring.

Senna and Prost clashed again at Suzuka, this time giving Senna the title. Then the quarrels began. Meanwhile Piquet led home a Benetton one-two ahead of Roberto Moreno who had replaced Nannini after the latter had severed a hand in a helicopter crash.

Benetton won again in Australia, through Piquet, with Mansell and Prost second and third. And, by dint of having scored two wins to Berger's none, Piquet claimed third overall.

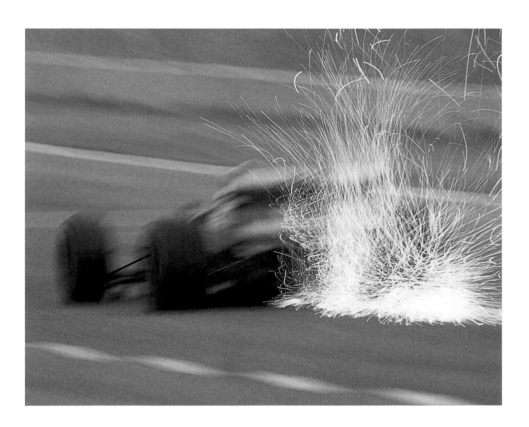

Left FAITHFUL RICARDO: PATRESE BACKED UP THIERRY BOUTSEN AT WILLIAMS TO RANK SEVENTH OVERALL.

Above FORMULA ONE SPECTACLE: TITANIUM SKIDPLATES GAVE PHOTOGRAPHERS SOME STUNNING OPTIONS.

SENNA LEADS FROM START

Ayrton Senna and McLaren made it two titles in succession, while Nigel Mansell elected not to retire but to race for Williams, offering a strong challenge.

Senna won the first four races. The first was at Phoenix, when he easily beat Alain Prost's Ferrari and Nelson Piquet's Benetton.

In Brazil, Senna beat Riccardo Patrese's Williams with McLaren team-mate Gerhard Berger close behind. Imola was easier, with only Berger on the same lap. Patrese led, but was slowed with engine problems, while Mansell went off after colliding with Martin Brundle's Brabham and Prost fell off on the parade lap.

Senna won at Monaco, and the closest anyone got was Stefano Modena with his best drive. But his Tyrrell's engine blew, also accounting for Patrese who went off

on its slick, so Mansell claimed second.

Mansell failed within sight of the line in Montreal. He was waving to the crowds, but his engine died and Piquet nipped by. Modena finished second, to atone for Monaco. Patrese hit the top in Mexico after a late-race challenge from Mansell. Senna followed them home, having recovered from flipping his McLaren in qualifying.

MANSELL COMES GOOD

Mansell took his first win of the year in the French Grand Prix, held at Magny-Cours for the first time. He swapped the lead with Prost, but was in front when it counted. Senna resisted a late challenge from Alesi for third. Mansell repeated his success at Silverstone, triggering wild scenes. Senna should have been second, but he ran out of fuel, letting Berger and Prost past.

Senna's points lead was reduced further at Hockenheim when Mansell made it three in a row. Patrese made it a Williams one-two ahead of Alesi. Senna ran out of fuel on the last lap again, losing fourth place.

With his points advantage over Mansell down to eight, Senna was delighted to win in Hungary. Indeed, with the power circuits ahead, it was to be his last likely victory for a while. Mansell pushed hard, but could find no way by on this narrow track.

Spa favours those with power, such as the Renault in Mansell's Williams. So it was a surprise to see Senna win after being outpaced by Mansell and then by Alesi, but both retired. Andrea de Cesaris was heading for second for Jordan, but his engine gave up. His team-mate that day was Michael Schumacher, making

LEFT **BRAZILIAN BLEND: SENNA STARTED HIS TITLE DEFENCE WITH FOUR STRAIGHT WINS, INCLUDING THIS ONE FOR McLAREN AT INTERLAGOS.**

217

his debut. He outqualified de Cesaris, but was out on lap one. However, we would hear a great deal more from him.

Mansell won at Monza to stay in the title chase. Senna led, but was eating his tyres in an attempt to stay ahead of Patrese then Mansell, so had to settle for second. Schumacher scored his first points for fifth place.

Patrese won again in Portugal, but this was handed to him when Mansell lost a wheel leaving the pits. The wheel was reapplied, but in an illegal place, so he was disqualified. Second place for Senna put him 24 points clear with three races to go. Giving his best, Mansell won at Barcelona from Prost and Patrese with Senna fifth. Berger won in Japan, albeit only after Senna let him past on the final lap. By then he no longer needed the extra four points as the title was already his, as Mansell had spun off. Sadly,

Senna took the occasion of his third title to attack outgoing FISA President Jean-Marie Balestre, raking over old ground.

Luckily, the season was brought to a happier end in Australia when Senna starred in torrential conditions in a race that was halted after 14 laps. There was further drama, as Prost had been fired by Ferrari. He was going anyway, tired of the politics. In view of the conditions, he probably wasn't disappointed.

THE BRITISH BULLDOG

This was the year when Nigel Mansell showed the world he could be a champion, not just a melodramatic challenger. And seldom has any driver dominated to such an extent.

Mansell planted his Williams on pole at Kyalami and led every lap from team-mate Riccardo Patrese. It was the same story in Mexico, with Mansell leading home a Williams one-two. Benetton's Michael Schumacher finished third. Mansell and Patrese were again first and second at Interlagos next time out, again with Schumacher third.

With Mansell dominant at Barcelona, Patrese spun out of second to elevate Schumacher. Jean Alesi brought his Ferrari home third.

The fifth of Mansell's wins came at Imola, with Patrese taking his fourth second place. Ayrton Senna fought his way around to third, but his input had been so great that it was 20 minutes before he could climb out of his McLaren.

Mansell's run came to an end in Monaco. But he was only 0.2 seconds from victory when he crossed the finish line after a monumental struggle to re-pass Senna after pitting when one of his tyres deflated.

Canada provided a surprise as Gerhard Berger won for McLaren ahead of Schumacher. Senna had led, but his electrics failed, by which time Mansell had spun out of second, elevating the Austrian.

The French Grand Prix should have heralded victory for Patrese, but it was halted by rain and he lost out on the restart as team orders forced him to wave Mansell past. Benetton's Martin Brundle finished in third place.

Mansell didn't just beat the opposition at Silverstone, he demoralized them with pole, fastest lap and victory by 40 seconds. Patrese was second and Brundle third after Senna pulled off. Mansell won again in Germany ahead of Senna, with Schumacher finishing third ahead of Brundle.

Mansell hoped to wrap up the title in Hungary with another win, but had to play second fiddle to Senna. Even so, there was typical drama when he had a puncture at three-quarters distance and had to fight his way past Berger for second. It was enough, though.

SCHUMACHER'S FIRST WIN
Schumacher scored the first of what would be many victories by winning in Belgium with a lucky break. Everyone

started on slicks in light rain. But the rain worsened and only Senna fought on with slicks, falling back as others pitted. If the rain had stopped it would have been a masterstroke, but it didn't and Senna would finish fifth. Schumacher was third, but ran wide and dropped behind Brundle. In an instant he noticed his team-mate's tyres were blistering and, reckoning his were doing likewise, dived into the pits. It proved the optimum moment and put him in the lead ahead of Mansell and Patrese by the time they too had pitted.

The Italian Grand Prix was overshadowed by two stories. Firstly, Mansell announced his retirement from Formula One. Secondly, Honda was pulling out, too. Mansell led, then ceded the lead so Patrese could win on his home patch, but both hit gearbox problems. Mansell

retired, while Patrese limped home fifth as Senna won the race from Brundle and Schumacher.

Mansell was back to winning form at Estoril, taking a record-breaking ninth win in a season. He was nearly caught out by debris after Patrese suffered a huge accident when he clipped Berger's McLaren. Berger continued to finish second, while Senna made it past Brundle for third.

Mansell played hero at Suzuka and waved Patrese into the lead, but his engine blew and so Berger and Brundle completed the top three.

The season ended in Adelaide with Berger grabbing victory ahead of Schumacher and Brundle in a race that lost Mansell and Senna in a shunt when the Brazilian was attempting to take the lead.

Above **TOKEN VICTORY: PATRESE WAS WAVED THROUGH BY TEAM-MATE MANSELL AT SUZUKA FOR HIS ONLY WIN OF 1992.**

Left **KICKING UP THE SPARKS: SCHUMACHER'S DRIVE TO VICTORY WAS THE HIGHLIGHT OF THE BELGIAN GRAND PRIX. HERE HE SPLITS HAKKINEN AND ALESI.**

PROST'S MASTERCLASS

This was another year of Williams domination, this time with Alain Prost taking the title, triumphing after a year away from the cockpit. Prost had spent 1992 commentating and it was known early in Nigel Mansell's championship year that Frank Williams was anxious to have him for 1993 in place of Mansell, precipitating the Englishman's departure to Indycars. Thus Williams began 1993 with Prost and Damon Hill upgraded from the test team.

Prost won at Kyalami after Senna had made the early running, with Mark Blundell a surprise third for Ligier. Then McLaren's Senna took a tactical win at Interlagos. Prost was leading when it rained and he hit a car that had spun. This put Hill in front, but he was to be Senna's prey in the Brazilian Grand Prix.

Rain struck the European Grand Prix at Donington Park, but Senna put on one of the drives of all time as he forced his way from fourth on the grid into the lead by the end of the opening lap, going on to beat Hill by over a minute, while Prost showed his dislike for the rain and was a lapped third.

Furious at the slating he received from the French press, Prost answered them with a controlled win at Imola, albeit only after Hill spun off. Senna was second when his hydraulics failed, so he yielded his position to Benetton's Michael Schumacher.

Hill was looking good at Barcelona until his engine blew, leaving Prost to win from Senna and Schumacher. Senna's team-mate, Michael Andretti – son of 1978 world champion Mario Andretti – finally finished a race, scoring points for fifth place.

Prost led at Monaco, but was given a stop-and-go penalty for jumping the start and magnified the punishment by stalling. This put Schumacher in front, but his hydraulics failed and so Senna won. Hill came second with Jean Alesi third for Ferrari. Then Prost won in Canada, as Schumacher benefited from Senna's late retirement to come second, with Hill third.

Williams scored a one-two at Magny-Cours. Hill led from pole, but was delayed in the pits and was bumped to second by Prost, with Schumacher third. In front from the start at Silverstone, Hill saw his efforts come to nought when his engine blew. Prost needed no second asking and motored on to his 50th win, with Benetton's Schumacher and Riccardo Patrese second and third.

LEFT **GLORIOUS SWANSONG: AFTER A YEAR WATCHING FROM THE SIDELINES, PROST RETURNED TO THE FAST LANE IN STYLE IN 1993, WINNING SEVEN TIMES AND CLAIMING A FOURTH WORLD TITLE.**

ABOVE **MR CONSISTENT: SCHUMACHER'S BENETTON WAS NOT THE BEST CAR, BUT HE WAS OFTEN ON THE PODIUM, WINNING IN PORTUGAL.**

RIGHT **LOTUS STRUGGLES: THIS ONCE-GREAT TEAM WAS AT THE WRONG END OF THE GRID THROUGHOUT 1993.**

HILL STARTS WINNING

Hill was set for success in Germany until a tyre cruelly blew two laps from the end. Prost, ten seconds behind after another stop-and-go penalty, flew past with Schumacher and Blundell second and third.

Hill finally won in Hungary. Despite qualifying behind Prost, Hill led all the way when Prost was forced to start from the back after stalling on the parade lap. Senna pressed Hill, but retired and left the way clear for Patrese and Berger.

The next two races had two things in common: both were won by Hill, and both witnessed shocking accidents. Alessandro Zanardi shunted while qualifying at Spa, rattling his Lotus off the barriers at Eau Rouge. Then at Monza,

Christian Fittipaldi clipped his teammate's car on the sprint to the finish line and flipped. Amazingly, his Minardi landed the right way up.

Schumacher won in Portugal, where Prost, one second behind, claimed the title and announced his retirement. Hill stalled and tigered through to third from the rear of the grid.

Senna won in style in Japan, but he threw a punch at Jordan's sixth-placed debutant Eddie Irvine who he felt had blocked him. Prost and Mika Hakkinen – in at McLaren in place of Andretti – were second and third.

The season ended in Adelaide, and victory for Senna helped McLaren pass Ferrari become the most successful team ever. Prost was second and Hill third.

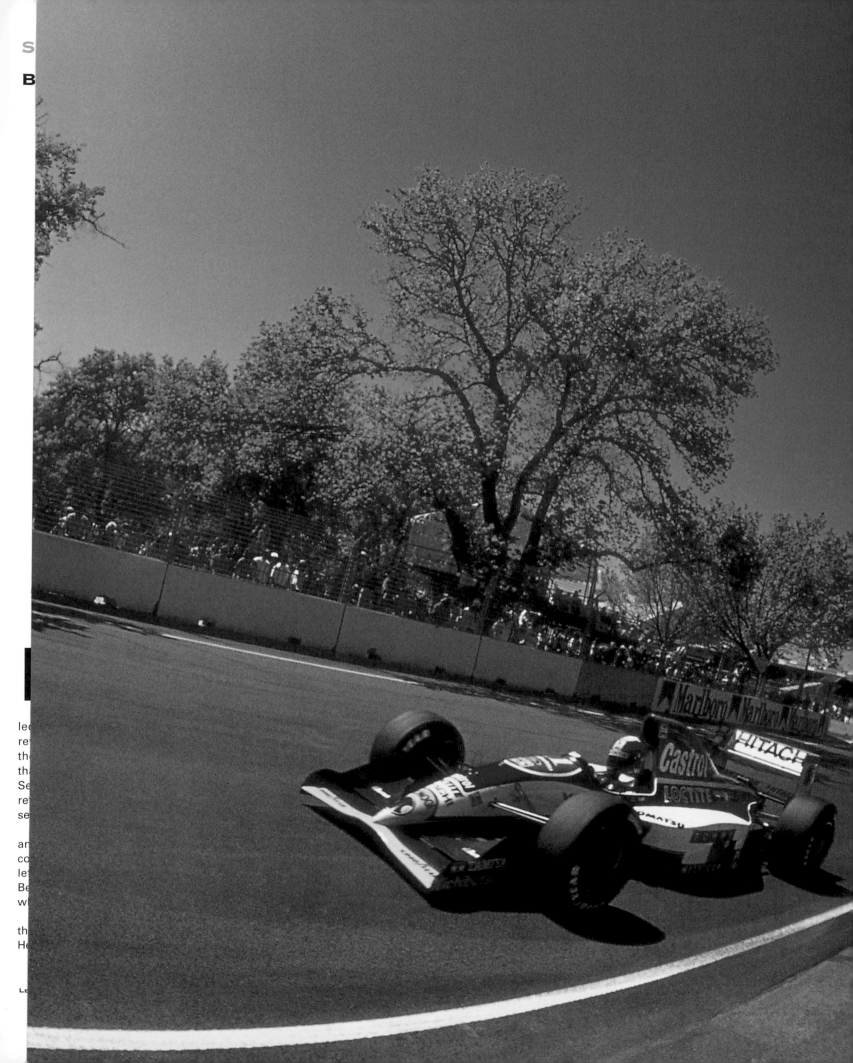

led
rev
the
tha
Se
rev
se

an
co
let
Be
w

th
He

fire that engulfed Benetton's Jos Verstappen who escaped with burns.

Schumacher and Verstappen sandwiched Hill in first and third in Hungary. Then controversy returned at Spa where Schumacher won from Hill and Hakkinen. But he had ground away too much of his 'plank' and was disqualified, elevating Verstappen to third.

Schumacher missed the next two races, so it was essential that Hill win both. At Monza he worked his way past the Ferraris and was heading a Williams one-two when David Coulthard's ran out of fuel on the last lap, letting Berger and Hakkinen claim second and third. Then, at Estoril, Hill overcame being flipped in qualifying to lead Coulthard home and close to within a point of Schumacher.

Schumacher beat Hill on his return at Jerez when the Williams wouldn't take on the right amount of fuel in a pit stop.

The Japanese Grand Prix was run in heavy rain. Schumacher led, but Hill stuck to his tail, nearly blind in the spray. But Schumacher chose to make two pit-stops, Hill just one. It was very close, but Hill held on to cut Schumacher's advantage to just one point.Schumacher and Hill dominated the Australian Grand Prix Adelaide. But Schumacher grazed a wall. Hill dived for a gap at the next corner and Schumacher, knowing his car was damaged, appeared to drive into Hill. Schumacher was tipped out of the race, but he had made himself champion, since Hill's car was too damaged to continue, leaving Mansell to win from Berger and Brundle.

Above **PIT STOP CRISIS: JOS VERSTAPPEN WAS ENGULFED IN FLAMES WHEN HIS BENETTON CAUGHT FIRE AT HOCKEN-HEIM, BUT ESCAPED WITH MINOR BURNS. IT WAS A MIRACLE.**

Left **MOMENT OF TRUTH: SCHUMACHER MOVES HIS DAMAGED BENETTON TO THE APEX AND INTO THE PATH OF HILL. BOTH RETIRED: SCHUMACHER WAS CHAMPION.**

LIKE FATHER, LIKE SON

It was a case of mission accomplished for Damon Hill. For, in 1996, he landed the title that Michael Schumacher had twice kept out of his grasp, making the might of Williams pay.

This was the season in which Hill was going to put the record straight. With 1994 and 1995 World Champion Schumacher moving to Ferrari, the idea was that there would be no-one who could stop the Englishman from emulating his late father, Graham Hill by becoming World Champion.

From the first race in Melbourne Hill found there was a threat, though, from new team-mate Indycar Champion Jacques Villeneuve who had enjoyed a good winter's worth of testing. The little Canadian even had the temerity to show Hill the way until an oil leak forced him to slow and finish second.

With Hill winning the Brazilian and Argentinian Grands Prix ahead of Benetton's Jean Alesi and Villeneuve respectively, Villeneuve had to wait until the fourth race, the Grand Prix of Europe at the Nurburgring, to hit the big time, winning a great chase to the line ahead of Schumacher.

Hill re-established his dominance at Imola ahead of Schumacher. But then came the shock of the year as Olivier Panis mastered changeable conditions to guide his Ligier to victory at Monaco ahead of McLaren's David Coulthard. Amazingly, this was the French team's first win since 1981. Hill had been leading when his engine failed, while Schumacher crashed out on lap one.

Schumacher atoned by driving masterfully in the wet to win at Barcelona on a day when he was clearly a cut above the rest, with Hill spinning out of contention as Alesi finished second ahead of Villeneuve.

Hill prevented team-mate Villeneuve from claiming a precious home win at the Montreal circuit named after his late father Gilles. Then Hill won again at Magny-Cours, again ahead of Villeneuve, to give himself a 25-point lead over Villeneuve. However, Hill had no such luck on home ground at Silverstone where he fell off when third and Villeneuve won from Benetton's Gerhard Berger and McLaren's Mika Hakkinen.

HILL UNDER PRESSURE

Hill's world appeared to cave in at the next race, at Hockenheim, when a story broke that he was to lose his ride at Williams to Sauber's Heinz-Harald Frentzen. He was able to leave Germany wearing a smile, though, as he picked up a fortunate win when Berger had his Renault engine blow with three laps to go, giving Hill a 21-point lead over Villeneuve.

This was soon whittled down, as Villeneuve won in Hungary by a short head from Hill, then reduced Hill's advantage to 13 at Spa as he placed second behind Schumacher with Hill fifth after a mix-up over when to come in for tyres. Then Williams announced that Frentzen

would be replacing Hill, leaving the world champion elect with few options as all the top drives were now filled.

HILL TRIPS UP

When Hill crashed out of the lead in Italy, matters looked serious. But Villeneuve also failed to score, so Hill was in a position to wrap it all up in Portugal, and he led until lap 48 of the 70-lap race distance. But then Villeneuve motored past him after a fabulous drive that saw him

pass Schumacher around the outside, and this took the title race to the final round in Japan, albeit with Hill needing just one point.

And Hill stamped his authority on proceedings at Suzuka and led all the way to sign out with a win ahead of Schumacher and Hakkinen. However, he had already become the first ever second generation world champion as Villeneuve had lost a wheel and crashed out of the race.

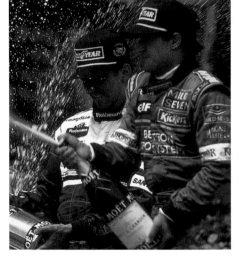

Above **FIRST TIME AT MELBOURNE: VILLENEUVE LEADS HILL ON THEIR FIRST RACE AS WILLIAMS TEAM-MATES.**

Above **REGULAR PODIUM FINISHERS: HILL AND ALESI DISPENSE THE BUBBLY AT THE CANADIAN GRAND PRIX.**

Left **LIGIER'S CONQUERER: OLIVIER PANIS SHOWS HIS DELIGHT AFTER BEATING THE CONDITIONS AND THE OPPOSITION TO WIN AT MONACO.**

Above SHATTERED HOPES: JACQUES VILLENEUVE'S BROKEN WILLIAMS LIES TRACK-
SIDE IN JAPAN AFTER LOSING A WHEEL ENDED THE CANADIAN'S SLIM TITLE HOPES.

VILLENEUVE: AT THE LAST

Michael Schumacher returned to the antics of 1994 when he tried to prevent Jacques Villeneuve passing him at the final round. But this time he failed and Villeneuve became champion.

So, instead of being applauded for taking challenging the Canadian's superior Williams-Renault package, Schumacher was sent away with his reputation sullied. The FIA confiscated all his points.

Villeneuve was on pole in Melbourne by 1.7 seconds from team-mate Heinz-Harald Frentzen. But he was taken off at the first corner by Schumacher's team-mate Eddie Irvine. Frentzen didn't push on his second set of tyres and fell behind David Coulthard then crashed out when a brake disc collapsed, leaving the Scot to score McLaren's first win since 1993, followed by Schumacher and his own McLaren team-mate Mika Hakkinen.

Status quo was re-established when Villeneuve won in Brazil, chased by Benetton's Gerhard Berger. He won again in Argentina, this time pushed by Irvine.

The pressure was starting to mount on Frentzen, but he responded at Imola to win from Schumacher as Villeneuve hit gearbox problems.

SCHUMACHER GETS GOING

Schumacher dominated at Monaco, as it rained, with his day being made by Williams coming away with nothing. Rubens Barrichello delighted Stewart by finishing second on only the team's fourth outing.

Barcelona brought tyre problems, but Villeneuve was in control for his third win. Olivier Panis was again impressive in finishing second, but his luck was to run out in Canada when his Prost thumped the barriers, breaking his legs. The race was stopped and Schumacher was declared winner, which was cruel luck on the dominant Coulthard whose engine stalled at his second pit stop, dropping him to seventh as the red flag flew.

Schumacher won in France, with Frentzen second and Villeneuve fourth. The British Grand Prix at Silverstone went to Villeneuve, but only after fighting back from a bungled pitstop and having Hakkinen lose the lead with a blown engine.

Berger had missed three races due to illness, and so his return at Hockenheim was even more amazing as he overcame a challenge from Jordan's Giancarlo Fisichella to win from Schumacher.

There was nearly an even bigger shock in Hungary as Villeneuve had to

LEFT **TWO ON THE TROT: JACQUES VILLENEUVE GOT HIS SEASON OFF TO A GOOD START. HE IS SHOWN HERE LIFTING THE WINNER'S TROPHY IN ARGENTINA.**

Aʙᴏᴠᴇ **DRIVER MISSING: VILLENEUVE'S CAR SITS ABANDONED AFTER ITS FIRST-CORNER ACCIDENT IN AUSTRALIA. WINNER COULTHARD DRIVES BY, FOLLOWED BY SCHUMACHER.**

Rɪɢʜᴛ **NOT A GOOD START: FRENTZEN WAS STILL OUT OF THE POINTS AFTER HIS RETIREMENT IN ARGENTINA.**

wait until half a lap before the end before passing Damon Hill's slowing Arrows to win, with Hill limping home second. Schumacher bounced back to win in Belgium from Fisichella as Villeneuve paid for a poor tyre choice in the rain and fell to fifth.

Coulthard triumphed at Monza. But it was a tight race decided by pitstops, during which McLaren eased him ahead of Alesi.

Prost was given a boost in Austria, as Panis's stand-in Jarno Trulli led half the race before Villeneuve moved past to win. Sadly, Trulli's engine blew and Coulthard bagged second.

Villeneuve was lucky to win the Luxembourg Grand Prix at the Nurburgring. Firstly, Ralf Schumacher took his brother out at the first corner.

Then Coulthard blew up mid-race when second and half a lap later so did leader Hakkinen.

Villeneuve was adjudged to have passed under a yellow in qualifying at Suzuka and, with a suspension hanging over him, was banned. He raced under appeal but struggled to fifth as Schumacher won. And so Schumacher went to Spain with a one-point lead.

The crunch at Jerez came as Villeneuve attempted to pass Schumacher. It caught the leader by surprise. He turned in on Villeneuve, but bounced into a gravel bed. Villeneuve led until he took the precaution of letting the McLarens past in the final metres, as third was enough for the crown. And so Hakkinen finally landed his first win.

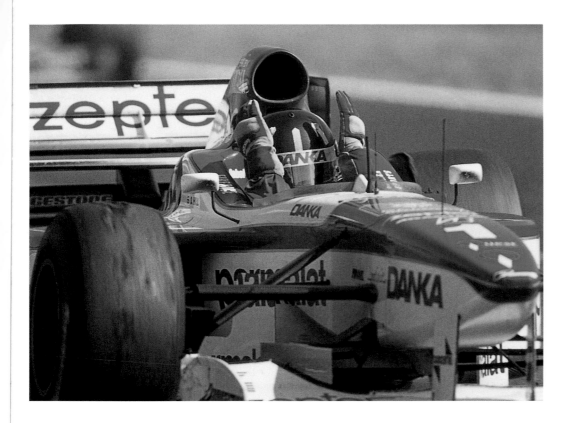

LEFT A TRACK LIKE NO OTHER: MONACO CONTINUES TO PROVIDE AN UNRIVALLED SPECTACLE WITH THE TRACK AROUND ITS STREETS AN ETERNAL LINK TO THE PAST.

ABOVE A SHOCK SHOWING: HILL ACKNOWLEDGES THE APPLAUSE AFTER LEADING MOST OF THE WAY IN HUNGARY AND FINISHING SECOND FOR ARROWS.

BELOW THE CHAMPIONSHIP CLINCHER: SCHUMACHER PULLS ACROSS ON VILLENEUVE AT JEREZ. THE GERMAN RETIRED, HIS CANADIAN RIVAL BECAME CHAMPION.

and second in Austria and Germany and could have repeated this in Hungary, but Ferrari's Ross Brawn put Schumacher on a three-stop strategy that worked for a famous win.

Schumacher slammed into the back of Coulthard in Belgium and ripped off a wheel, throwing away a 30s lead over Damon Hill's Jordan which went on to the team's first win ahead of team mate Ralf Schumacher and Jean Alesi's Sauber. Schumacher was gifted a win on home ground at Monza, though, when Coulthard retired from the lead and Hakkinen fell to fourth with brake problems. Although he led at the Nurburgring, Hakkinen came from behind to win. Schumacher had to win the final round at Suzuka with Hakkinen third or lower to be champion, but he stalled at the start and was forced to take the restart from the back. Hakkinen duly raced off to his eighth win and the title.

There was a three-way shoot-out for third in the constructors' cup between Williams, Benetton and Jordan. Yes, the 1997 cup-winning team had fallen from grace, with Williams struggling with ex-works Renault engines badged as Mecachromes. Indeed, so were Benetton, and both suffered from a lack of grunt. Villeneuve and Frentzen struggled, finishing no higher than third, while Fisichella scored Benetton's best results with two second places. But Jordan's one-two in the crash-torn Belgian Grand Prix and a run of strong results in the second half of the season helped them pass Benetton into fourth place overall.

Above ARGY BARGY: MICHAEL SCHUMACHER (LEFT) BASHES DAVID COULTHARD'S McLAREN OUT OF THE WAY EN ROUTE TO VICTORY IN ARGENTINA.

Left ONE-TIME WINNER: COULTHARD WAS FORCED TO BE HAKKINEN'S NUMBER TWO AT McLAREN AND WON ONLY AT IMOLA.

LEFT **ROLLERCOASTER RIDE: ALEXANDER WURZ'S BENETTON IS INVERTED AT THE ABORTED START OF THE CANADIAN GRAND PRIX .**

RIGHT **JOY FOR JORDAN: DAMON HILL SLITHERS TO JORDAN'S FIRST VICTORY IN THE BELGIAN GRAND PRIX.**

BELOW **JOB WELL DONE: COULTHARD LOOKS UP TO HAKKINEN AFTER HIS TEAM-MATE HAD CLINCHED THE WORLD TITLE IN THE FINAL ROUND AT SUZUKA.**

A GOLDEN FIFTIETH

This was always going to be another battle between Mika Hakkinen and Michael Schumacher. And so it proved, until Schumacher broke a leg in the British GP and team-mate Eddie Irvine stepped up to the breech. Ultimately, Irvine failed, but he made Hakkinen wait until the final round before he made it two titles on the trot.

As in 1998, the speed of the McLarens in the first round at Melbourne was remarkable and they seemed set to dominate. Fortunately for the other 10 teams, both McLarens retired. So, Ferrari took the honours, though not through Schumacher who started from the rear of the field and failed to score but Irvine, narrowly leading home Heinz-Harald Frentzen on his first outing for Jordan and Ralf Schumacher on his maiden run for Williams.

Rubens Barrichello led in Brazil for Stewart, but he wasn't running to the same tyre strategy as the McLarens and Ferraris and retired as Hakkinen overcame a gear selection problem to pass Michael Schumacher and win. Frentzen emphasised how competitive he was at Jordan by coming third.

The third race, at Imola, should have been a Hakkinen benefit. But, amazingly, he crashed into the barrier coming onto the start/finish straight. Schumacher proved more effective in traffic than Coulthard and gave the tifosi the win they craved. Then Schumacher and Irvine respectively got the jump on Hakkinen and Coulthard off the grid at Monaco, and Irvine moved up to second when Hakkinen slid up an escape road.

McLaren re-established control at Barcelona, a race notable for Jacques Villeneuve running third for the new BAR team ahead of the Ferraris. As in all the previous races, the Canadian retired and it was Mika Salo – standing in for Ricardo Zonta who had injured an ankle at Interlagos – who became the first driver to get a BAR to the finish line.

It was Michael Schumacher's turn to have a red face at Montreal as he crashed out of the lead. With Hakkinen leading, Coulthard and Irvine clashed after the safety car peeled off for the third time and fell down the order. Irvine made it back to fourth which became third when, with four laps to go, Frentzen crashed out of second, elevating Benetton's Giancarlo Fisichella to his best result of the year.

Rain hit Magny-Cours and made qualifying a lottery that was won by Barrichello who set his time early on. Coulthard took the lead after six laps, but,

LEFT **A MAN ON A MISSION: MIKA HAKKINEN FOCUSES ON THE JOB IN HAND ON HIS WAY TO
COMPLETING BACK-TO-BACK WORLD CHAMPIONSHIPS.**

253

yet again, his car was to fail him. Hakkinen moved from 14th to take the lead before the first pitstops when Stewart did a better job and put Barrichello back into the lead. Hakkinen spun and fell to seventh as he tried to regain the lead. Michael Schumacher hit gearchange problems and so Frentzen scored his first win for Jordan.

It was at the British GP that the season turned as Michael Schumacher speared off on lap one at Stowe corner. He broke his right leg and would miss six races. Hakkinen ought to have won, but

his right rear wheel didn't go on properly, requiring a slow lap and a further stop. Later, it fell off for good. This put Irvine and Coulthard clear, and the Scot won, helped by the Ulsterman overshooting his pit as he was unsighted by the McLaren crew working on Hakkinen's car.

Then Coulthard spun his team-mate Hakkinen out of the lead on the opening lap of the Austrian GP. His drive back to third from stone last was outstanding, but he certainly didn't shake the Scot's hand on the podium. Not that Coulthard was smiling as he was outraced by Irvine who won

after a mid-race charge put him ahead.

The tide turned Ferrari's way at Hockenheim as Hakkinen hit refuelling trouble and Coulthard was stuck behind Salo's Ferrari – the Finn now acting as Schumacher's stand-in – and had to pit for a new nose. Having fallen to fourth, Hakkinen crashed coming into Agip Kurve when a rear tyre failed, leaving Salo to hand the lead to Irvine and complete a Ferrari one-two.

Hakkinen won the Hungarian GP, with Coulthard passing Irvine for third. When Coulthard beat polesitter Hakkinen to the

ABOVE **FORD'S FLIER: RUBENS BARRICHELLO PUSHED STEWART AND FORD TO THE FRONT BY LEADING HIS HOME GRAND PRIX IN BRAZIL.**

LEFT **SUPER SCOT: DAVID COULTHARD STILL HAD TO PLAY SECOND FIDDLE TO 1998 CHAMPION MIKA HAKKINEN.**

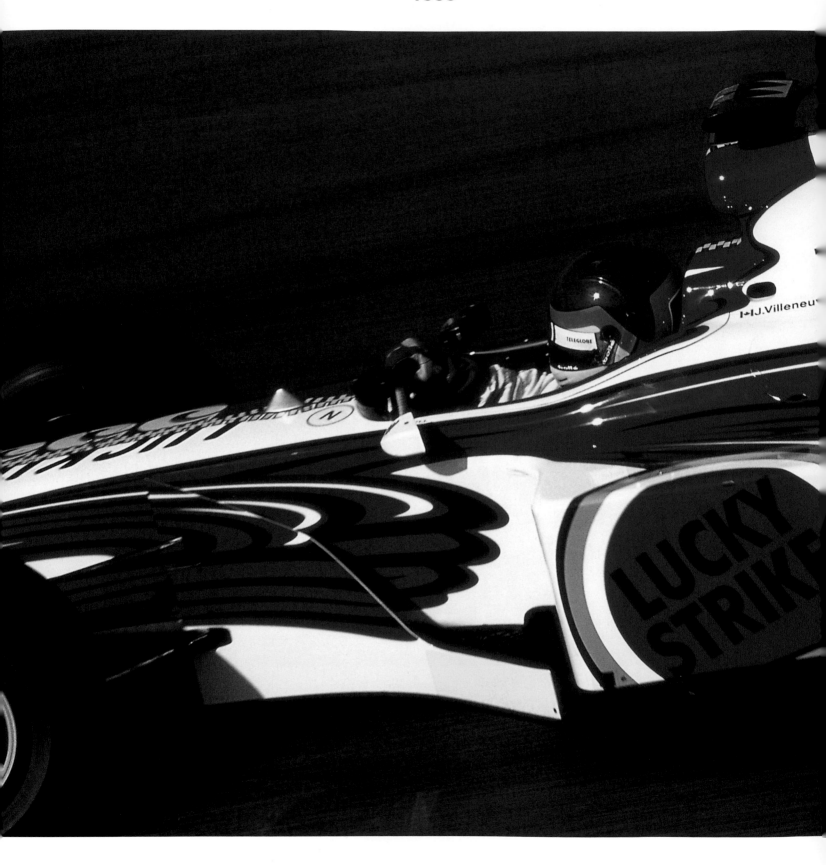

first corner at Spa-Francorchamps and went on to win, many said that McLaren boss Ron Dennis should have ordered Coulthard to move aside, but he replied that no team orders would be issued. When Hakkinen spun out of the lead at Monza, Dennis must have reconsidered those words. Fortunately for Hakkinen, Irvine was able to finish only sixth as Frentzen won from Ralf Schumacher and Salo.

There was a great battle for the lead between Frentzen and Coulthard in the European Grand Prix at the Nurburgring. But Frentzen pulled off and then Coulthard slid off the wet track. Fisichella did likewise and through it all came Johnny Herbert to give Stewart its first, and only, win.

Schumacher returned for the first ever Malaysian GP and did a great job by shielding Irvine from Hakkinen and finishing a dutiful second. Post-race, there was a scare as the Ferraris were disqualified for a technical irregularity, but they were reinstated. With a win vital for either driver in the final round at Suzuka, it was Hakkinen who delivered and Irvine who trailed home a distant third.

Of the support players, Frentzen rebuilt his reputation by completely overshadowing team-mate Hill, Ralf Schumacher built his and his team-mate Alex Zanardi dropped right out of the reckoning in a massive comedown after his two Champ Car titles. BAR also failed to impress, failing to score a single point.

Above **GOLDEN MOMENT: EDDIE IRVINE FINALLY HIT THE BIG TIME BY WINNING THE AUSTRALIAN GRAND PRIX FOR FERRARI.**

Left **OPPOSITE EMOTIONS: MICHAEL SCHUMACHER CONTAINS HIS PLEASURE AFTER BEING BEATEN BY MIKA HAKKINEN IN BRAZIL.**

Far Left **NEW KIDS ON THE BLOCK: JACQUES VILLENEUVE QUIT WILLIAMS TO JOIN FORMULA ONE'S NEWEST TEAM, BRITISH AMERICAN RACING.**

THE NOUGHTIES

FERRARI DOES IT AT LAST

Quite how Ferrari had failed to land a drivers' title since Jody Scheckter was first in 1979 will always be something of a mystery. But, in 2000, thanks to Michael Schumacher, it finally all came together.

As in 1998, the battle was between him and arch-rival Mika Hakkinen and the German's tally of nine wins from the 17 rounds to the McLaren racer's four meant that the treasured title was his with a round still to run.

For the second year running, all cars were on Bridgestone-spec tyres, meaning that any advantage had to be found through the teams' engines, chassis and their drivers. In short, Michael was exemplary, making up for the leg-breaking interruption to his 1999 season that undoubtedly delayed his crowning by a year. There were very few changes at

Ferrari, save for Eddie Irvine being replaced in the (very much) number two car by Rubens Barrichello. Irvine moved on to Jaguar, the team formed from what had been Stewart before, with Johnny Herbert as his team-mate. At Williams, Alex Zanardi had been dropped to make way for last-minute selection Jenson Button, straight from Formula Three, and BMW engines replaced the Supertec V10s.

MICHAEL'S FLYING START
Three wins from the first three grands prix set Michael's show on the road. Conversely, two retirements in the first two outings with engine-related problems when leading tipped Hakkinen off course. In fact, the points he lost in Melbourne and Interlagos were more than the difference between being

champion and being runner-up. Victory by a second over Hakkinen at Imola made it three.

Muscle flexing by the FIA saw the organisers of the British GP punished for some slight or other by the race being shunted forward from July to April, something that caused a huge problem as Silverstone's car parks were waterlogged after a wet winter, causing fans to be turned away from Saturday's qualifying. At least there was a home win to cheer on the following day, as David Coulthard led home Hakkinen.

Then Hakkinen hit the front at Barcelona for another McLaren one-two before Michael usurped him at the Nurburgring, with even third-placed Coulthard lapped.

Jarno Trulli showed great promise by running second to Michael at Monaco,

LEFT **LIKE LOTUS'S COLIN CHAPMAN AND JIM CLARK BACK IN THE 1960S, TEAM BOSS JEAN TODT AND LEAD DRIVER MICHAEL SCHUMACHER FORGED AN UNPRECEDENTED LEVEL OF SUCCESS TOGETHER AT FERRARI, WINNING RACE AFTER RACE AND WORLD TITLE AFTER WORLD TITLE.**

267

TWO IN A ROW

If Michael Schumacher had to fight for that first world title in 2000, it was totally different in 2001 as he ended up with almost double the points tally of the second-ranked driver, McLaren's David Coulthard.

There was little change among the top teams, save for Michelin breaking Bridgestone's monopoly on the tyre front as Williams, Benetton, Jaguar, Prost and Minardi threw in their lots with the French firm.

The other new arrival was Champ Car star Juan Pablo Montoya at Williams, in place of Jenson Button who joined Giancarlo Fisichella at Benetton, for whom Renault had now placed its name on the flanks of the engine before a full takeover in 2002.

For all this, Michael and Ferrari won the opening race and followed this with victory in Malaysia, although this owed

a lot to fortune as rain fell just after he'd slipped off the track, with the fitment of intermediate tyres – when others fitted wets – proving inspired. In a class of his own, Michael won on seven more occasions, wrapping up his fourth title with four races still to run.

Rubens Barrichello emerged more from Michael's shadow but was forced to play a supporting role again and failed to win a race. Only when Michael had been crowned did Ferrari start to help his challenge to beat Coulthard and Ralf Schumacher to be runner-up.

Coulthard was inspired in victory in Brazil, but underdeveloped launch control left him stranded at the start at Barcelona. He then qualified on pole at Monaco, only to have his launch control fail. Despite winning the French GP, David spent the rest of the year in Michael's wake. Team-mate Mika

Hakkinen was spooked by a suspension breakage that pitched him off in Australia and mechanical failure in the Spanish GP when he was half a lap away from victory, allowing Michael to win. He was reinvigorated by winning at Silverstone. Then, one race after announcing his intention to take a sabbatical, he won again at Indianapolis.

Running on Michelins was a gamble for Williams. Yet, with powerful engines from BMW – which were to become the most powerful of all – they were confident. Off the pace when conditions were cool, they struggled at Imola, until it warmed and Ralf romped clear of the McLarens for his first win. This was repeated at Montreal and at Hockenheim. Montoya muscled his way past Michael Schumacher in Brazil, later being deprived of victory at Hockenheim. But his day of days came at Monza when he

LEFT: **SO COMPLETELY DOMINANT WAS MICHAEL SCHUMACHER, SCORING NINE WINS FOR FERRARI, THAT HE WRAPPED THE 2001 FORMULA ONE TITLE UP AS EARLY AS THE 13TH OF THE 17 WORLD CHAMPIONSHIP GRANDS PRIX.**

Above JUDGING BY THEIR FACES,
YOU CAN TELL WHO WAS THE WINNER
AT MONZA. IT'S MONTOYA, NOT
BARRICHELLO OR RALF SCHUMACHER.

Right IN GENERAL, MIKA HAKKINEN HAD
A DISAPPOINTING YEAR BUT HIT TOP
FORM TO WIN THE US GP, A RACE THAT
STANDS AS HIS FINAL TRIUMPH.

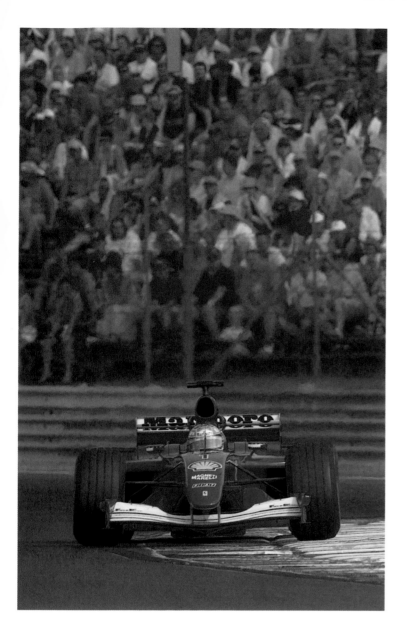

LEFT MICHAEL SCHUMACHER
CONTROLLED PROCEEDINGS AT WILL
TO LEAD HOME A FERRARI ONE-TWO
AT THE HUNGARORING.

BELOW NICK HEIDFELD PUSHED HIS
SAUBER AS HARD AS HE DARED AND
WAS REWARDED WITH THIRD PLACE
AT THE BRAZILIAN GP.

scored his maiden win.

Sauber ranked fourth. Running with Ferrari engines from 2000 – badged as Petronas engines – allowed Nick Heidfeld to shine. Rookie team-mate Kimi Raikkonen arrived with 23 car races to his name, having bypassed Formula Three and Formula 3000, and placed sixth on his debut.

Jordan ended up fifth only after Jarno Trulli's disqualification from fourth at Indianapolis was overturned. Heinz-Harald Frentzen was dropped before the year was out to make way for Jean Alesi.

Benetton ran wide-angle Renault engines, but were close to the rear of the grid in the first half of the year. However, they upped the power and both scored points in the German GP. Two races later, in Belgium, Fisichella ran second before being demoted by Coulthard.

Like Jordan, BAR lacked grunt from their Hondas, but their main worry was the chassis, leaving Jacques Villeneuve and Olivier Panis to scrap for points. Jaguar also failed to shine, with boss Bobby Rahal being shown the door to

make way for Niki Lauda. Eddie Irvine claimed a surprise third at Monaco, but neither he nor Pedro de la Rosa had much to smile about.

Arrows lacked both power and budget, but Jos Verstappen often showed well early in races, although this could be seen as artificial as he'd be running with a light fuel load. While the arrival of airline magnate Paul Stoddart saved Minardi, Alain Prost's team folded shortly after the final race.

TOTAL DOMINATION

Michael Schumacher and Ferrari dominated as never before, appearing to win almost so easily that it belittled the stature of his achievement as he landed the drivers' title at the French GP in July, with six grands prix still to run. Rival teams simply couldn't wait for the season to end so that they could concentrate on making sure that they could take the battle to Ferrari in 2003.

The only real change at the front was that Mika Hakkinen was to be found at home by a lake in Finland, with fellow Finn Kimi Raikkonen taking his seat at McLaren. Renault was hoping to escape from the midfield, having meta-morphosed from Benetton, with Jenson Button joined by Jarno Trulli, who'd swapped with Giancarlo Fisichella, who crossed to Jordan. The seat vacated at Sauber by Raikkonen went to Brazilian

Felipe Massa, while Prost had failed to last the winter, with Toyota keeping the numbers up with its brand new and well-funded team.

Michael set the ball rolling in Australia after a dramatic start when brother Ralf's Williams got airborne over Rubens Barrichello's pole-sitting Ferrari and the mêlée took out six other drivers. Juan Pablo Montoya finished second for Williams, but had Raikkonen not made a slip-up, he'd have claimed the position, having to make do with third instead. Debutant Mark Webber raced home fifth for little-fancied Minardi as only eight of the 22 starters made the finish.

Ralf made amends in Malaysia, followed home by Montoya for Williams' first one-two since 1996, despite having a drive-through penalty for "causing an avoidable incident" after a first corner clash with Michael.

FERRARI UPS THE ANTE
With Ferrari delaying the introduction of its F2002 chassis until the third round, Michael produced a run of four wins in four races, at Interlagos, Imola, Barcelona and the A1-Ring.

At the last of these, Ferrari's top brass ended up with egg on their faces as they ordered Barrichello – fastest all weekend – to let Michael through to win, even though this was at the sixth of the 17 rounds, not the 16th.

Montoya had reason to regret running too close to Michael in Brazil, losing his nose, which left him in fifth place behind Ralf and McLaren's David Coulthard. Ralf put up a brave charge at Imola, but fell to third behind Barrichello. Then Montoya gave it his best shot to come second in Spain, 35 seconds behind Michael.

LEFT **FERRARI WAS IN CONTROL THROUGHOUT THE 2002 WORLD CHAMPIONSHIP, BUT RUBENS BARRICHELLO AND THE FERRARI-POWERED SAUBERS FELL AT THE FIRST HURDLE IN AUSTRALIA WHILE MICHAEL SCHUMACHER RACED ON TO THE FIRST WIN OF HIS TRIUMPHANT CAMPAIGN.**

Above IN ATTEMPTING TO STAGE
A DEAD-HEAT IN THE US GP,
SCHUMACHER GOT IT A BIT WRONG
AND IT WAS BARRICHELLO WHO
TOOK THE WIN.

Right KIMI RAIKKONEN SHOWED HIS
SKILLS BY KEEPING MICHAEL
SCHUMACHER IN HIS WAKE IN THE
FRENCH GP UNTIL A LATE SLIP-UP.

McLAREN FIGHTS BACK

McLaren came up trumps at Monaco, with Coulthard getting the jump on poleman Montoya, then leading every lap, with Michael rising to second after Montoya's engine failed.

Michael resumed his winning ways in the Canadian GP in Montreal, chased by Coulthard and Barrichello as engine failures left the Williams drivers on the sidelines.

A good start for Barrichello at the reshaped Nurburgring and a spin for Michael ensured that he triumphed. After winning at Silverstone, Michael profited from a slip by Raikkonen with five laps of the French GP remaining, his win leaving him with an unassailable tally of 96 points.

Michael won at Germany's other reshaped track – Hockenheim – before, perhaps as a payback for Austria, he played second fiddle to Barrichello at the Hungaroring, thus easing Barrichello into second overall as Montoya failed to score. Arrows was unable to pay for its engines so failed to race in Hungary and was never to appear again.

Ferrari kept on winning, with Michael dominating at Spa and Barrichello

BELOW **ALL IS CALM ON THE RUN TO THE FIRST CORNER IN THE OPENING RACE IN AUSTRALIA, WITH BARRICHELLO LEADING RALF SCHUMACHER'S WILLIAMS AND THE TWO McLARENS. BUT THEN RALF CLIPS THE REAR OF HIS FERRARI AND IS SUDDENLY HEADING SKYWARDS. CHAOS ENSUES...**

leading him home at Monza. The sight of former Ferrari racer Eddie Irvine up there with them was a shock, as his Jaguar hadn't been competitive all year.

The penultimate race, at Indianapolis, was another Ferrari one-two, but Michael tried to stage a dead-heat and Barrichello nosed ahead for victory.

Michael completed his season by winning at Suzuka – amazingly this was his 11th win from 17 starts – in a race in which the crowd went wild as Takuma Sato scored his first points, finishing fifth for Jordan.

ABOVE **TOYOTA WAS THE FIRST NEW TEAM FOR YEARS, COMPLETE WITH A HUGE BUDGET, BUT IT FAILED TO MAKE MUCH OF A SPLASH.**

RIGHT **TAKUMA SATO CHOSE THE RIGHT PLACE TO SCORE HIS FIRST POINTS, AT THE JAPANESE GP AT SUZUKA IN FRONT OF MANY ADORING FANS.**

MICHAEL BY A NOSE

Two things stand out from 2003. Firstly, that it was extremely close between the top teams, with Michael Schumacher claiming the title only in the closing laps of the final round and, secondly, that this was the year in which likely future champions finally took the battle to Schumacher, with Kimi Raikkonen and Fernando Alonso throwing down the gauntlet.

There was a major change to qualifying as each driver was sent out on a one-at-a-time run of one flying lap each, running in an order determined by their speed in a session on Friday.

Jaguar, Sauber and Toyota also occasionally sent their drivers out with a light fuel load to ensure a superior grid position if not a better race chance. Points were awarded for the first time to the first eight drivers rather than just to the first six, with a 10-8-6-5-4-3-2-1 scoring system.

With the six drivers across the top three teams – Ferrari, Williams and McLaren – remaining the same, there was no change at the front, with the arrival of Alonso, stepping up from testing duties at Renault, the main change.

COULTHARD STARTS WELL

The opening grand prix was a shambles and David Coulthard was fortunate to come away as victor. However, he lost deserved wins in Malaysia and Brazil. The race at Sepang went to team-mate Raikkonen, this his first, while the one at Interlagos was a masterful performance by the Scot in changing conditions that was brought to a premature end when Mark Webber crashed his Jaguar just after Coulthard had made his final stop,

leaving him fourth at the premature end. Raikkonen was declared the winner, but the countback ruling proved that Jordan's Giancarlo Fisichella had finally scored a grand prix win.

And Michael? He simply wasn't competitive as he waited for the arrival of the 2003 car. However, he made amends by winning at Imola ahead of Raikkonen.

The arrival of the F2003-GA brought Michael victory in Spain, albeit only after a battle with Alonso, who added 20,000 fans to the crowd.

Another win followed in Austria, but then it was Juan Pablo Montoya's turn for glory, giving Williams victory at Monaco, which started a run of results for him and team-mate Ralf Schumacher.

Michael resisted a limp challenge from Ralf in Canada. Then Ralf struck back to win at the Nurburgring and

LEFT FERRARI DIDN'T HAVE THINGS ALL THEIR OWN WAY IN 2003, WITH WILLIAMS AND McLAREN A THREAT. THIS IS MONTOYA.

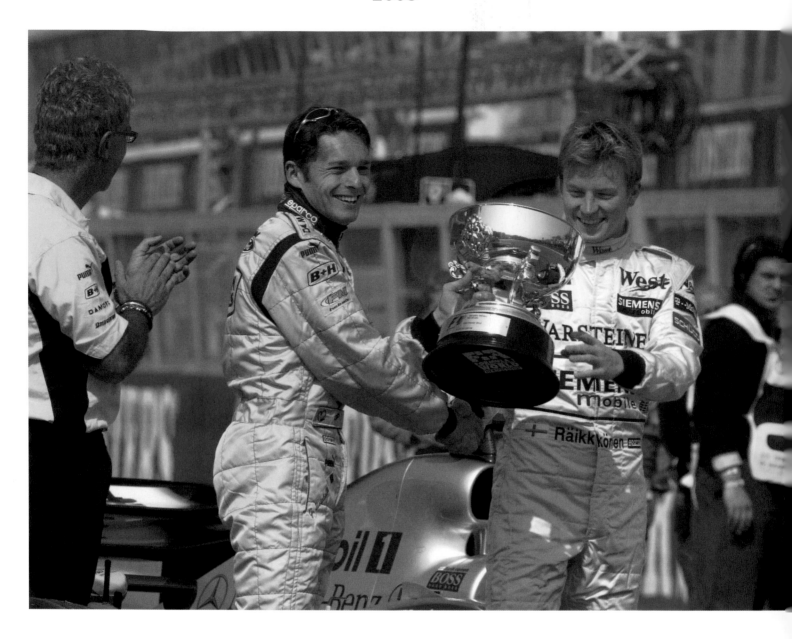

Above **OVER TO YOU: KIMI RAIKKONEN HANDS OVER THE BRAZILIAN GP TROPHY TO GIANCARLO FISICHELLA AT THE FOLLOWING RACE AT IMOLA.**

Magny-Cours. At the first of these, Raikkonen had blown up when in front and Michael spun when Montoya passed him, falling to fifth. The second of these was Ralf from start to finish.

THE RACE OF THE YEAR
Barrichello won a British GP that had its order scrambled when the safety car came out while a track invader was escorted off and then saw him pass Raikkonen in a move that lasted four corners... Montoya also passed the Finn to finish second. Montoya went one better to dominate the German GP, a race that was spoiled when Ralf,

Barrichello and Raikkonen clashed at the first corner and Michael suffered a late-race puncture.

Renault was then rewarded for its improving form when Alonso triumphed in Hungary, becoming the youngest driver ever to win a grand prix at the age of 22 years and 26 days. Michael finished eighth after he stalled in a pit stop, his points lead down to one over Montoya, two over Raikkonen.

McLaren talked of unveiling its 2003 chassis, the MP4-18, but it was shelved and Raikkonen and Coulthard struggled at Monza where only Montoya could challenge Michael. The three-way title

Below FERNANDO ALONSO HIT GOLD WITH A DOMINANT MAIDEN WIN FOR RENAULT AT THE HUNGARORING. MARK WEBBER RAN SECOND.

Bottom KIMI RAIKKONEN CELEBRATES HIS FIRST-EVER WIN, AT SEPANG. HE WASN'T TO WIN AGAIN, THOUGH HE FINISHED SECOND SIX TIMES.

fight lost Montoya at Indianapolis when he was given a drive-through penalty for a clash with Barrichello. A damp track favoured the Michelin runners, but as soon as the rain intensified Michael was in a class of his own.

At Suzuka, Michael had only to finish eighth for his record-setting sixth title. Raikkonen had to win, but Barrichello stepped up a gear and won to help Michael to the title, which was fortunate as Michael drove a wretched race from 14th on the grid. Raikkonen's second-place finish was his seventh in 16 starts. In reality, though, it was only the revised points system that had kept it close.

GUESS WHO?

Michael Schumacher recorded a fifth drivers' title in a row and Ferrari landed its sixth consecutive constructors' crown as Ferrari took an iron grip on a championship that offered little in the way of challenge. In short, Ferrari and tyre supplier Bridgestone were just too good for the rival teams. It came as little surprise, then, that negotiations raged throughout the close-season as the other teams sought ways to reduce the seemingly limitless testing that Ferrari carried out as they tried to peg back both the Italian team's speed advantage and have budgets pegged as they lagged behind.

In fact, only one team – Toyota – had a budget to match Ferrari's, but this counted for little as the German-based Japanese team struggled to score more than a few points. For the record, Ferrari outscored closest rival BAR two to one.

TWO TOP TEAMS STUMBLE

Perennial Ferrari challengers McLaren and Williams ended up with egg on their faces in 2004.

McLaren came out with its second duff chassis in two seasons and only improved after notable modifications in the second half of the season. Williams took an aerodynamic leap with a high-nose, twin-keel front – dubbed a 'walrus nose.' It didn't work and time was wasted before a more normal front was introduced.

In their stead, it was left to Renault to take up the challenge, with Fernando Alonso finishing third behind the Ferraris at the Australian opener before BAR's Jenson Button came on strong. He was twice on the podium at the next two races.

No-one, though, could live with Michael's pace as he won the first five

races, the third of which was in the inaugural Bahrain GP. He was going for a record sixth straight win when, in Monaco, he was taken out by Juan Pablo Montoya's Williams during a safety car period. This left the way clear for Jarno Trulli to score his first win for Renault.

That Michael bounced back to win the next seven rounds, with team-mate Rubens Barrichello finishing second in three of these, rubbed salt in their rivals' wounds.

McLAREN FINDS ITS FEET AGAIN

Michael wrapped up the title at the Belgian GP, but the headlines were filled by the driver who beat him across the line. This was Kimi Raikkonen who gave McLaren's updated MP4-19B chassis its first win.

The Ferrari team leader then proved that he was human after all by having

LEFT **MICHAEL SCHUMACHER, FERRARI AND BRIDGESTONE WERE TRULY IN A CLASS OF THEIR OWN IN 2004 AS THE GERMAN RACED TO HIS FIFTH STRAIGHT FORMULA ONE TITLE, WINNING 13 OF THE 18 ROUNDS.**

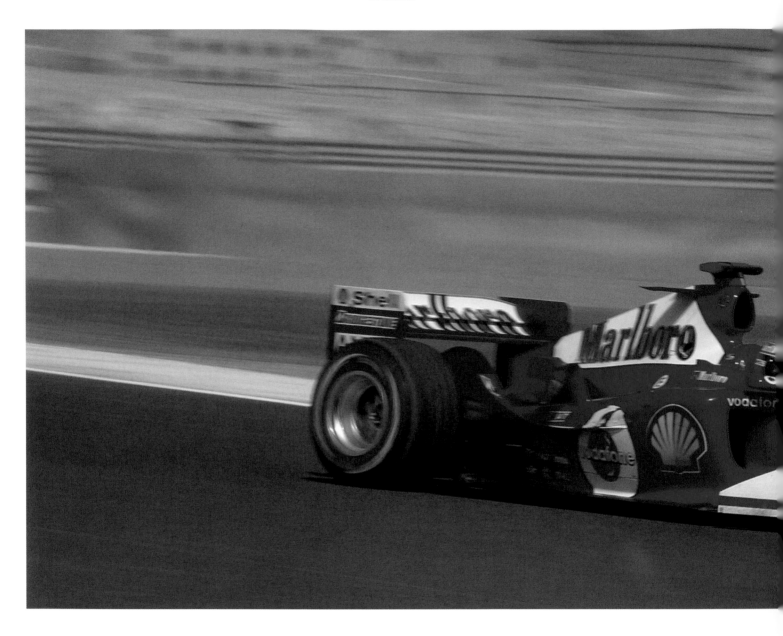

Above MICHAEL SCHUMACHER HIT THE
GROUND RUNNING AND HIS WIN IN
THE INAUGURAL BAHRAIN GP WAS
THE MIDDLE OF A FIVE-WIN RUN.

Right THE FIRST NEW PORT OF CALL FOR
FORMULA ONE WAS BAHRAIN, ITS PALM
TREES AND DESERT PROVIDING
A VERY DIFFERENT BACKDROP.

Far right FORMULA ONE WENT TO CHINA
FOR THE FIRST TIME AND RUBENS
BARRICHELLO DROVE A MASTERFUL
RACE TO BE THE FIRST WINNER THERE.

two off races in a row, spinning down the order at Monza, albeit before powering back through to second place as track conditions favoured his Bridgestones, and then on Formula One's first visit to Shanghai where he floundered around to finish 12th. Barrichello triumphed in both races as he tends to when Ferrari let him off the leash once Michael has the drivers' title in the bag.

This spurt of points made it clear to Button that third would be as high as he could rank overall, but the Briton had worked wonders for BAR, boosted by ever stronger engines from Honda. He and Takuma Sato gathered sufficient

points to outscore Renault, which inexplicably ditched Trulli for the final three races and replaced him with Jacques Villeneuve – back from a year out.

The last laugh went to Williams and Montoya, though, as he won a wonderfully exciting championship-closer at Interlagos. Once more Barrichello was frustrated when his home race escaped him yet again.

Despite his win in Belgium, Raikkonen could rank only seventh and David Coulthard only 10th, before being dropped to make way for Montoya for 2005. This left the 1998 constructors'

champions only fifth overall behind Williams. Williams had lost continuity with the loss of Ralf for six races after he suffered a back injury in a monumental collision with the wall in the US GP. Antonio Pizzonia proved more effective than Marc Gene as a stand-in. Impressively, Ralf raced to second at Suzuka on his second race back.

Fall of the year went to Jordan which scored but five points then had to be bought out over the winter of 2004/05 to ensure its future. Likewise, Jaguar would only continue after being bought by Red Bull and renamed accordingly.

ABOVE **JENSON BUTTON LEADS AWAY FROM POLE AT IMOLA, BUT IT WAS MICHAEL SCHUMACHER (BEHIND) WHO POWERED THROUGH TO WIN.**

RIGHT **QUALIFYING ON POLE AT MONACO, JARNO TRULLI CONTROLLED THE RACE FROM THERE FOR HIS FIRST WIN.**

THE FIRST OF THE NEW BREED

It had seemed that the day would never come, but someone other than Michael Schumacher became World Champion in 2005, with Renault's Fernando Alonso ending the German's run of five straight titles. In so doing, he became the youngest World Champion ever, at 24 years and 58 days, to break Emerson Fittipaldi's record set in 1972.

Perhaps Ferrari and Bridgestone's slide from dominance was down to a rule change that dictated that there would be no tyre changes during pit stops. Yet its difficulties were multiplied by being the only top team on Bridgestone tyres, and the lack of comparative testing hampered Bridgestone's quest to maximize their tyres' performance as their Michelin-shod rivals worked towards a more competitive package for this new format.

There was a further rule stating that engines must last two grands prix. So, perhaps there were grounds for Michael to explain why not only was he beaten by two rivals, but that one outscored him more than two to one and the other ended up 50 points clear.

The dominant duo were Alonso and McLaren's Kimi Raikkonen, two drivers already at the vanguard of Formula One's next generation of champions.

RENAULT'S FAST START

Third in 2004, with less than half of Ferrari's points tally, Renault was on the pace from the outset. The wet/dry/wet weather helped Giancarlo Fisichella to benefit from a new one-at-a-time qualifying system to claim pole in Australia. He was out when the track was at its driest, leaving Juan Pablo Montoya back in ninth, Raikkonen 10th, Alonso 13th and Schumacher 18th on the 20-car grid. Fisichella made the most of this and won from Ferrari's Rubens Barrichello, but Alonso's charge from the back to third was ominous. Schumacher came away with nothing after clashing with Nick Heidfeld's Williams.

If that opening race had an element of lottery about it, the writing was on the wall at the second round, in Malaysia, as Alonso and Fisichella qualified first and third, split only by Toyota's new signing Jarno Trulli. Michael Schumacher again qualified outside the top 10, with Barrichello also struggling, to prove that Ferrari had work to do.

The team wasn't alone in having to find speed from somewhere as Alonso

A LEGEND RETIRES

Inspired by his first world title in 2005, Renault's Fernando Alonso added another, this time pushed by a resurgent Michael Schumacher rather than Kimi Raikkonen as Ferrari rediscovered its form while McLaren fell away and failed to win a race.

Schumacher announced his retirement from racing during the season, as had been expected, bringing to an end the most garlanded career in Formula One history. He finished with a tally of 91 wins and seven world titles in 250 grand prix starts.

Another notable moment in 2006 was Jenson Button giving Honda its first win since 1967. It was a fitting reward for the Japanese manufacturer. Honda took over BAR, which had been winless in its seven years in the sport despite launching itself with the fatuous catchline of "a tradition of excellence."

After Ferrari had been caught out by the rule changes for 2005, there was another round of changes for 2006, with teams again allowed to change tyres during races, helping Ferrari and Bridgestone to get back to the front. Perhaps the major change, though, was that engines were downsized from 3000cc V10s to 2400cc V8s.

Qualifying was also reconfigured, with the slowest six drivers being eliminated after the first 15 minutes to fill 17th to 22nd positions on the grid. After a further 15 minutes, the six slowest of the remaining 16 drivers would be eliminated, leaving the fastest 10 to take a tilt for pole.

ALONSO GETS A FLYER
Renault was fast from the outset, with Alonso and team-mate Giancarlo Fisichella winning the first three races. Alonso kept up the pressure by adding wins at Barcelona, Monaco, Silverstone and Montreal to take a 25-point advantage midway through the 18-race season.

Then down and down came the gap between Alonso and Schumacher as the Ferrari ace won at Indianapolis, Magny-Cours, Hockenheim, Monza and Shanghai. With two races remaining, Schumacher and Alonso were level on points and a record-extending eighth world title for Ferrari man was very much on the cards.

Amazingly, something almost unheard of during his 11 years with Ferrari happened when Schumacher was controlling the Japanese GP from the front: his engine blew. This boosted Alonso from second place and left him with a 10-point lead heading to the final round, the Brazilian GP, where he would have to score just one point in case Schumacher won.

LEFT **FELIPE MASSA FINDS HIS FERRARI IN THE THICK OF THE FIRST CORNER MAYHEM AT THE AUSTRALIAN GP IN MELBOURNE, ALONG WITH NICO ROSBERG'S WILLIAMS, CHRISTIAN KLIEN'S RED BULL AND RUBENS BARRICHELLO'S HONDA.**

Felipe Massa, a winner already in Turkey, was in sparkling form on his home track, Interlagos, but second place was enough for Alonso to be champion.

SCHUMACHER'S FINAL CHARGE

Schumacher's already faint chances were scuppered when his fuel pressure dived as he went out for his final run, leaving him 10th. Determined to end his career on a high, he went on a charge but clashed with Fisichella as he passed for fifth and suffered a puncture that dropped him to last of the 18 remaining cars before he drove one of the races of his life to make it back to fourth. It wasn't enough, but it was a magnificent way to sign out and even went a long way to erase the memory of his unsporting manoeuvre in qualifying at Monaco where he apparently

blocked the track to prevent Alonso from usurping his pole time. Schumacher's punishment from the stewards was to be put to the back of the grid.

Fisichella and Massa spent the year in their team-mates' shadows, while McLaren wasn't quite up to the challenge and Raikkonen was the first to come unstuck in the new-for-2006 qualifying format. Starting 22nd wasn't the dream way to get his season underway and although flashes of speed were there, a pair of second places were to remain his best results. McLaren's season was also interrupted by the departure of Juan Pablo Montoya for a new career in NASCAR stock cars. His replacement, Pedro de la Rosa, finished second in a tospy-turvy Hungarian GP, but wasn't able to match Raikkonen.

JENSON'S ON THE BUTTON

Button finally rewarded Honda's input by winning in Hungary, his first win at his 114th attempt. He achieved it from 14th on the grid in an unusual race. It started on Friday when Schumacher and Alonso were given 2s qualifying penalties, so they started from 11th and 15th.

The track was damp at the start. Pole-sitter Raikkonen led, but was distracted as de la Rosa closed in on him and vaulted over Red Bull's Vitantonio Liuzzi who had pulled over to let himself be lapped. By pitting late, Alonso looked to have pulled off a masterstroke, but a wheelnut came loose and he crashed, leaving Button to win from de la Rosa by half a minute. Button also finished on the podium in Brazil, but team-mate Rubens Barrichello failed to get on with the RA106.

ABOVE MICHAEL SCHUMACHER
PRODUCED A SCINTILLATING RUN IN
HIS FINAL GRAND PRIX, IN BRAZIL,
RECOVERING FROM A FLAT TYRE THAT
HAD LEFT HIM LAST TO FINALLY
FINISH FOURTH.

TOP RIGHT THE RENAULT CREW HOLD
FERNANDO ALONSO ALOFT AFTER
SECOND PLACE IN BRAZIL ROUNDED
OUT HIS SECOND STRAIGHT TITLE-
WINNING YEAR.

Boosted by BMW money, Sauber improved as the campaign progressed. They took a big step forward when Robert Kubica replaced Jacques Villeneuve with six races to go to. He finished third in only his third outing, at Monza, equalling Nick Heidfeld's best result, to help BMW Sauber rank fifth.

Conversely, Toyota slid to sixth, with technical director Mike Gascoyne fired after only three races. Emphasising that Japanese corporate culture doesn't always fit with the individual ways of the top brains, Geoff Willis was then ousted from Honda.

Third place for David Coulthard at Monaco was the highlight of Red Bull's year, but it lagged behind technically so the team chose to focus its efforts on its car for 2007. Christian Klien was replaced in the team's second car by Robert Doornbos before the season was out.

Williams had a torrid season, having to make do with running a non-works engine rather than a manufacturer-supplied one. The Cosworth V8 was much admired, but Cosworth's budget was tiny against their rivals, and poor reliability often thwarted Mark Webber, though he did produce a powerful drive to third place in Monaco. Team-mate Nico Rosberg starred by finishing seventh on his debut, with the fastest lap, but he was in the points only once more.

Scuderia Toro Rosso, formerly Minardi, was allowed to run rev-restricted V10s, upsetting some rivals, but Red Bull's money bought just one point when Liuzzi came eighth at Indianapolis. Team-mate Scott Speed had been denied a point for eighth at the Australian GP when he was penalised 25s for passing Coulthard under yellow flags.

The team that had been Jordan, MF1 Racing, changed its name again before the year was out, becoming Spyker after being bought out by Michiel Mol and renamed after the Dutch sports car manufacturer. Neither Christijan Albers nor Tiago Monteiro scored.

Super Aguri was an all-new team, created by former racer Aguri Suzuki at the 11th hour, largely to stem criticism of Honda in Japan that Takuma Sato had been kicked out of BAR when it was rebadged as Honda Racing. Its first car was brought to the opening round in Bahrain with next to no testing and was way off the pace. But the car improved as development parts finally came on-stream until Sato raced to 10th place in the final round. Sato's three team-mates – Yuji Ide, Franck Montagny and Sakon Yamamoto – all struggled.

TOO CLOSE TO CALL

No script writer would have dared come up with a storyline of three drivers heading into the final round of the season with a shot at the title, with the championship going to the least favoured of the three having been handed victory by his team-mate. Yet, this is what happened in 2007, much to the delight of Formula One ringmaster Bernie Ecclestone.

The new champion was Ferrari's Kimi Raikkonen, who overcame team-mate Felipe Massa and McLaren's duo of astonishing rookie Lewis Hamilton and reigning champion Fernando Alonso.

However, to go with all the excitement, there was plenty of acrimony. After a strong start with McLaren, Alonso fell out with the team. Many believed that Hamilton's sheer speed had upset the defending champion, thus preventing him from being seen as the team's de facto number one – irrespective of the fact that McLaren never designates its drivers as one and two, as it prides itself in running equal cars.

It was undeniable that Hamilton, who been team chief Ron Dennis's protégé for a decade, was very quick and also was well liked within the team. The matter came to a head during qualifying for the Hungarian GP, after which it was clear that the Spaniard's sojourn at McLaren would last one year and no more.

SPYGATE
However, McLaren were involved in a considerably more serious matter, one that cost the team all of its points in the constructors' championship. Ferrari accused McLaren of industrial espionage after Mike Coughlan, McLaren's chief designer, was found with Ferrari technical drawings in his possession, supposedly passed to him by disenchanted Ferrari race and test technical manager, Nigel Stepney.

Whatever the reality of the situation, McLaren was punished severely by the FIA, the governing body removing all of the team's points – past and future in 2007 – and hitting the team with a $100m fine. Renault, which was also said to have another team's technical details – McLaren's – escaped without punishment.

HAMILTON WOWS THEM
This was a shame, as the racing in 2007 was magnificent, something that became clear from the opening round when Hamilton showed an exciting lack of respect for his elders by passing Alonso

301

before the first corner at Melbourne, even after a poor getaway. There was clearly a new ace in the pack.

That first day belonged to Raikkonen, who got his Ferrari career off to a winning start, from pole, proving the best on the new spec tyres – Bridgestone had signed a deal during the offseason to be sole supplier of rubber. But Alonso showed his grit by passing Hamilton to finish second and he won as he pleased next time out, at Sepang. Ron Dennis's smile was made even wider as Hamilton finished second, well clear of Raikkonen. It appeared this would be McLaren's year and Alonso's third title in a row.

Racing doesn't always run to plan, though, and Ferrari's Felipe Massa gave the Italian team hope by winning in Bahrain and Spain. Alonso put McLaren back on track by winning at Monaco, in a race that Hamilton felt could have been his. After an unprecedented five consecutive podium finishes at the start of a Formula One career, Hamilton claimed his first win, at Montreal, staying cool at the head of a race interrupted by safety car periods.

When Hamilton won again, at Indianapolis, he led the championship by 10 points and Alonso was really rattled. Raikkonen won again at Magny-Cours, then at Silverstone too. Despite failing to score at the Nurburgring, Hamilton was still two points clear of Alonso and 11 up on Massa, with Raikkonen, who had retired, seven further back.

ALONSO'S FRUSTRATION BOILS OVER
But then came the Hungarian GP when Alonso and Hamilton got personal in qualifying. Alonso was demoted five places for impeding Hamilton, who was thus promoted to pole and would go on to win, from Raikkonen, who had been bottled up behind him all race.

Massa was dominant in Turkey, where a puncture dropped Hamilton to fifth. At Monza, Hamilton was outraced by Alonso, who reduced his lead to three points. Next up was the Belgian GP and Raikkonen led another Ferrari one-two. However, when Hamilton showed the world how to drive in the (very) wet on Formula One's return to Fuji, he was 12 points clear with two races to go and seemed set to be Formula One's first rookie World Champion. But it wasn't to be...

Above left **BMW SAUBER'S ROBERT KUBICA WAS LUCKY TO SURVIVE THIS HORRIFIC CRASH IN THE CANADIAN GP.**
Left **LEWIS HAMILTON THREATENED TO WIN FROM HIS DEBUT AND TOOK HIS FIRST IN CANADA IN ROUND SIX.**
Above right **LEWIS HAMILTON LOST OUT IN BRAZIL, WHERE VICTORY FOR KIMI RAIKKONEN (BEHIND) WAS ENOUGH FOR THE TITLE.**

The image of Hamilton's McLaren beached in the pit entry gravel trap at Shanghai will remain with his fans for years. He had just been passed for the lead by Raikkonen, and didn't need to win, but McLaren declined to bring him in for new tyres, even though his were threadbare. McLaren's plan, it appeared, was to wait for a change in the weather, but it backfired and Hamilton's failure to score any points left him just four clear of Alonso going to the final round, with Raikkonen a further three behind.

Hamilton started second behind Massa in Brazil, but was passed by Raikkonen going into the first corner, then got blocked and fell behind Alonso. This would have been fine, but Hamilton attempted to fight back, only to go wide and drop to eighth. Six laps later, after regaining two places, a gearbox problem slowed Hamilton's car and dropped him to 18th before it could be righted.

That left him with a mountain to climb, and it proved too much. Massa led for much of the race but handed victory to Raikkonen. Alonso was a lacklustre third while Hamilton could climb back only to

seventh, so Raikkonen was champion.

BMW Sauber were next best behind Ferrari and McLaren, with Nick Heidfeld and Robert Kubica deserving of more. Their best result was Heidfeld's second place in Canada. McLaren's removal from the constructors' championship table left Mario Theissen's team second overall.

Renault's form plummeted, with rookie Heikki Kovalainen taking half the season to find his feet before outperforming Giancarlo Fisichella. Conversely, Williams made ground, but its form was still inconsistent, making it hard for Nico Rosberg and veteran Alex Wurz. The team's only podium finish was Wurz's on a crazy day in Montreal.

Red Bull Racing was even more up and down en route to fifth in the constructors' championship, with its RB3 increasingly fast but fragile. Mark Webber lost several strong point scores and was outscored by David Coulthard. Toyota slipped to sixth, its meagre points tally the most expensive in the sport's history. The team's TF107 defeated both Jarno Trulli and Ralf Schumacher.

Toro Rosso was going nowhere fast,

then hit the points in the penultimate round when rookie Sebastian Vettel (who crashed out of third in the previous race) finished fourth and Vitantonio Liuzzi took sixth.

The team that was once Minardi finished ahead of Honda and this summed up how excruciating life must have been for Rubens Barrichello and Jenson Button. At least a fifth place finish for Button saved the embarrassment of being ranked behind the Super Aguri team to which Honda provides engines.

Super Aguri could even have landed a podium finish, in Canada, but a marmot bent Anthony Davidson's front wing and the crew weren't ready when he pitted. However, the race yielded sixth for Takuma Sato when he passed Alonso on merit.

Underfinanced Spyker brought up the rear and, when rookie Adrian Sutil calmed down, it made progress. Markus Winkelhock started the European GP at the Nurburgring on wet weather tyres and took the lead on lap 2 when everyone dived for the pits, then stayed there for six laps, which wasn't bad for his debut and was more than his late father, Manfred, managed during his Formula One career in the 1980s.

THE FINAL ACT OF THE FINAL RACE

The 2008 Formula One World Championship had the most exciting conclusion ever. At the end of the final race, first one driver won the title, then, 30 seconds and one overtaking manoeuvre later at the last corner, it was plucked from his grasp. Felipe Massa was the vanquished party and Lewis Hamilton the victorious one, in so doing breaking Fernando Alonso's record from 2005 to become the youngest ever World Champion, at just 23 years 300 days.

There was a major rule change: the banning of electronic driver aids, much to the delight of purists who felt that these had narrowed the gap between the good and the best. A standard engine 'brain', the ECU, was made mandatory and a gearbox was now to last for four sets of grand prix Saturdays and Sundays, with a five-place grid penalty if one needed to be changed. Engines

continued to be expected to last for two Saturdays and Sundays.

There were also two new venues. A street circuit around the docks in Valencia became the new home of the European GP, but it was eclipsed by Singapore's street circuit that hosted Formula One's first night-time grand prix, offering novelty and a stunning backdrop.

EARLY SURPRISES

Hamilton helped McLaren emerge from its winter of discontent by racing from pole to an easy victory in the Melbourne opener, with Nick Heidfeld second for BMW Sauber. Reigning champion Kimi Raikkonen had started 16th after a fuel pump problem, but made it back to eighth. Raikkonen then waltzed to victory at Sepang, with BMW Sauber's other driver, Robert Kubica, second, giving Stefano Domenicali his first win since

taking Ferrari's reins from Jean Todt. He was pleased again, when Massa won in Bahrain, from Raikkonen, with Hamilton clashing with Fernando Alonso's Renault. Third and fourth put BMW Sauber top of the points table.

The fourth race, in Barcelona, will be remembered for three things: first, Raikkonen led home Massa in another Ferrari one-two; second, Heikki Kovalainen survived a massive accident in the second McLaren; and third, it turned out to be the final appearance for Super Aguri before the team folded.

A fourth straight Ferrari win, this time for Massa in Turkey, might have been bad news for McLaren, but Hamilton was on his tail after running an aggressive three-stop pit strategy because of tyre concerns. Kovalainen reckoned that he might have won the race, but a first lap clash with Raikkonen left him with a puncture.

LEFT **LEWIS HAMILTON CELEBRATES AFTER HE REGAINED THE POINTS LEAD GOING INTO THE FINAL CORNER OF THE LAST LAP OF THE TRULY DRAMATIC BRAZILIAN GP TO CLAIM THE WORLD TITLE AHEAD OF FERRARI'S FELIPE MASSA.**

A NEW ORDER

A change in the rules often produces a season of excitement, with something of a reshuffling of the pack, but it's hard to recall if there has ever been such a changing of the order as in 2009, with erstwhile pace-setters McLaren left struggling to emerge from the midfield and Ferrari scoring not a single point In the first three Grands Prix.

Yet more remarkable than that, the team that won three of the first four Grands Prix, in Australia, Malaysia and Bahrain, wasn't even in existence at the 11th hour in the run-up to the first race. This was Brawn GP, the team that had been Honda Racing until late November 2008 when the Japanese manufacturer pulled the plug, mindful of the global economic recession. Indeed, several manufacturers had to balance their F1 programmes against laying off staff at their factories as sales of road cars fell. Technical director Ross Brawn took the helm and agreed reluctantly for the team to be called Brawn GP, and the new car's speed from its handful of pre-season tests was startling. This was of extra delight for drivers Jenson Button and Rubens Barrichello who had looked to be out of F1 until the team was given its reprieve.

It is true that Brawn had focused on the 2009 car at the expense of development of the 2008 challenger that was good enough to leave the team only ninth overall, but many of the sport's insiders pointed to the pace of the white Mercedes-powered cars and that of the Williams and Toyota duos as being down solely to the shape of their diffusers, claiming that they were bending the rules by running a double-diffuser set-up. The FIA rejected this charge, leaving the other teams to copy the concept or lose out, with aerodynamic benefits coming from the gap in the transition between the two diffusers being used to direct airflow out the back of the car above the diffuser tunnel.

PRESS KERS TO PASS

If the grids looked strange in Melbourne, almost reversed, the cars looked even more odd, as they sported the new aerodynamic packages that left them with wide, driver-adjustable front wings, no bargeboards or any of the multifarious winglets that used to adorn their flanks, and a narrow, high rear wing. On the plus side, these changes were made to make it easier for a driver to follow then pass another car and the cars were fitted with slick tyres, back for the first time since 1997. Under the skin, cars were allowed to run with a KERS system that stores energy generated by braking then releases it to boost acceleration. The downside is its weight, and some teams started the year with a system far better than others who chose to wait and develop their KERS further.

With Brawn and Toyota being the standard bearers in the first two races, with flashes of speed from Williams' Nico Rosberg, there was an early opportunity for the stewards to get busy, and it sprang from an innocuous moment when Jarno Trulli ran off the track behind the safety car and reigning champion Lewis Hamilton slipped past before letting him back by. Trulli was given a 25s penalty, but Hamilton was later found to have been at fault and was disqualified. His reputation took a knock, but it was worse for McLaren sporting director Davey Ryan who was fired, while Ron Dennis chose to stop all of his involvement with McLaren's F1 team and focus on its road car division instead.

LEFT **AFTER THAT OPENING WIN IN AUSTRALIA, BUTTON AND BRAWN GP KEPT ON WINNING. THIS IS BAHRAIN.**

THE TEENS

Above MINARDI TEAM OWNER PAUL STODDART AND MARK MOUNT THE PODIUM TO CELEBRATE MARK'S FIFTH PLACE ON HIS F1 DEBUT, SUITABLY IN AUSTRALIA.

Top right MARK'S SECOND TEAM WAS JAGUAR RACING, BUT HIS SECOND SEASON WITH THEM, IN 2004, PRODUCED JUST SEVEN POINTS.

Opposite top AFTER A TWO-YEAR SPELL WITH WILLIAMS, MARK JOINED RED BULL RACING AND LANDED HIS FIRST F1 VICTORY AT THE NURBURGRING IN 2009.

Opposite bottom MARK COULDN'T MATCH THE PACE OF TEAM-MATE SEBASTIAN VETTEL IN 2011, BUT HE GOT THE BETTER OF HIM TO WIN THE FINALE IN BRAZIL.

and, although he claimed his first podium, Mark was anxious to move up the grid. This meant re-joining a team he'd raced for before, albeit as Red Bull Racing for 2007. What was the main difference? "Adrian Newey," Mark quips. "Having a decent budget helped too. The team did a lot of head hunting."

This suggests a team in turmoil, and Mark is a fan of continuity, as he explains: "Ferrari got the results it got in the 2000s with Michael Schumacher because it had continuity. It was working as one and things tend to work when everything is going well and a team's personnel are working without one-upmanship. Since Adrian has left McLaren, it's been tough... What a good team needs is for its heads of department to be beacons, to fight for their corner. If you're not winning, though, people start questioning your work."

It was at Red Bull Racing that Mark worked his way to the front of the field, with his first win coming in 2009 at the Nurburgring. Ranked fourth, as Jenson Button dominated for Brawn GP, Mark then scored four wins in 2010, but was overhauled at the final round by team-mate Vettel, and so it was that the enemy was within for the next three years as Vettel

collected three more titles and Mark had to settle for third overall in 2010, 2011 and 2013.

One of the issues in this time was the spectre of team orders, something that Vettel famously ignored at Sepang in 2013.

"There's a lot of paranoia surrounding team orders. It's very difficult to keep both drivers happy," says Mark. "Team orders are only an issue when your team is in a position of dominance and the team doesn't want to shit in its nest. Also, people don't like to see manipulation. Some might wonder why Rubens [Barrichello] appeared to have so many sticky pitstops with Ferrari... And a team can do you on the starts too, if it wishes."

Ask Mark about which drivers he rates across his time in F1 and he doesn't go straight for vaunted team-mate Vettel. "Fernando [Alonso] is pretty complete and has been good across all the regulation changes," he starts, "whereas Sebastian and Kimi [Raikkonen] didn't like their cars in 2014. Fernando is also very precise and consistent. Is he as quick as Ayrton Senna was over a lap? Absolutely not. Michael [Schumacher] was the Sunday afternoon computer."

"The best way to beat Sebastian is mentally. If you could get him rocking, he might not deal with a situation well, like I did in early 2012 when we were running with the non-blown floor. When he gets confident, though, he's very, very potent. In 2014, you've seen him with a car he doesn't like and this doesn't help him find a set-up as he can't feel the car as he wants."

Assessing his own strengths as a driver, Mark replies: "One of my strengths was fast corners. Look at some of the tracks now, like Abu Dhabi, with so many second gear bends, where are you supposed to make time up? Give me Copse, Maggotts, corners like that."

This brings Mark to his thoughts about F1 cars today compared to the ones when he started in F1. "Back in the first half of the 2000s, F1 was much more physical. You see the drivers get out after a Grand Prix now and they don't even look tired. Also, cars then looked as though they were on fast-forward through the corners. Sure, they're fast on the straights now, but not so much in the corners. F1 was such a major step up from any other racing formula then. Nowadays, sportscars are almost as fast and GP2 only a few seconds slower."

Track safety wasn't as good back in 2002, though. "Racing at Le Mans remains the most dangerous thing I've done, as there are many old school elements to the lap and also more variables," Mark grimaces. Yet he appears to thrill at the challenge. New tracks leave him a little cold: "I think that the tracks built in the last decade, like in Bahrain, are horrendous and they certainly don't reward you like the old ones do," comments Mark. "Everyone raved about Abu Dhabi, but if you strip away the flashy buildings it's a very ordinary track. We don't want second and third gear bends, we want seventh gear bends. Give us a little camber too, then we can play with our lines. I've always said that the track that tows the best produces the best racing. Look at Turn 11 in Turkey, at Blanchimont at Spa and at 130R at Suzuka.

"You need undulations too and variations in track width that make it hard to get the right line in qualifying let alone in the race."

"I had two big shunts in F1, in Brazil in 2003 and Valencia in 2010, and I was thankful for F1's safety requirements of high cockpit sides. Composites have helped too. I wouldn't have wanted to go back to Jackie Stewart's day in the 1960s and 1970s, and getting rid of the threat of fire was brilliant, but drivers really don't get punished for mistakes any more."

What about F1 as a showpiece? Mark doesn't think F1 it's great currently: "No, it's too clinical and the fans can see that. With all the instruction over the radio, it's not just distracting but a little demeaning. After all, can you imagine Roger Federer being told to serve left or right? No one can see what we're going through in the car. They certainly can't see our emotions. Also, wouldn't it be great if drivers were allowed to grab a flag after winning?"

Max Verstappen will make F1 history as its youngest driver when he races for Toro Rosso in 2015 at the age of 17. Does Mark think this rise of youth is a good thing? "Absolutely not. It's not good for the drivers either, as not all will make it and nobody talks about the young ones whose careers have crashed and burned, like Jaime Alguersuari. Take Jan Magnussen too. On the other hand, look at Kevin Magnussen's career and it's unbelievable.

"The young drivers have got to earn their stripes. They've got to build their physicality and people should start to worry that it's possible for a 17-year-old to get the most out of an F1 car. Put them in a 2004 Ferrari and it would snap them in half.

"This young generation now wants things very quickly and they can try them too, on simulators. Was I ready for F1 at 18? No. At 20, probably not..."

Finally, what does Mark think of F1's constant: Ferrari, a team he came close to joining after Red Bull?

"You'll have to wait for my book to discover how close I came... What I will say is that if you were at a winter test at 21:00, the Pom mechanics would be working away, which I like, and the Italian mechanics would be smoking behind the garages...

"The lure of joining Ferrari was a change of environment, but did I still have the motivation in my 30s to learn 700 people again? The passion for Ferrari was a draw, and you only have to visit Italy to feel their love for F1. Ferrari is definitely good for the sport."

RIGHT **MARK WON HIS 'OTHER HOME RACE', THE BRITISH GP, TWICE, WITH THIS WIN IN 2012 BACKING UP THE ONE HE SCORED AT SILVERSTONE IN 2010.**

CHANGE AT THE LAST

One element that was always going to focus the teams' minds for 2010 was the banning of refuelling. Pit stops continued for tyre changes, but this rule change meant that the cars had to carry up to 180kg of fuel at the start of each race rather than around 60kg as before. To accommodate this change, each car had to be fitted with a larger fuel tank and this forced the designers to move the engine and gearbox further back to accommodate it, with the obvious effect on the car's balance plus an encouragement for the manufacturers to make their engines more fuel-efficient so that they could start with a lighter fuel load.

Other changes included a move to narrower front tyres, down from 270mm to 245. The cars also had to run with a higher minimum weight, up by 15kg to

620. These changes were across the board, but the teams that had developed KERS through 2009 – Ferrari, McLaren and Renault - were disheartened by the dropping of the energy release system, costing them a hard-earned advantage.

As with all periods of change, though, F1 continued to be a hotbed for ingenuity and one of the developments of 2010 was the F-duct introduced by McLaren. It worked by piping air through a duct on the top of the nose to the rear wing, with the driver operating this by moving his left knee to cover a slot in the pipe in the cockpit side when on the straights to allow all the air to flow towards the rear wing. This extra air then stalls it – separating airflow from the wing element to make it less effective and so reduce drag – before releasing it as they brake. It wasn't easy for others to copy, as they

had to make space for the ducting through their already tight monocoque design.

QUALIFYING BY ELIMINATION

Aimed to make the Grand Prix meetings more exciting, the format of qualifying was changed, with the slowest seven drivers eliminated after the first qualifying session then the seven slowest at the end of the second session also made to drop out, leaving just 10 drivers for the final session. In this, they had to take into consideration that they would have to start the Grand Prix on the tyres they fitted for this final tilt at pole.

To give the races extra spice, too, points were now awarded to the top 10 finishers rather than just the top eight, with a win no longer worth 10 points but 25, making the difference between first and second seven points rather than two.

LEFT **VETTEL WINS THE ABU DHABI GP.**

VETTEL SHOWS HIS CLASS

f Red Bull Racing laid its foundations in 2009 and then built on those in 2010, then it unveiled its masterpiece in 2011 as its cars won 12 of the 19 Grands Prix and Sebastian Vettel left even his closest rival trailing by 122 points by season's end.

The Renault-powered Red Bull RB7 was obviously the class of the field, but it was in qualifying that it was at its most deadly, with Vettel and his team-mate Mark Webber claiming pole position at every race bar one, with the German more often than not then proving able to dominate from there.

Perhaps a bigger surprise was the extent to which Webber was outperformed by Vettel after they had been so closely matched in 2010. After the opening nine rounds, Vettel had six wins and three second places, whereas the Australian

had just one second place and four thirds to his name. The reason for this appeared to be that he didn't like the RB7's behaviour on the new Pirelli tyres, but also that he made poor starts in the early races and also the fact that he's 10kg heavier than Vettel meant that the team had more choice where it placed ballast in the German's car. Add to this the fact that Vettel simply seemed to be continuing to develop his craft and the slight but crucial performance difference can be explained. Previous talk of Vettel being the 'new Michael Schumacher' was very much something of the past, as he was certainly his own man, forging his own place in F1 history. Webber's form did improve in the second half of the year, culminating in victory in the final round at Interlagos, but this was only enough to promote him from fourth overall to third.

INDIA JOINS THE F1 SHOW

Vettel had to make do with second place in that final race, but he had long before clinched his second title, doing so at the 15th round, the Japanese GP at Suzuka. He then underlined his superiority by winning on F1's second visit to Korea and then on its first to India. This was one of the landmark moments of the 2011 season and the teams were hugely impressed by the all-new Buddh International Circuit outside capital city New Delhi, if less so by the exceptional degree of bureaucracy that seemed to override every action.

After the 19 rounds, Jenson Button, in his second year with McLaren, proved himself to be the best of the rest, this time getting the upper hand over team-mate Lewis Hamilton, showing how his personable ways could augment his

LEFT **PRINCE ALBERT CONGRATULATES SEBASTIAN VETTEL AFTER THE GERMAN RED BULL DRIVER'S FIRST MONACO VICTORY.**

VETTEL BY A NOSE

Three-time World Champions are rare enough in Formula One, but drivers who have won three titles in consecutive years are rarer still, which made Sebastian Vettel's feat in 2012 all the greater. The only others to have achieved this feat are Juan Manuel Fangio and Michael Schumacher, putting the 25-year-old's achievement into stark perspective. Certainly, Red Bull Racing provided him with a great car in the RB8 and built its attack around him, but he had to deliver, which he did, then resist a late-season charge from Ferrari's Fernando Alonso, which he also did.

Pirelli's new tyres produced more grip, resulting in teams having to manage their fuel load better, and a new maximum height for the car's nose, helped to create the unusual situation in which seven different drivers won the season's first seven Grands Prix. Indeed, it was not until the end of June before the season had its first two-time winner. Fittingly, it was Alonso at Valencia in the European GP who achieved it. In a season in which he performed with consistent excellence, Alonso was fortunate as only alternator failure prevented Vettel from becoming the first two-time winner.

What was clear through 2012 was the excellence of Alonso's attack, as his Ferrari was seldom even the second best car, which was usually the McLaren, but he kept on pressing and not only won three rounds – at Sepang, Valencia and Hockenheim – but usually appeared on the podium if he didn't win. Felipe Massa looked set to be dropped from the second Ferrari seat, but upped his form in the second half of the season to keep his ride for 2013.

A SEXTET OF CHAMPIONS

One historic first in 2012 was that the grid contained six F1 champions for the first time thanks to the return of 2007 World Champion Kimi Raikkonen to pit his talents against Michael Schumacher (1994 and 1995 then 2000 to 2004), Alonso (2005 and 2006), Lewis Hamilton (2008), Jenson Button (2009) and Vettel (2010 and 2011). The Finn was back after a two-year foray into rallying after quitting Ferrari. This time, he was driving for Lotus Renault GP. To avoid confusion, this was the team that had been Renault in 2011 but had taken over the Lotus name from Tony Fernandes's team that was now known as Caterham. These name changes were not popular, especially as neither of these teams had any connection with the original Team Lotus that ran in F1 from 1958 until 1994. Furthermore, the 'new'

LEFT **SEBASTIAN VETTEL LEADS THE FIRST US GP AT THE CIRCUIT OF THE AMERICAS, CHASED BY LEWIS HAMILTON AND MARK WEBBER.**

329

FOUR IN A ROW

Looking back on 2013, Sebastian Vettel's fourth World Championship-winning campaign, his rivals can at least say that he didn't win the opening race in Australia, as he finished third in Melbourne. This, though, is grasping at straws, as there was little else that Vettel failed to win, and his streak of nine victories in the final nine rounds shows just how superior he and his Renault-powered Red Bull RB9 were. Thirteen wins across the year's 19 rounds are all the proof that you need of the advantage that the team offered him and the way in which he made the most of it.

That he had done enough by the 16th round – the Indian GP at the Buddh International Circuit – to secure his fourth F1 title in succession in the 2010s proves just how dominant he had been.

McLAREN STRUGGLES
The opening round in Melbourne had been a real wake-up call for the teams as they were shocked just how rapidly their Pirelli tyres went off in the race, with some drivers describing their car's performance as having 'fallen off a cliff'. Canniest of all, though, was Kimi Raikkonen who triumphed for Lotus as even Red Bull found that its tyre performance was extraordinary. Fernando Alonso finished second for Ferrari and Vettel third for Red Bull. Of McLaren, though, there was no sign at the sharp end of the field and Jenson Button did well to finish ninth in a car that was 2.5s off Vettel's pole time. Journalists even enquired of team principal Martin Whitmarsh whether the team would go back to its 2012 chassis.

Yet, things changed very quickly through the opening rounds as teams reacted to the behaviour of the latest Pirellis and, unusually, it was Vettel who was among the most displeased, calling them "chocolate tyres". Red Bull chief technical officer Adrian Newey said that they were "very sensitive to high load conditions, so you couldn't go through high-speed corners without destroying them". Then, just when rivals thought that they might have a chance of toppling Vettel, Red Bull Racing returned from the summer break to win the Belgian GP then did so in every other race from then until the end of the season. Vettel's eventual tally of 397 points left him 155 clear of his closest rival, Alonso.

This sequence for Vettel shattered the records. It might have been helped slightly by some rival teams taking their eye off continued development as they prepared instead for the comprehensive set of

LEFT SEBASTIAN VETTEL ROUNDED OUT HIS 2013 SEASON WITH A 13TH WIN. MARK WEBBER WAS SECOND AND FERNANDO ALONSO THIRD.

MERCEDES TAKES CONTROL

With a comprehensive change in the technical regulations – the replacement of 2.4-litre V8 engines by 1.6-litre turbocharged V6s and the introduction of hybrid power, plus the banning of exhaust-blown floors and the reduction in the width of nose wings – it was always possible that one team would get it more right than the others and so find an advantage.

One might have thought that Adrian Newey and the design team at Red Bull Racing would continue their dominance, but it was Mercedes that came good, and how.... By dint of applying themselves to the task sooner than their rivals, Mercedes not only produced the best engine, but also mastered the best way to package this along with the hefty energy recovery system. That the teams that used the new Mercedes V6 all rose towards the top emphasized just how good the motor was, with teams using Renault or Ferrari engines finding themselves some way adrift.

A NEW DRIVING STYLE

The teams were worried after their minimal close-season testing that they might not be able to meet the new fuel economy figures that required them to race with a third less fuel, but their engineers did the job and they all mastered that from the very first round. What was not so easy was the challenge that faced the drivers, as these cars were very different to drive when ERS was employed and offered an extra 160bhp for as much as 33s per lap, with braking having to be handled differently and the loss of exhaust-blown downforce making the handling even trickier than before.

Nico Rosberg won that opener in Australia in a race that might have gone to his Mercedes team-mate Lewis Hamilton but for an engine failure on the third lap. That the British driver bounced back by winning the next four on the trot, with Rosberg second each time, showed how the title fight would be between only them.

In fact, such was their performance advantage that it took the pair of them hitting mechanical trouble in Canada before any other driver got a look in.

Through the course of the season, Rosberg surprised people by being more than a match for Hamilton in qualifying, taking pole on 11 occasions to the British driver's seven. In the races, though, Hamilton was the sharper tool. There was considerable concern when they went to Yas Marina for the final round that despite

LEFT **LEWIS HAMILTON CELEBRATES TAKING THE POINTS LEAD WITH THE FOURTH WIN OF HIS CAMPAIGN AT THE SPANISH GP.**

HAMILTON AT A CANTER

Having proved the most adept at building a car to the new regulations that introduced 1.6-litre turbocharged V6 engines and hybrid power in 2014, Mercedes started 2015 as the favourite and duly delivered.

Such was the competitive advantage enjoyed by Lewis Hamilton and his team-mate Nico Roberg that not only did they finish the season as champion and runner-up respectively, but their combined tally of 703 points gave Mercedes an eventual margin of 275 points over its closest rival: Ferrari. Between them, the Mercedes drivers won 16 of the 19 grands prix, with Sebastian Vettel taking the other three for Ferrari in his first season with the Scuderia.

The balance of power lay with Hamilton, as he claimed his third F1 drivers' title by winning the opening round in Australia and then adding another nine victories, in China, Bahrain, Canada, Britain, Belgium, Italy, Japan, Russia and the USA. He made it look easy.

Rosberg spread three wins through the season and then assumed the upper hand to win the final three grands prix, all from pole position. However, there appeared to be little support for Hamilton from within the team in these races as it refused to let him adapt his strategy during the race in the hope of passing Rosberg. Those three wins were enough to ensure that the German overhauled compatriot Vettel to be runner-up.

What couldn't be disguised, though, was the near open warfare inside the Mercedes camp, with Hamilton and Rosberg scarcely talking, most notably after Hamilton barged his team-mate aside on the opening lap of the United States GP. That the team appeared to favour Rosberg after that might have been their way of redressing the balance.

FERRARI BACK ON FORM

Ferrari appeared to be rejuvenated by the arrival of Vettel from Red Bull Racing, taking over the lead seat from Fernando Alonso. He settled in easily and found life easier than it had been at Red Bull in 2014 when Daniel Ricciardo outraced him as his Ferrari team-mate Kimi Raikkonen stuck to his mantra of avoiding PR duties, being completely contained and so not interested in trying to ensure he had any advantage. Indeed, the Finn simply did what he likes best, driving. Importantly for Vettel, Raikkonen was consistent rather than blazingly fast and so he was comfortable in knowing that he'd always be that little bit faster. Vettel's wins came at the second round in Malaysia when the

LEFT **LEWIS HAMILTON LEADS THE WAY IN SOCHI FOR MERCEDES TO MAKE IT TWO RUSSIAN GP WINS IN SUCCESSION.**

LIKE FATHER, LIKE SON

It was all Mercedes all over again in 2016 and a guide to how the team from Northamptonshire still held all the trump cards was the way that its cars claimed pole position at all but one of the season's 21 grands prix. By the end of the year, its silver F1 W07s had won all but two of the races and romped home just short of 300 points ahead of its closest rival: Red Bull Racing. So, it was another year of excellence. There were glimpses that both Red Bull and Ferrari might be able to challenge, but Ferrari in particular lost momentum.

One of the most positive elements of the 2016 World Championship was that F1 reversed a trend and added a new team to its ranks. This was Haas F1 and, better still, it was an American team, offering a rare chance for American fans to have a team of their own to cheer on.

Add to that the fact that the World Championship expanded from 19 rounds to 21 with the addition of races in Azerbaijan, strangely under the guise of the European GP, and at Hockenheim with the welcome return of the German GP, and F1 looked in better health than it had for a while.

However, the arrival of Haas F1 was then given a counterbalance by a weaker team falling to its knees, with Manor shutting shop after the season-closing grand prix in Abu Dhabi to go and contest the FIA World Endurance Championship instead.

A CHANGE AT THE TOP

Nico Rosberg and Lewis Hamilton go back a very long way. Not just the four years they'd spent together at Mercedes, but all the way back to their karting days

when they operated from under the same awning. Although their race to the top moved at a different pace, with Nico nosing ahead to get to F1 first, it was Lewis who started 2016 as a three-time World Champion and Rosberg as the bridesmaid. Having been with Mercedes for four years before Hamilton arrived, Rosberg could have felt cowed by Hamilton becoming champion in 2014 and 2015. Indeed, many felt that he was, but 2016 seemed to be contested by a different Rosberg, one who was applying himself even more, giving his everything to topple his rival.

The battle between them became even more fraught, but this time Rosberg showed more mettle and he did it from the outset of the season. Having ended 2015 by winning the final three rounds, Rosberg set to and

Left **NICO ROSBERG LEADS MERCEDES TEAM-MATE LEWIS HAMILTON IN AUSTRIA, BUT IT WAS THE BRITISH DRIVER WHO WENT ON TO WIN.**

345

triumphed at each of the first four rounds. They then clashed on the opening lap of the fifth round, in Spain, and both retired on the spot. This was no quarter given stuff. Finally, at the sixth time of asking, Hamilton won at Monaco. And so the great catch up began. Further victories in Canada, Austria and Britain got him back into the hunt. Winning in Hungary moved Hamilton into the points lead, but this is where Rosberg showed that he was not going to be beaten without a fight and wins in Belgium, Italy and Singapore boosted his title hopes.

It was clear that the title would be settled by small margins and a major blow to Hamilton's hopes came when his engine failed when he was leading at Sepang. When only one team is on the pace, a chasing driver has meagre chance to reduce the deficit. Indeed, Hamilton won each of the final four rounds, but the 18 points for second place were going to be enough for Rosberg to be crowned. This forced Hamilton to do everything in his power in the final race in Abu Dhabi to slow Rosberg enough for Vettel to pass him for second, but Rosberg just resisted this fate and so became the second second generation World Champion nine years after Damon Hill made history.

Then, not long after the dust had settled, Nico shocked everyone by announcing that he was retiring from racing, his ambition achieved.

While Mercedes was dominating,

Red Bull Racing did its best to stay in touch and it was this team from Milton Keynes that landed the two races that didn't go Mercedes' way. The first was the Spanish GP, when the Mercedes duo clashed. The win didn't go to Daniel Ricciardo, though, as he was hampered by a strategic call the team made to thwart Ferrari, but to Max Verstappen who had just been promoted to the team in place of Daniil Kvyat who had failed to impress sufficiently in the opening four rounds. His win, at 18 years and 227 days, made him the youngest ever F1 winner. Ricciardo did take one scalp, though, winning in Malaysia after Hamilton's engine blew.

Ferrari could have won the opening race of the year, in Australia, and Sebastian Vettel led but the team opted for the wrong compound of tyre during a red flag stoppage and blew his hopes of victory. Then, in a replay of earlier moments of Ferrari political plays over the decades, the management saw fit to get rid of technical director James Allison and duly lost its way. Vettel was less than impressed and his gradual loss of competitiveness left him able to finish only fourth overall behind Ricciardo. By season's end, he was only just ahead of Verstappen who, don't forget, started the year with Scuderia Toro Rosso.

WORKING WONDERS
Force India puts most other teams to shame. Its budget is a fraction of many of its rivals and yet it keeps doing things simply, doing things right and moving

up the order. Fourth place overall was one place and 37 points better than it had managed in 2015 as it overhauled Williams in the battle to be the best-placed of Mercedes' customer teams. Sergio Perez built on a strong 2015 campaign to claim two third-place finishes, in Monaco and on the streets of F1's newest venue, Baku in Azerbaijan. Team-mate Nico Hulkenberg also showed well, if with fewer tangible results.

Valtteri Bottas was again Williams's better-placed driver, albeit three places further back than in 2015, the Finn peaking with third place in Canada. Team-mate Felipe Massa was notified that this would be his final season and did a respectable job.

One can point out that McLaren made marked progress in 2016 as it advanced from ninth in 2015 to a less woeful sixth position overall. Yet, for a team of McLaren's pedigree, this was still way below acceptable. Fernando Alonso's best finish was fifth place, which he achieved in both Monaco and the United States, while Jenson Button managed sixth in Austria, but Honda still fell way short of its part of the bargain. By year's end, Ron Dennis, the man who made the team great in the 1980s, was sent on his way.

That Scuderia Toro Rosso finished just 13 points behind, was mainly down to Carlos Sainz Jr collecting a trio of sixth place finishes and he outshone Kvyat after the Russian's demotion.

HAAS F1 MAKES A SPLASH
People said that newcomers Haas F1 was onto a hiding to nothing, especially as it was looking to buck the trend by basing itself in the USA. Yet Romain Grosjean gave it a dream start with sixth place on the team's debut and then backed that up with fifth next time out. This was astonishing, but he scored on three more occasions, although team-mate Esteban Gutierrez came away empty-handed as the team ranked eighth in its debut season.

F1 can be confusing at times, as there was a team called Renault in the World Championship once more, but this was simply the team that had raced in 2016 as Lotus after yet another rebranding. Drivers Kevin Magnussen and Jolyon Palmer stood little chance, as the budget was tiny and development work for 2016 had been stopped during 2015. The Dan's seventh place in the Russian GP was its one shining light.

At least Sauber's traditional struggle resulted in points in 2016, with Felipe Nasr racing to ninth place at the penultimate round to, crucially, move it ahead of the Manor team which had been sitting in 10th overall – vital for prize money – since Pascal Wehrlein had finished 10th in the Austrian GP some 11 rounds earlier.

TOP **DANIEL RICCIARDO WAS IN POSITION TO WIN IN MALAYSIA AFTER LEWIS HAMILTON'S MERECEDS SUFFERED ENGINE FAILURE.**

Right **THE CHAMPION ROSBERG FAMILY CELEBRATES IN ABU DHABI AS PARENTS KEKE (LEFT) AND SINA (RIGHT) JOIN WIFE VIVIAN AND NICO.**

Below **IT'S THE NEW VERSUS THE OLD AS MAX VERSTAPPEN LEADS KIMI RAIKKONEN BEHIND HIM AS HE RACES TO HIS MAIDEN WIN IN SPAIN.**

IT'S HAMILTON AGAIN

It was all change for 2017 as the sport's governing body decided to give F1 more fan appeal. Their aim was to make the cars faster and more exciting. To achieve this, they gave them wider front and rear wings, fatter tyres, longer underbody diffusers and reprofiled body aerodynamics up their flanks. The target was more than visual and the FIA brains trust hoped that this would slash their lap times by as much as 6s per lap to get the speeds back to where they were in the days when the cars were propelled by 3.0-litre V10s up until 2005.

Lap times did improve, but not by as much as predicted, but one thing that didn't change was the name of the team at the front: Mercedes. Its tally wasn't as dominant as in 2016, but 12 wins from 20 rounds was still hugely impressive. With Lewis Hamilton winning nine of those, his fourth F1 title was clearly going to be a formality as the season progressed and the British driver had it all wrapped up with two rounds to go.

With Nico Rosberg shocking Mercedes by announcing his retirement just after landing the 2016 title, the team had to scramble to find a replacement and convinced Williams, a team it supplies with engines, to hand over Valtteri Bottas. The Finn adjusted well, scored his first win at the fourth time of asking, in Russia and, despite a mid-season dip in form, added wins from pole in both Austria and Abu Dhabi to rank third overall. Their combined efforts gave Mercedes the reward of a fourth consecutive constructors' championship title.

VETTEL LEADS THE WAY

The driver who split them was Ferrari team leader Sebastian Vettel who opened his campaign with victory in Australia. He then kept Hamilton on his toes in China, and added a second win in Bahrain to lead the points table. Winning in Monaco left his tally as three wins and three second places from six starts, and consistent scoring kept Hamilton behind him until round 13 in Italy. Of all the places for a Ferrari driver to be toppled… A crazy move on the run to the first corner next time out in Singapore which took out team-mate Kimi Raikkonen and Max Verstappen, revealed the pressure he was under and his non-score there hurt his chances. That wasn't Vettel's worst move of the year, though, as that went to his lunge at Hamilton's Mercedes behind a safety car in Azerbaijan, from which he was fortunate to escape without a ban.

Victory for Vettel in the Brazilian GP boosted Ferrari's points tally, but the war

Left **FORMER PRESIDENT BILL CLINTON JOINS LEWIS HAMILTON AND KIMI RAIKKONEN ON THE PODIUM AFTER HAMILTON WON THE US GP.**

349

FORMULA ONE RECORDS

DRIVERS' WORLD CHAMPIONSHIP 2005

POS.	DRIVER	NAT.	CONSTRUCTOR	PTS
1	FERNANDO ALONSO	ESP	RENAULT	133
2	KIMI RAIKKONEN	FIN	McLAREN-MERCEDES	112

All scores counted

CONSTRUCTORS' CUP

POS.	CONSTRUCTOR	PTS
1	RENAULT	191
2	McLAREN-MERCEDES	182

DRIVERS' WORLD CHAMPIONSHIP 2006

POS.	DRIVER	NAT.	CONSTRUCTOR	PTS
1	FERNANDO ALONSO	ESP	RENAULT	134
2	MICHAEL SCHUMACHER	GER	FERRARI	121

All scores counted

CONSTRUCTORS' CUP

POS.	CONSTRUCTOR	PTS
1	RENAULT	206
2	FERRARI	201

DRIVERS' WORLD CHAMPIONSHIP 2007

POS.	DRIVER	NAT.	CONSTRUCTOR	PTS
1	KIMI RAIKKONEN	FIN	FERRARI	110
2	LEWIS HAMILTON	GBR	McLAREN-MERCEDES	109

All scores counted

CONSTRUCTORS' CUP

POS.	CONSTRUCTOR	PTS
1	FERRARI	204
2	BMW SAUBER	101

DRIVERS' WORLD CHAMPIONSHIP 2008

POS.	DRIVER	NAT.	CONSTRUCTOR	PTS
1	LEWIS HAMILTON	GBR	McLAREN-MERCEDES	98
2	FELIPE MASSA	BRA	FERRARI	97

All scores counted

CONSTRUCTORS' CUP

POS.	CONSTRUCTOR	PTS
1	FERRARI	172
2	McLAREN-MERCEDES	151

DRIVERS' WORLD CHAMPIONSHIP 2009

POS.	DRIVER	NAT.	CONSTRUCTOR	PTS
1	JENSON BUTTON	GBR	BRAWN-MERCEDES	95
2	SEBASTIAN VETTEL	GER	RED BULL-RENAULT	84

All scores counted

CONSTRUCTORS' CUP

POS.	CONSTRUCTOR	PTS
1	BRAWN-MERCEDES	172
2	RED BULL-RENAULT	153.5

THE TEENS

DRIVERS' WORLD CHAMPIONSHIP 2010

POS.	DRIVER	NAT.	CONSTRUCTOR	PTS
1	SEBASTIAN VETTEL	GER	RED BULL-RENAULT	256
2	FERNANDO ALONSO	ESP	FERRARI	252

All scores counted

CONSTRUCTORS' CUP

POS.	CONSTRUCTOR	PTS
1	RED BULL-RENAULT	496
2	McLAREN-MERCEDES	454

DRIVERS' WORLD CHAMPIONSHIP 2011

POS.	DRIVER	NAT.	CONSTRUCTOR	PTS
1	SEBASTIAN VETTEL	GER	RED BULL-RENAULT	392
2	JENSON BUTTON	GBR	McLAREN-MERCEDES	270

All scores counted

CONSTRUCTORS' CUP

POS.	CONSTRUCTOR	PTS
1	RED BULL-RENAULT	650
2	McLAREN-MERCEDES	497

DRIVERS' WORLD CHAMPIONSHIP 2012

POS.	DRIVER	NAT.	CONSTRUCTOR	PTS
1	SEBASTIAN VETTEL	GER	RED BULL-RENAULT	281
2	FERNANDO ALONSO	ESP	FERRARI	278

All scores counted

CONSTRUCTORS' CUP

POS.	CONSTRUCTOR	PTS
1	RED BULL-RENAULT	460
2	FERRARI	400

DRIVERS' WORLD CHAMPIONSHIP 2013

POS.	DRIVER	NAT.	CONSTRUCTOR	PTS
1	SEBASTIAN VETTEL	GER	RED BULL-RENAULT	397
2	FERNANDO ALONSO	ESP	FERRARI	242

All scores counted

CONSTRUCTORS' CUP

POS.	CONSTRUCTOR	PTS
1	RED BULL-RENAULT	596
2	MERCEDES	360

DRIVERS' WORLD CHAMPIONSHIP 2014

POS.	DRIVER	NAT.	CONSTRUCTOR	PTS
1	LEWIS HAMILTON	GBR	MERCEDES	384
2	NICO ROSBERG	GER	MERCEDES	317

All scores counted\

CONSTRUCTORS' CUP

POS.	CONSTRUCTOR	PTS
1	MERCEDES	701
2	RED BULL-RENAULT	405

DRIVERS' WORLD CHAMPIONSHIP 2015

POS.	DRIVER	NAT.	CONSTRUCTOR	PTS
1	LEWIS HAMILTON	GBR	MERCEDES	381
2	NICO ROSBERG	GER	MERCEDES	322

All scores counted

CONSTRUCTORS' CUP

POS.	CONSTRUCTOR	PTS
1	MERCEDES	703
2	FERRARI	428

DRIVERS' WORLD CHAMPIONSHIP 2016

POS.	DRIVER	NAT.	CONSTRUCTOR	PTS
1	NICO ROSBERG	GER	MERCEDES	385
2	LEWIS HAMILTON	GBR	MERCEDES	380

All scores counted

CONSTRUCTORS' CUP

POS.	CONSTRUCTOR	PTS
1	MERCEDES	765
2	RED BULL-TAG HEUER	468

DRIVERS' WORLD CHAMPIONSHIP 2017

POS.	DRIVER	NAT.	CONSTRUCTOR	PTS
1	LEWIS HAMILTON	GBR	MERCEDES	363
2	SEBASTIAN VETTEL	GER	FERRARI	317

All scores counted

CONSTRUCTORS' CUP

POS.	CONSTRUCTOR	PTS
1	MERCEDES	668
2	FERRARI	522

RIGHT A MAGICAL MOMENT FOR LEWIS HAMILTON AS HE IS CARRIED ALOFT BY THE WILDLY PATRIOTIC CROWD AT SILVERSTONE IN 2017 AFTER RACING TO HIS FIFTH BRITISH GP VICTORY WHEN NO ONE COULD GET CLOSE TO HIS PACE IN HIS MERCEDES.

The publishers would like to thank the following sources
for their kind permission to reproduce the pictures in this book:

Action Images: /Sporting Pictures; **Diana Burnett; Getty Images; LAT Images:** 352-353, 360; /Lorenzo Bellanca:
263R, 295R, 298-299, 300, 302B, 312-313, 342; /Sam Bloxham: 340, 346, 347TR; /Charles Coates: 1, 307T, 311T,
317B, 322B, 323, 343B, 350T; /Glenn Dunbar: 265, 299R, 306, 326T, 326B, 338, 339R, 348, 351T, 359; /Jakob
Ebrey: 10; /Steve Etherington: 261, 262, 263L, 294, 296, 307B, 308, 311, 316R, 320, 327, 331B, 335, 339T, 339B,
343TR, 343R, 347R; /Andrew Ferraro: 258-259, 302T, 319, 322T, 324, 328, 330, 332; /Andy Hone: 2, 8-9, 315,
331T, 347B, 350B, 351L; /Alastair Staley: 310, 334T, 336; /Steven Tee: 4, 6-7, 292, 295L, 303, 304, 317T, 334B,
344; **Ludvigsen Library Ltd; Mirrorpix.com; ©Phipps Photographic; Nigel Snowdon.**

Every effort has been made to acknowledge correctly and contact the source and/copyright holder
of each picture, and Carlton Books Limited apologises for any unintentional errors or omissions,
which will be corrected in future editions of this book.

Extended thanks are due to Zoë Schafer at LAT Photographic whose efforts greatly rendered the
burdens of picture research. Also to David Phipps for all his help and co-operation with this project.

Above **MICHAEL SCHUMACHER DID A LOT OF CELEBRATING IN 2002. THIS IS AFTER HE BEAT FERRARI
TEAM-MATE RUBENS BARRICHELLO AND HIS BROTHER RALF IN THE SAN MARINO GP AT IMOLA.**